# ✳ Oratorical Culture in Nineteenth-Century America ✳

## ✳ Transformations in the Theory and Practice of Rhetoric ✳

### ✳ Edited by ✳

*Gregory Clark and*

*S. Michael Halloran*

Southern Illinois University Press
*Carbondale and Edwardsville*

Printed in the United States of America
Production supervised by Natalia Nadraga
96  95  94  93     4  3  2  1


Library of Congress Cataloging-in-Publication Data

Oratorical culture in nineteenth-century America : transformations in the
theory and practice of rhetoric / edited by Gregory Clark and S. Michael
Halloran.
       p.   cm.
    Includes bibliographical references and index.
    1. Speeches, addresses, etc., American—History and criticism. 2. Rheto-
ric—United States—History—19th century.   3. Oratory—United States—
History—19th century.   4. United States—Civilization—19th century. I.
Clark, Gregory, 1950–   .  II.  Halloran, S. Michael.
PS407.067   1993
815'.0109—dc20                                                      92-42230
ISBN 0-8093-1739-7                                                       CIP


The paper used in this publication meets the minimum requirements of
American National Standard for Information Sciences—Permanence
of Paper for Printed Library Materials, ANSI Z39.48-1984. ⊚

# Contents

# Introduction ✳

## Transformations of Public Discourse in Nineteenth-Century America

✳ *Gregory Clark and S. Michael Halloran*

✳In his history of the discipline of English studies, Gerald Graff speaks of an "oratorical culture" that grounded the study of language and literature in American colleges through the first half of the nineteenth century (1987, 36–51). In his view, this oratorical culture "pervaded the college and linked the classical courses with the courses in English rhetoric and elocution, with the literary and debating societies, and with the literary culture outside" (35). It consisted of the oral exercises—disputation, declamation, forensic oration, and the like—that were a part of the traditional arts curriculum, as well as the literary and debate societies and the literary magazines that were increasingly prominent in the extra-curriculum of American colleges from the mid-eighteenth century on. According to Graff, this collegiate oratorical culture lent some vitality to the study of literature in English, though it supported a view of literature as "a public or civic discourse fit for socializing future citizens" (42), a view he takes as falling short of the true "literary" understanding that began to emerge with the dawn of "the professional era" in English studies in the last quarter of the century (53). "What finally should be the verdict on the literary education provided by the old-fashioned college?" he asks, replying that "in many ways it was worse than a waste of time, a form of unredeemed drudgery carried on in the name of archaic social ideals" (50).

As Graff's reference to "archaic social ideals" hints, "oratorical culture" in fact pervaded more than college life in the early nineteenth century. American politics and society during this period were in-

1

formed by a discourse inherited from the Revolutionary period, a discourse drawn self-consciously on the model of classical Roman rhetoric. In principle, this discourse enacted the neoclassical assumption that moral authority in a community is located in the public consensus of its members rather than in their individual private convictions. It took the form of the classical rhetorical kinds—deliberative, forensic, and epideictic—as practiced by orators such as John Adams, John Hancock, Thomas Jefferson, Timothy Dwight, John Witherspoon, Daniel Webster, Edward Everett, and a host of others. This neoclassical rhetorical discourse is likewise illustrated by the voluminous periodical and pamphlet literature of the era, of which the Federalist Papers and Paine's *Common Sense* are probably the most familiar examples. Its consistent purpose was to form and sustain a public consensus, intellectual and moral, as the basis of civic action.

What we now call "literature" this rhetoric treated as a species of epideictic discourse whose end was to "teach and delight," to pass on the established values of the culture and thus to sustain the common ground upon which arguments about particular issues could be conducted. Robert Ferguson shows in *Law and Letters in American Culture* (1984) how the fiction and poetry of such writers as Charles Brockden Brown, Washington Irving, and William Cullen Bryant were shaped by ideals of civic humanism and legal eloquence drawn from Cicero and contemporary legal authorities. He lists a number of prominent periodical editors who were educated in the law (71) and argues that for many of them, what we would privilege as their "literary" endeavors were epiphenomena of their primary vocation. The didactic voice of the lawyer can be heard in their poetry, the lawyer's organizational genius read in their prose. Those who taught rhetoric in the colleges during this period quite naturally adopted pedagogical practices time-honored in the liberal arts curriculum and traceable ultimately to Isocrates and Quintilian, the original inventors of an educational system aimed at producing the eloquent and morally informed leader of society, "the good man skilled in speaking," of which the lawyer of the Revolutionary and Federal period was a particular instance.

Graff is thus correct when he says that oratorical culture "pervaded" American colleges of the early nineteenth century but is somewhat misleading when he says that oratorical culture linked the college curriculum and extra-curriculum with "the literary culture outside." The culture outside during the early years of the nineteenth century was not "literary" in our sense of that term, but oratorical. Its most prized symbolic work was that of the orator. Its social ideals may from the perspective of the late twentieth century seem archaic and were from that perspective exclusionary, but they deserve an effort to understand them in their own terms.

This book tries both to understand those social ideals and to show how they gave rise to the radically different ideals of the later professional culture within which Graff's history is situated. Our purpose in this introductory essay is to explore the oratorical culture that characterized the United States at the beginning of the nineteenth century and show how that culture was transformed by an emerging individualistic spirit that, in diverse social and institutional forms, challenged the traditional principle of collective moral authority by establishing as a new principle the moral authority of the individual. We will suggest that, once established, this authority of the individual was itself transformed by the political and economic complexities of a rapidly expanding nation into the authority of the expert and that it was this new public morality of expertise that defined the professional culture we see characterizing the United States by the end of that century.

We describe this change as a "transformation" in Kenneth Burke's sense of that term: a process through which "the position at the start can eventually be seen in terms of the new motivation encountered enroute" ([1945] 1969, 422). That is, we use the term to suggest that as the political and economic realities of the American community changed during the nineteenth century, its public discourse, in theory as well as in practice, changed as well. The term *transformation* enables us to bear in mind Burke's advice that, while such a change in motivation may appear to observers (such as historians) as "a kind of jolt or inconsistency," to those who experienced the change it appeared to be simply the natural progress of things (422). In doing so it provides us with the method we are using both to understand oratorical culture in its own terms and to remain skeptical of any teleologically grounded explanations that we might want to impose as we examine the ways in which that culture changed.

We are not the first to use this term to explain the changes that occurred in rhetorical theory during the nineteenth century. In Thomas M. Conley's *Rhetoric in the European Tradition*, the nineteenth

century in both Europe and America is described as a period of
"political and social transformations" that made it "a watershed
between the old society of hierarchy and caste and the new culture of
industrialism" (1990, 236). Conley describes American colleges in
particular undergoing a "transformation" that secularized and democratized them as their purpose shifted from initiating "the young
into polite society" to preparing them for "a fruitful occupation and
individual self-realization" (248). Nan Johnson's *Nineteenth-Century
Rhetoric in North America* uses the term more specifically to characterize "the adaptive dynamics of rhetorical theory and practice" (1991, 4),
describing change in the theoretical materials she examines as a
"process of responsive transformation" (6). And Johnson's statement
of her guiding historiographical assumption can illuminate ours:

> To investigate the configuration of any rhetorical tradition necessarily
> obliges us first to recognize that throughout the history of rhetoric,
> rhetorical theory and pedagogy have displayed a dynamic tendency
> toward responsive transformation. An account of the nature of the
> nineteenth-century rhetorical tradition implies an investigation of the
> philosophical assumptions, theoretical models, and cultural mandates
> that shaped nineteenth-century theory and practice. (7)

The essays in this volume examine change as transformation in
the practice of rhetoric in nineteenth-century America as well as in its
theory and pedagogy. In doing so, they explore the methodological
resources that this notion of transformation provides for situating
change in the context of the cultural forces to which rhetorics are
always a response. A historiography guided by this notion requires
that a place of beginning—in the case of this introductory essay, the
discursive culture we are characterizing as oratorical—not be privileged as an origin. Rather, it becomes a point on a line of descent that
enables us to identify and evaluate historical forces that contributed to
the construction of its descendant—here the inherited discursive
culture we are characterizing as professional. In doing so, this essay
presents a particular narrative of transformation providing what we
believe is a useful explanation of what happened to the theory and
practice of rhetoric in the United States during the nineteenth century. We present this narrative as a "representative anecdote" in the
sense that Burke ([1945] 1969) uses that term—as a case that exem-

plifies what we mean by transformation used as a guiding methodological term.

The essays that follow all focus on specific moments in nineteenth-century American rhetoric and use the concept of transformation in a variety of ways to explain the patterns of change they
present. In doing so, of course, they expose the limitations inherent in
the particular narrative of transformation that this introductory essay
presents. Oratorical culture as we render it here was distinctly limited
in the gender and class of its participants, and while its individualist
and professional transformations as we describe them gradually
expanded the scope of participation in public discourse, almost all
women and many men still remained at its margins. Further, oratorical culture was not the only form of public culture in America early in
the century and what we are calling professional culture not its only
transformation at the century's end. Some of the essays that follow
confirm and elaborate this introductory narrative, while others point
to limitations of it and to cultural issues such as these that it ignores.
In doing so, they complicate and even conflict with it in ways that,
fully examined and developed, could overturn it. So while the immediate purpose of this essay is to present one narrative of transformation, its larger purpose—the purpose shared by the essays that
compose this volume—is to explore the concept of transformation
itself as a historiographical trope that enables constructions of the
past that are skeptical of teleological assumptions about its relation to
the present. We explore this concept in the hope of developing
narratives of the history of rhetorical theory and practice in nineteenth-century America that assert neither decline nor progress.
Reminding us of Burke's motto that always "it's more complicated than
that" ([1961] 1970, 277), a historiography of transformation commits us
to histories that acknowledge losses and gains while tempering the
impulse to assign praise or blame.

Our narrative of transformation in this introductory essay ends
in a description of a culture in which the locus of public morality is the
expert and autonomous individual rather than a communal consensus. Indeed, that is the primary characteristic of the culture that Graff
describes as "literary." What we describe is a process of transformation that brought public culture in the United States to that point at
the end of the nineteenth century. Our thesis is that both the theory of
rhetoric taught in the schools and the practice of public discourse

sustained outside them were transformed during the nineteenth century from those of the neoclassical oratorical culture into those of the professional culture we see characterizing both colleges and communities by its end. What Graff calls "literary culture" is but one expression of this new professional culture, albeit the one most apparently like the older oratorical culture. Burke observes that the problem with any such specialized culture is that it tends to treat its activities as "autonomous," as unconnected to those of the larger community in which it is situated ([1950] 1969, 27). Such a culture makes morality something to be determined in terms of the effectiveness and efficiency of the activity alone rather than in terms of the function of that activity within that larger community. This transformation in the motivation of rhetoric in America during the nineteenth century suggests a diminishing ability of American public culture to function collectively—for us, one of the losses. However, the emergence of these specialized communities gave access to the theory and practice of public discourse to people who had never had access before—for us, one of the gains.

## Rhetoric in the Oratorical Culture

The rhetoric taught in American colleges at the beginning of the nineteenth century was strongly neoclassical, which is to say that it was a rhetoric of general citizenship closely tied to the public discourse practiced in pulpit, bar, and senate of the larger society. Some prominent teachers of rhetoric, such as John Quincy Adams of Harvard and Timothy Dwight of Yale, were in fact simultaneously practitioners in one or more of those rhetorical forums. Adams served as senator from the state of Massachusetts from 1803 to 1808, a period that overlapped his tenure as Boylston Professor of Rhetoric at Harvard. Dwight, as president of Yale from 1795 to 1817, made his pulpit one of the most prominent political lecterns in New England as he sustained the cause of Puritan theocracy well into the second decade of the nineteenth century. The commitment of these men to the practice of rhetoric in this classical sense of oratorical discourse on civic issues was paralleled in the theory they taught. The statutes for the Boylston Chair were drawn directly from John Ward's English language compendium of Ciceronian rhetoric (1759; Reid 1959), and Adams's *Lectures on Rhetoric and Oratory* (1810) were likewise virtually pure Cicero. Dwight's senior course in rhetoric, although influenced by Hugh Blair's *Lectures on Rhetoric and Belles Lettres* (1783) and so less purely classical than Adams's work, still directed his students insistently to use the art of deliberative, forensic, and epideictic discourse to address civic matters.

At the center of this neoclassical rhetoric was an American version of the traditional rhetorical ideal, "the good man skilled in speaking" whose civic duty it was to articulate an established wisdom and focus it on particular issues. The ideal had been expressed and exemplified a generation earlier by John Witherspoon, president of the College of New Jersey at Princeton from 1768 to 1794 and author of what has been called "the first complete rhetoric by an American" (Guthrie 1949, 100). Witherspoon spoke in his posthumously published *Lectures on Moral Philosophy and Eloquence* (1810; Miller 1990a) of a "complete orator," and he enacted in his own life the ideal of theory and practice, contemplation and action combined. He was active in both civil and church politics while serving as president of Princeton and was the only clergyman to sign the Declaration of Independence. He also encouraged his students' inclinations to become involved in issues surrounding the Revolution. Like Cicero and Quintilian, Witherspoon rejected the idea of a contemplative life divorced from the concerns of the public forum, arguing that "when statesmen are also scholars, they make upon the whole greater orators and nobler writers than those who are scholars merely, though of the greatest capacity" (Miller 1990a, 260). The insistent refusal to draw a sharp line between contemplation and action, between the academy and the public forum, was in fact a key element of his "complete orator," as it had been of Cicero's and Quintilian's "good man skilled in speaking." From the classical and this neoclassical point of view, a central purpose of academic life was to preserve and articulate a moral consensus for application by citizens in the public forum.

Witherspoon's complete orator was not motivated by the ideal of striving for individual advancement that would become central to middle-class culture in the nineteenth century. As Burton J. Bledstein shows in *The Culture of Professionalism*, Americans of the eighteenth century did not have a middle class in the modern sense, though they were inclined to see themselves as "persons of middling ranks" (1976, 8). They understood this phrase in a sense that drew implicitly on the Aristotelian ideal of the mean: neither too rich nor too poor, governing their lives by shared interests and a concern for community welfare and values. To become a "complete orator" was not a personal achievement but the public responsibility of citizenship. The underlying ethos was communitarian, though in a limited and exclusive sense. While their particular shared interests and common concerns authorized a kind of participatory democracy, they limited participation—citizenship, essentially—to educated, white males. Both women in general and men who weren't "middling"—who lacked the education that developed those interests and concerns or who were poor or recent immigrants or black or native American—were denied the public responsibility and opportunity of citizenship so defined.

By mid-century, the concept of oratorical public discourse and its communitarian ethos as taught and practiced by figures such as Witherspoon, Adams, and Dwight had begun to erode in the United States, both outside the academy and within. As Americans became more conscious of the invitations to individual autonomy inherent in their physical and social settings, they became increasingly self-absorbed. And this self-absorption is characteristic of the individualistic rhetoric that was emerging in both the college classroom and in public practice. By the end of the century, "rhetoric" as a college-level subject had little overtly to do with the traditional rhetorical forums. This was a consequence of two closely related factors: the growth of individualism as a central cultural value and the increasing specialization of knowledge leading to a similarly specialized academic discourse. Teachers and practitioners of rhetoric alike came to conceive public life primarily as a context for individual self-definition and action. Knowledge became increasingly arcane and specialized and came under the control of narrowly defined professions and disciplines. Citizens were no longer people who brought general knowledge to bear on broad public issues so much as specialists who attended to their own sharply limited domains.

The dynamic of this transformation is illustrated by an episode in the early history of one of the new nineteenth-century professions, engineering. The first American school to grant degrees in engineering was Rensselaer Polytechnic Institute, founded as The Rensselaer School in 1824 for the purpose of training itinerant lecturers who would travel the countryside, teaching farmers, merchants, and mechanics to apply science in their own pursuits (Rezneck 1968, 3–8). Its philosophy might be characterized as "populist applied science" in that it understood the new scientific knowledge as common property to be spread widely for the general improvement of the populace. Like the lyceum movement, formally established by Josiah Holbrook just two years after The Rensselaer School's founding, it was an expression of an individualistic idealism that envisioned every American (at least every white male American) able to prosper in private affairs and participate fully in public affairs by virtue of a general moral and intellectual improvement. And like the lyceum movement, it was inexorably transformed into something quite different. By mid-century, The Rensselaer School was training professional engineers who would market their knowledge of applied science as a specialized ability, doing for hire what the general populace was now presumed incapable of doing. And the lyceum movement was well on its way toward becoming a medium of entertainment.

We will have more to say below on the general theme of professionalization, and the essay by Frederick Antczak and Edith Siemers traces the transformation of a successor to the lyceum movement, the Chautauqua. The example of The Rensselaer School raises the tantalizing (and probably unanswerable) question of whether there was some inevitability in the move from what we have called the populist model to the professional model for the new scientific knowledge. Could the individualist vision of a morally and intellectually elevated public have survived in the changing cultural climate of nineteenth-century America? We don't claim to be able to answer that question, but we will turn now to a more detailed consideration of how the individualist vision developed.

## Individualistic Transformations of Oratorical Culture

A powerful physical aspect of the American setting invited a shift in the culture of the United States from a social morality grounded in the community to one grounded in the individual. In the course of the nineteenth century, the expansive landscape of the continent became more accessible to many white Americans who perceived within it unlimited space and resources theirs to claim. And while such a perception seems to have been characteristic primarily of men during the first half of the century (Kolodny 1984), later in the century, as settlement moved closer to the barrier of the Pacific, some women began to act upon that perception for themselves. Indeed, Myra

Jehlen argues that in availing both space and resource to the exertions of individual enterprise, this seemingly unlimited landscape made the individualism for which the liberal philosophy of the eighteenth century had argued appear "natural" and materially necessary (1986, 3). Liberal individualism became material in the form of the private property that the American landscape offered to its citizens, property that, for them, warranted individual claims of natural rights and political autonomy. As Jehlen puts it, the very word "America" came to connote "not only the strenuous spirit of individualism, but also . . . its material effectiveness in the real world" (15). Extending Jehlen's thesis that conceptions of America were shaped more by the material reality of that landscape itself than by philosophy, we can suggest that as that landscape became increasingly accessible to individual settlement and enterprise, American concepts of self became increasingly individualistic and autonomous.

Philip Fisher (1985) documents this shift in his study of the social setting in which the American novel developed. Using terms appropriate to our discussion, Fisher argues that the public world in America during the nineteenth century shifted from a "polis" to an "economy"—a shift that itself can be read as a transformation, as Burke puts it, of the motives of "economic necessity" into "moral purpose" ([1950] 1969, 422). Social life, in Fisher's analysis, "became economic rather than political, atomized rather than centered, focused on money rather than on power, and based in the lives of individuals rather than families" (1985, 16). What Fisher documents is the cultural impact of the unprecedented expansion of American settlement and the rapid emergence of a manufacturing and commercial economy that resulted in the capitalism that came to dominate all aspects of American life. Capitalism in this early form—relatively small-scale and utterly unregulated—seemed to present every American with opportunities for both economic advancement or disaster, opportunities that were, in either case, accessible to the individual alone. Richard Sennett (1977) observes that as the economic experience of Americans grew increasingly treacherous and seductive, individuals withdrew from each other for protection and advantage to become rivals in an inherently competitive and risky game. The public realm that had once been the place where those who had access to it collaborated in constructing a social order became a stage where they attempted to define, assert, and aggrandize themselves as

autonomous beings. These individuals who had conceived themselves as both contributors to and beneficiaries of the public good
came to see themselves as autonomous moral agents responsible first
and last for their own survival (19–22). Consequently, increasing
numbers of Americans adopted a moral stance that Alasdair MacIntyre (1984) describes as "bureaucratic individualism." Caught within
institutions and organizations that seemed to wield power imper-
sonally and were apparently answerable to no one, people intensified
their allegiance to the very ideology of self-interest of which they were
victims, one that justified withdrawal from others in order to protect
and provide for themselves (34–35).

The intellectual setting for this intensifying individualism was a
later version of the liberalism in which American rhetorical theory
and practice had merged in an eighteenth-century neo-Ciceronian
synthesis: the consensual conviction that every individual has a
natural right to freedom of conscience and action. Under the influence
of Lockean and Cartesian epistemologies that grounded knowledge
in individual experience, moral authority shifted gradually from
institutions to individuals. This shift was affirmed publicly in the
American Revolution, which was in large part a rejection of traditional institutional authority. During the years that followed the Revolution and the adoption of the Constitution, this philosophical individualism was tempered politically as individual moral authority was
directed, by the consensus that established it, toward communitarian
ends. The rhetorical theory and practice of Witherspoon, Adams, and
Dwight, for example, addressed the articulation of shared individual
values that would support common, cooperative action. But our point
is that discourse such as this was gradually rendered obsolete by the
more materially based individualist consensus that began to develop
in the rhetoric that was taught as well as practiced as the public
discourse of the nineteenth century.

Particularly instructive in the development of the ideology of
liberal individualism to a point where it almost left the community
behind was the Massachusetts poet and essayist Ralph Waldo Emerson. Extending the individualist epistemologies of Locke and Des-
cartes, Emerson made absolute spiritual truths accessible to individual perception alone. Jehlen describes Emerson's project as resulting in
"an intensification of consciousness so powerful that the material
universe dissolves into . . . a [personal] knowledge that claims, be-

yond interpretation, to be simply vision" (1986, 77). In doing so, he authorized his fellow citizens to reject history and heritage and to redefine both themselves and their world in autonomous personal terms. It is of course more than a bit paradoxical for us to claim that Emerson "authorized" such a move, since his views on the autonomy of the individual mind and conscience, taken literally, would have made any such "authorization" extraneous. Few among privileged Americans were prepared to go to Emerson's individualist extreme, fewer still were capable, and one who did suggested, as the story goes, that Emerson himself pulled up short of living out the values he espoused. Jailed for refusing to pay a tax in support of the Mexican War, Emerson's friend Henry David Thoreau is said to have asked Emerson why he was not himself in jail—why Emerson had bowed to government authority by paying the tax he too opposed as unjust. Thoreau articulated this position in his influential essay on "Resistance to Civil Government," which asserted the moral and political autonomy of the individual conscience in the statement that "there will never be a really free and enlightened State, until the State comes to recognize the individual as a higher and independent power, from which all its own power and authority are derived, and treats him accordingly" ([1849] 1990, 1981).

While perhaps atypical in the extreme to which they carried the ideology of individualism, Emerson and Thoreau and a few others like them nonetheless represented an important tendency in American thought and culture. Sennett observes that the role of the public realm was shifting during the early nineteenth century from the setting for the formation of social order to the setting for the formation of individual personality (1977, 22). For the New England Transcendentalists, the public realm became the place for self-culture, for development of an individual vision that would energize the consciousness and the conscience that would ensure in the enlightened self correct thought and action. For them, social reform began with this reform of the individual. And while for Emerson and Thoreau it seemed to end with the individual as well, for others, like Margaret Fuller, it came to require participation in political public discourse. In "The Great Lawsuit" (1843), her long essay in the Transcendentalist journal *The Dial*, Fuller put the concept of self-culture into the service of the women's rights movement. While she believed with Emerson and Thoreau that moral reform in America must begin with reform of the self, she located that self in relationships that are inflected by ineq-uities of power. In doing so, she parted ways with them by making self-culture explicitly a political practice. Specifically, Fuller argued that relationships between men and women should be changed to enable women not "to learn their rule from without" but, like men, "to unfold it from within" (16–17). She suggested that to enact this argument, women must "lay aside all thought . . . of being taught and led by men" (45). It was Fuller's position as a woman in a culture dominated by men that led her to transform the politics of self-culture from one that designates the individual a majority of one into one that makes the individual an activist working to establish a new majority coalition.

Another element in this general shift of the public realm from a setting for socialization to a setting for individuation is the increasing secularism—or at least the decreasing practice of traditional, formal religion—of a people who insisted upon assigning moral respon-sibility to conscience alone. Through the nineteenth century, religion in the United States became less a public concern of institutions and more the private matter of individual conscience. Even those Ameri-cans who continued to practice formal religion shifted increasingly to evangelical movements led by lay ministers who left matters of piety and moral judgment to the private person. That this change in the location of even spiritual authority to the individual was representa-tive of a more general cultural transformation during the early nine-teenth century is demonstrated at the grass roots of American politi-cal life that shifted, with Andrew Jackson's 1828 defeat of John Quincy Adams, from the centralized and patrician leadership of an elite to the decentralized and democratic leadership of the common man. More than any preceding president, Jackson was innocent of a classical education, and his victory over the one-time Harvard chair-holder Adams can be taken as a figure of the declining importance of oratorical public discourse and of the collectivist assumptions about moral authority on which it was based.

### Individualistic Transformations of the Rhetoric of Oratorical Culture

As the nineteenth century progressed, the rhetoric that emerged both within and outside the academy in America expressed this increasing individualism. Sennett describes the change as a shift in the role of the individual American to whom public discourse is addressed from that of judging reasons advanced to observing the performance of an exemplary, representative self (1977, 261). In examining that shift, Frederick Antczak (1985) has traced the growth of what he calls the rhetoric of identification that was affirmed in the election of Andrew Jackson. Jackson defeated Adams by presenting himself to the voters as a representative personality, using rhetoric that addressed its audience not as citizens who must judge but as spectators observing a version of themselves. This rhetoric of identification was not necessarily a pandering to or indulgence of the audience. Rather, its purpose was what Antczak calls "popularization": A speaker would present to an audience a personality that was recognizable yet idealized and thus would invite them each to become their own versions of that better self (9). But his examples of such rhetorical popularizers—Emerson, Mark Twain, and William James on the public lecture circuit—demonstrate that this rhetoric tended to turn people inward, making public discourse a drama through which spectators define themselves as an assemblage of autonomous individuals. It did so by presenting no arguments, and, as Antczak's essay with Edith Siemers in this volume suggests, public discourse of this sort came to function primarily as entertainment.

That this rhetoric presented no arguments marks a significant change. Arguments, as Lloyd Bitzer (1978) shows, function as essentially collaborative exchanges that construct public knowledge. In hearing arguments, an audience is invited to judge and make a public commitment—intellectual, emotional, and moral—to something common. In place of arguments, Antczak's popularizers presented their personalities alone, expecting the personalities of their auditors to develop in response. Their invitation was not to some specific and shareable commitment but to the acceptance of individual moral responsibility generally. Sennett makes a case against public discourse of this sort, associating it with the cult of charisma in which leaders are judged not by their policies and accomplishments but by the "sincere" intentions their personalities convey (1977, 265). Our concern here, however, is that the representative personalities were often inherently inaccessible to many of the people who may have heard them speak—women, for example, and men of different and less privileged class, race, or culture than the speaker. In its public practice, such a rhetoric appears to have been as socially exclusive as the neoclassical.

Within the nineteenth-century academy, the neoclassical rhetoric of public discourse taught by professors/statesmen like Witherspoon, Adams, and Dwight was transformed into a rhetoric that would address the "practical, accumulative, . . . acquisitive" purposes of the late nineteenth-century American university that, as Richard Hofstadter and DeWitt Hardy wrote, emerged to serve primarily the interests of "business and technology" (1952, 36). In the early decades of the century, the Scottish rhetorics of Hugh Blair (1783), George Campbell (1776), and Alexander Jamieson (1820) became widely popular as textbooks. According to Sharon Crowley, "The crucial move made by [these] modern discourse theorists was their centering of invention [i.e., the discovery of what to say in a discourse] in the minds of individual authors" (1990, 54), an innovation for which she gives primary credit to Campbell (15). The significance of this move, which Crowley places at the heart of the rhetoric that came to dominate American colleges in the nineteenth century, is that it locates the experience of the private individual where the public moral consensus had once been. The most popular version of this tradition in the United States was that of Hugh Blair, whose *Lectures on Rhetoric and Belles Lettres* was for decades the most widely used textbook in its colleges. Blair is also the major source for the first rhetoric text published by an American, Samuel Knox's *A Compendious System of Rhetoric* (1809). Knox's book was not a commercial success, but neither were the two more classically based texts published the following year, Adams's *Lectures on Rhetoric and Oratory* and Witherspoon's *Lectures on Moral Philosophy and Eloquence*. The popularity of Blair's "belletristic" rhetoric coincided with a growing interest in the creation of a distinctly American literary culture to refocus scholarly attention away from deliberative, forensic, and epideictic discourse and toward poetic discourse.

When a commercially successful text was finally published (Samuel P. Newman's *Practical System of Rhetoric* [1827]), it was clearly in the mold of Blair, Campbell, Jamieson, and Knox. As Crowley shows, its treatment of rhetorical invention emphasized the role of private experience and neglected classical methods of scanning the common wisdom of the public mind. Moreover, two of its five chapters were organized around the concept of "taste," an idea that occupied in belletristic rhetoric a position roughly equivalent to that of "eloquence" in classical and American neoclassical rhetoric. As a rhetorical virtue, taste was to some extent based in what Bitzer would call public knowledge and thus connected with the communitarian view of moral responsibility that grounded classical rhetoric. Indeed, Nan Johnson notes that the doctrine of taste assumed that its principles "embody 'natural' inclinations" that, when nurtured in the members of a community, would bring them to a common recognition of higher laws (1991, 56). And Hans-Georg Gadamer shows that, in the pre-Kantian version that was adopted by Newman from the Scottish belletrists, "taste" was a kind of knowledge of objects shared by members of a community and thus was part of the *sensus communis*, the common understanding that provided the ground for moral and political judgment (1975, 33–39). In distinct contrast to eloquence, however, taste was an inward response rather than a manifest expression and hence inherently more private. Further, as Gadamer also shows, that belletristic notion of taste had already been invalidated by the time of Newman's writing. Kant's *Critique of Judgment* (1790) denied any status as knowledge to the judgment of taste, thus stripping it of moral and political implications and providing a theoretical basis for the understanding of "literature" as an arhetorical, aesthetically autonomous mode of discourse. Newman's text was thus symptomatic of academic rhetoric's turn inward and prophetic of its eclipse in the academy by the emerging discipline of literary studies.

The tendency to ground rhetoric in the private experience of the individual is likewise evident in the *Lectures Read to the Seniors at Harvard College* (1856) by Newman's contemporary, Edward T. Channing, one of Emerson's teachers at Harvard. In comparison with Newman, Channing showed considerably more interest in the classical forms and forums of rhetoric, but his lectures nonetheless focused on individual moral experience in a way that was more in tune with the thinking of Locke, Hume, and the belletristic rhetoricians— Newman included—than with the American neoclassicists such as Witherspoon who, as we have already noted, had echoed Cicero's and Quintilian's concept of "the good man skilled in speaking." Like others of the Revolutionary and Federal periods, Witherspoon assumed the state of American society to be closely analogous to that of ancient Athens and Rome and so appropriated classical rhetoric as a means of imposing moral leadership on a mob who needed it. By contrast, Channing argued in his opening lecture that American society was politically very different: "A modern debate is not a contest between a few leading men for a triumph over each other and an ignorant multitude; the orator himself is but one of the multitude, deliberating with them upon common interests, which are well understood and valued by all" ([1856] 1968, 17). As a consequence, sound arguments and high eloquence would not be enough for the modern leader:

> It is his virtues, his consistency, his unquestioned sincerity that must get the orator attention and confidence now. He must not rely too much upon the zeal or even the soundness with which he treats a question under immediate discussion. His hearers must believe that his life is steadily influenced by the sentiments he is trying to impress on them, — that he is willing to abide by principle at any hazard, and give his opinions and professions the full authority of his actions. (23)

In effect, Channing was teaching the kind of rhetoric that Antczak describes in practice.

Channing's faith that the audience could be relied upon to understand and value common interests flew in the face of abundant contradictory evidence. Presidential election campaigns of the 1820s through the 1850s—all of which Channing witnessed—more often than not were won by crass and mindless appeals to prejudice and factional loyalty. What Channing illustrates, then, is an ideological commitment to an ethos of the sincere individual—in Antczak's terms the "representative personality," in Sennett's the "charismatic man." Like the rhetorical practice of Andrew Jackson, the rhetorical theory taught in the colleges turned away from the public knowledge of the community and inward toward the experience of the individual as the locus of moral authority.

## The Rhetoric of a Culture of Professionalism

An often noted development in nineteenth-century American academic life is the emergence of distinct academic disciplines. Certain specialties—natural and moral philosophy, rhetoric, mathematics, the classical languages—were well established in American colleges of the seventeenth, eighteenth, and early nineteenth centuries. These were understood as separate areas of study, and some division of faculty labor was organized around them. Under this system, it was customary for the college president to assume responsibility for rhetoric and moral philosophy, and individual professors might each present a "course of lectures" in mathematics or natural philosophy or some other "department" of knowledge. But it was still the tutors who did most of the actual teaching of students, and they were likely to be responsible for the full range of subjects included in the curriculum. Not infrequently, one person would serve as "professor" of a particular discipline and as tutor for the range of disciplines as well. It was assumed that an educated person should and could know everything being taught—that the professor who happened to lecture on moral philosophy would be equally qualified to teach mathematics or Greek grammar. Thus, when Timothy Dwight needed someone to fill a professorship of chemistry and natural philosophy at Yale in 1801, he selected a twenty-two-year-old law student with little specific training in science named Benjamin Silliman (Reingold 1964, 1). Essentially, this was a system in which the unity of the knowledge comprehended by the arts curriculum was emphasized far more than the distinct areas into which it could be divided.

Benjamin Silliman would go on to found the country's premiere scientific journal and establish Yale as its leading center for scientific education; when a failed lawyer named Amos Eaton took up the career in applied science that would eventually lead to his appointment as the first director of the Rensselaer School, it was Silliman to whom he went for instruction (Rezneck 1968, 10). Silliman's career thus figures the inexorable shift of curricular emphasis in the nineteenth century toward specialized knowledge and the distinctness of disciplines. In part, this was a simple matter of division of labor resulting from the growth of the colleges. With increasing numbers of students and faculty, it became necessary to divide the curriculum among a larger number of people and hence possible to divide it into a larger number of more formally differentiated disciplines. This simple process of division coincided in the latter half of the nineteenth century with a pattern of specialization and professionalism that was developing both inside the academy and out, transforming the knowledge of each loosely defined department from part of the common ground of educated people to the property of a specially trained elite. And in the minds of many leading educators, that transformation worked in the interest of the public good. When President Eliot of Harvard, for example, became alarmed by the tendency he saw in public culture to embrace "loose and inaccurate statements," he restructured his undergraduate curriculum as an elective system of courses taught by specialized departments and his graduate curriculum as training in specific professional disciplines (Bender 1984, 89).

That similar restructurings were widespread in the American academy late in the nineteenth century is evident in the nearly universal development of a system of specialized examination and grading. At the beginning of the century, examination was for the most part a matter of oral public performance before the assembled college community, which on certain occasions would include the trustees and even persons having no formal affiliation with the college other than a self-defined interest in its activities. Judgment of the students' performance—and in the case of disputations, participation in the questioning—was open to all present, not just to persons specially qualified in the subject matter at hand. The process assumed all educated persons to be fully qualified in all subjects of the arts curriculum. By the end of the century, separate written examination in particular subjects, with each examination under full control of disciplinary specialists, was the norm. Where they endured, public oral examinations were more and more a quaint ritual. The emphasis had shifted decisively from common to specialized knowledge, from liberal arts to the disciplines and professions.

In *Writing Instruction in Nineteenth-Century American Colleges*, James Berlin shows the relevance of this development to the current-traditional rhetoric that emerged after about 1870, characterizing the trend as a scientizing of the entire curriculum, rhetoric in particular (1984, 62). Central in Berlin's interpretation is the science of faculty psychology, which relegated invention to the empirical procedures of nonrhetorical disciplines, insisted on the distinctness of modes of discourse, and reduced arrangement and style to mechanical processes. Crowley likewise emphasizes the role of faculty psychology in the development of current-traditional rhetoric, though she moves the beginnings of current-traditional rhetoric back several decades to the early years of the nineteenth century and associates its inventional component with the experience of the private individual rather than with disciplinary procedures. While both Berlin's and Crowley's discussions of current-traditional rhetoric are insightful, neither the scientific spirit in general nor the specific science of faculty psychology seems adequate to account fully for the emergence of this new

"rhetoric" in the closing decades of the nineteenth century. As Douglas Sloan shows in *The Scottish Enlightenment and the American College
Ideal* (1971), science was a lively force in American colleges of the
eighteenth century. The science of which Sloan speaks included
faculty psychology, some traces of which are evident in the neoclassical rhetoric of John Witherspoon, who brought into the Princeton
curriculum, as Dwight did to the curriculum at Yale, other aspects of
the new science as well. Further, the faculty psychology that was
scientifically current in the time of Witherspoon was outmoded by the
time that A. S. Hill, John F. Genung, and Barrett Wendell are supposed to have based a scientized rhetoric upon it. If eighteenth-
century neoclassical rhetoric could coexist with the scientific spirit
and even draw upon a then-current scientific psychology, one must
ask why this same psychology would give rise to a radically different
rhetoric after it had been scientifically discredited.

The point is that while late-eighteenth-century science was in
most aspects "modern," it was not yet "professional." The knowledge
it produced was still morally tinged, rooted in the tradition of belles
lettres, and thus presumed to be the common property of educated
people. Within the professional culture that developed in the nineteenth century, scientific knowledge became a neutral commodity,
and its practical value to the community thus made it an economic
asset to those who possessed it. Once the pursuit of amateurs whose
passion gave its products the moral valence of traditional philosophy
and rhetoric, science as a profession became a vehicle for the social
and economic advancement of the individual. As Bledstein shows, the
professional ethos went hand in hand with the rise of a true middle
class motivated by the drive to move up in a competitive socioeco-
nomic hierarchy. Expertise, whether specifically scientific or not,
came to be understood in the new professional sense as a privately
held commodity and was for many in the new class the means of
advancement. Eliot Friedson (1986) has documented the consequences
of this transformation upon American public culture, observing that
the division of labor into specialized activities relocated public knowledge, as Bitzer uses that term, to the separate and diverse territories of
the various professional specialists, out of a realm held in common by
citizens. As such, Friedson observes, when that knowledge is used to
determine public policy, "decision-making on its basis is not democratic, not open to the active participation of all" (5), a situation that

directs the community "toward rule by technique rather than rule by public debate" (8).

Whether the professionalization of science was simply the unfolding of tendencies implicit in its origins or a distinct cultural development is an open question. It is worth noting that specialized educational programs and professional societies appeared in such nonscientific fields as law, librarianship, social work, and the humanistic disciplines at about the same time as in the sciences. Athletics likewise took on the trappings of "professionalism" in the same period (Bledstein 1976, 81–86). These developments coincide very closely with the emergence of current-traditional rhetoric in the last four decades of the nineteenth century. Whatever its relationship to "science," we believe it was the professional ethos, not science or faculty psychology alone, that set the stage for current-traditional rhetoric. By defining knowledge-bearing communities as private enclaves of specialists and knowledge as an economic commodity rather than a moral virtue, this professional ethos created the need for a rhetoric of morally neutral and exclusionary discourse, and current-traditional rhetoric arose to fill this need. Its neglect of classical invention was an inheritance from the rhetoric of Blair and Campbell and thus genetically linked to faculty psychology. But its real basis was the new authority granted to professional expertise in matters of public policy.

John Witherspoon had identified four "objects or ends" of rhetoric—information, demonstration, persuasion, and entertainment—and noted that the term "persuasion" could legitimately be used in a sense that would make it the overriding end of all discourse (Miller 1990a, 290). This perspective would in our own century be expressed by the neoclassicist Richard Weaver (1963) in the adage "language is sermonic." Persuasion is central in classical and the various neoclassical rhetorics because they see language as inherently suasory and society as an arena of collective moral and political inquiry and suasion. But in the professional ethos of current-traditional rhetoric, language becomes something more like a calculus and the public forum an arena of more or less individual calculation and force. From this perspective, argument is the marshalling of evidence according to morally neutral rules of logic. With argument so perceived, public discourse becomes not a place to debate the common good but, as MacIntyre puts it, "a place where bargaining . . . is conducted" (1988,

338). In this setting, persuasion becomes a distinct, mostly optional, and often dubious function of exciting the passions.

This radically new understanding of language and the public forum expresses itself in the new prominence given by such textbook writers as A. S. Hill and Barrett Wendell to "exposition," prose meant to inform the reader in a clear, dispassionate, untendentious fashion. The expository essay, as taught by the new rhetoric, was essentially a knowledge-bearing object, an academic version of the technical report in which a professional would present his findings. Discussions of current-traditional rhetoric, from Albert Kitzhaber (1953) on, have tended to focus on exposition as its most important feature, though few have considered its relationship to the emergence of professional culture. But the current-traditional view of argument and persuasion may illustrate more forcefully the transformation of oratorical culture into professional culture, given the centrality of these genres to neoclassical rhetoric. We thus turn to George Pierce Baker, one of the earliest and most influential of the late nineteenth-century argumentation theorists. His *Principles of Argumentation*, first published in 1895, was cited well into the 1920s as an authoritative text on its subject. Like Whately's *Elements of Rhetoric* (1828), Baker distinguished sharply between argument proper, whose end is intellectual conviction, and persuasion. Unlike Whately, however, he had virtually nothing to say about the latter. While he acknowledged the importance of persuasion in moving an audience to act on the implications of an argument, most of his text is devoted to the purely logical argument to convince. Another early and influential argumentation text by Gertrude Buck (1899) made no mention at all of persuasion, treating argument as applied logic, pure and simple.

Baker's stated reason for saying so little about persuasion is that there are no general principles, comparable to the "universal laws" of logic, to govern its operation. But he also betrays the conviction that in a somewhat better world persuasion would be unnecessary. "Unfortunately," he writes, "to be convinced of the truth of an idea does not mean that he who is convinced will act promptly in accordance with that idea" (343); and later, "The expression of strong emotion . . . has *especially for a cultivated audience*, something a little repellent in it: it is too uncontrolled" (358; emphasis added). Baker's ideal audience would conduct themselves like the members of a profession, weighing the evidence pro and contra by the strictest of rules of rationality, with no consideration for preferences and interests and most importantly with no passion. Other writers on argumentation would be even stronger in expressing the view that a proper argument should contain only as much emotional persuasion as necessary for the particular audience, and a proper audience should need none at all. Ideally, an argument should be pure applied logic, a structure of evidence devoid of the tendentiousness that had been inherent in classical and neoclassical rhetoric. Ironically, Baker himself abandoned the study of argumentation just a few years after writing *Principles*, moving into the field of drama, which he saw as a realm of emotional expression. He went on to found the Yale School of Drama, where his students included Eugene O'Neill.

The problem with Baker's rhetoric, as with professional culture in general, is that when knowledge is commodified as specialization and professional communities claim the authority to develop and apply that knowledge, few rules of rationality can be found that will apply across this fragmented spectrum. Rationality, as Friedson notes, becomes definable for each of those communities in terms of the "functional efficiency" of its particular project (1986, 3). MacIntyre characterizes those terms as a "politics of effectiveness" that addresses "how far rival interests can be promoted and yet reconciled and contained within a single order" (1988, 39). In other words, when not only knowledge but rationality itself are at least partly constituted by the specific and specialized interests of a professional community, the discussion of common problems that cross the boundaries of those communities—problems of public policy, for example—is transformed, as MacIntyre observes, from a process of cooperative common inquiry to an exchange of conflicting convictions based upon differing if not conflicting assumptions and justifications (5–6). What happens in practice in the public discourse of a pluralistic culture, such as the one MacIntyre characterizes, is that conflicts of public consequence may never be fully confronted. Instead, they are dismantled and their elements appropriated by the various specialists who claim authority to address them. Oratorical culture, built upon the common ground of the shared public knowledge of the relative few who had access to the public discourse, enabled them to confront their conflicts constructively. Professional culture, while providing to Americans who had never had it before access to knowledge and discourses of public consequence, is structured by boundaries of expertise that fragment public knowledge and prevent some significant conflicts in the community from ever being addressed collectively at all.

The pluralistic public culture of professionalism, with all its benefits and handicaps, enacts in its discourse the economic and institutional consequences of the ideology of liberal individualism in which the United States began its political life as a nation. During the nineteenth century, these consequences emerged in the form of a political culture that was primarily economic, one in which public power was brokered by people who claimed the authority of professional expertise. That this professional culture can be treated as a manifestation of American liberal individualism and the economy of individual enterprise it implies is suggested in this statement by Andrew Abbott:

> We have professionalism . . . because our market-based occupational structure favors employment based on personally held resources, whether of knowledge or wealth. Such employment is more secure, more autonomous, and usually more remunerative, partly because it is organized in "careers," a strategy invented in the nineteenth century to permit a coherent individual life within a shifting marketplace. . . . Professionalization thus offered continuously independent life chances. (1988, 324)

The professionalization of American public culture provided access to those chances to a far broader range of American citizens than had the oratorical culture that preceded it, though by definition it excluded many others who lacked requisite expertise. What appears to have been lost in the transformation is some of the ability of those citizens to think and act collectively beyond the boundaries of their professional subcultures.

## Conclusion

We have argued that the earliest nineteenth-century American rhetoric was neoclassical because American culture at this time was in an important sense an oratorical culture. What this means is that at the beginning of the century, the orator had a central cultural role: to articulate a public moral consensus and bring it to bear on particular issues through forms of discourse—spoken or written—that were more or less classical. During the course of the nineteenth century, both the oratorical culture and the neoclassical rhetoric that was central to it were transformed, first by individualism and later, and more radically, by its material consequence, professionalism. Individualism challenged the old assumptions about a communal moral consensus and gave rise to a rhetoric of the charismatic or representative personality whose role was to exhibit a private moral commitment. Because that private commitment was one with which the people addressed were expected to identify, the establishing of a general moral consensus remained the primary purpose of public discourse.

With the development of professionalism, the theory and practice of rhetoric were again transformed as Americans began to treat knowledge as a morally neutral commodity. Such knowledge was considered the property of specialists whose job was to apply it to particular problems through a discourse of strictly logical argument sustained among themselves. While this distinction between the first transformation and the second is perhaps overstated, it points to persistent tendencies. The rhetoric of identification does not necessarily preclude all logical argument, though it does tend to deemphasize it. The rhetoric of professional expertise does not suppress all passion and moral commitment, though it tends to undermine their legitimacy. These rhetorics did not counterbalance each other so much as the latter grew out of the former as the cultural situation of life in the United States changed. Our immediate argument in this essay is that by the end of the nineteenth century, the dominant aspects of American culture in general and the theory and practice of its public discourse in particular had been transformed by the emergence of the practical and seemingly apolitical ideals of professionalism. The larger argument explored in this book, however, is that the concept of transformation itself—rather than the teleological concepts of decline or progress—can explain cultural change in a way that enables us to understand why it occurred and to assess the legacy of theories and practices left to us as its consequence.

Some of the essays that follow illustrate aspects of the particular transformation we have traced, while others suggest the shape of other transformations that might explain changes in nineteenth-century American culture and in the theories and practices of public discourse that sustained it. Collectively, these essays suggest that American neoclassical rhetoric wasn't simply replaced by something different but rather was transformed by changing cultural realities that required shifts in theories and practices of public discourse in order to meet changing cultural needs. The essays in Part One by Ronald F. Reid on Edward Everett, Gregory Clark on Timothy Dwight, Russel Hirst on the conservative homiletician Austin Phelps, and P. Joy Rouse on Margaret Fuller examine aspects of this transformation in terms of a variety of neoclassical forms and forums of rhetorical theory and practice. Those in Part Two by Nan Johnson on self-instruction manuals in rhetoric and elocution, Nicole Tonkovich on rhetorical instruction in *Godey's Lady's Book*, Catherine Peaden on the rhetorical practice of Jane Addams, Frederick J. Antczak and Edith M. Siemers on the Chautauqua, and S. Michael Halloran on the picturesque examine public discourse in theory and practice as it was transformed later in the nineteenth century in terms of the individualism and ethos of expertise that we have argued here came to dominate American public culture.

Together the essays in this collection should suggest to historians directions for further study that examine connections between shifts in the theory and practice of rhetoric and the larger process of cultural change. We will reflect on those directions and on the primary purpose of such work—to inform our critique of our current theory and practice of rhetoric in particular and our public culture in general—in a brief afterword.

# Part One ✳ Classical Forms and Forums in the Nineteenth Century

# 1

# Edward Everett and Neoclassical Oratory in Genteel America ✳ *Ronald F. Reid*

✳Contemporary admirers often compared Edward Everett (1794–1865) to Cicero. "Fortunate it is," declared one critic of his ceremonial oratory, "that Everett has trod in the paths of Cicero" (Loring 1853, 525). Another said his oft-repeated lecture on Washington "suggests a comparison with the great Roman, not only as an orator, but also as a finished scholar, and a consummate master of style" (clipping in Everett diary, April 18, 1856, Everett papers).[1] When Everett was supporting Lincoln's war policy by touring the Union with a speech on "The Causes and Conduct of the Civil War," the president's supporters praised "the Cicero of America" (*Buffalo Morning Express* 1861, 3).

In contrast to the enthusiasm expressed by his contemporaries, Everett is scarcely remembered today. When he is, it is in a paradoxical way that illustrates the nation's changing oratorical culture. On one hand, Everett is remembered chiefly for his oratory. For example, the longest biography on Everett is subtitled *Orator and Statesman* (Frothingham 1925); and a student of his diplomatic career acknowledges that Everett is remembered not because of his diplomacy but because he was "primarily the great orator" (Stearns 1928, 6:137). On the other hand, Everett's speech making is usually scorned. A leading historian calls it "nickel-plated eloquence" (Commager 1936, 59), and a prominent literary critic dismisses it as "grandiloquent" (Buell 1986, 137–65).

Admittedly, the decline of Everett's reputation was not due entirely to the nation's changing attitudes toward oratory. Another reason was his habit of changing careers before he could make a lasting impression in any one of them. Still another reason can be expressed by the cliche "Winners write history," for Everett was a so-called Cotton Whig who was usually on the losing side of political struggles. Yet the contrast between Everett's contemporary fame as the "Cicero of America" and the tendency of later generations to rebuke him as "grandiloquent" leads to an inescapable conclusion: Everett exemplifies the declining reputation of neoclassical oratory.

Everett was a paradoxical figure. He lived through many of the cultural transformations that Halloran and Clark discuss in the Introduction to this book; but he exemplified the oratorical culture that prevailed before the transformations began. His academic career is almost forgotten, but he was an important academician whose career highlights the changes that were taking place within American universities. As a politician-orator, he was admired mostly by the old-fashioned genteel Americans; but he was also popular among the general public, thereby indicating that antebellum America had not entirely abandoned the ideals of the oratorical culture into which he was born. Yet Everett's failures, which were as numerous as his successes, reflect an inability to adapt to the demise of that culture. He recognized the changes that were taking place and sometimes tried to adapt, but he generally disapproved of the changes and refused to adapt.

These paradoxes will appear and reappear as I examine (1) the successes and failures of his career in relation to the changing oratorical culture, (2) how his reputation as a "Ciceronian" was essentially correct but partially inaccurate, (3) how his academic career reflects changing times and his educational philosophy, (4) how his theory of discourse was essentially neoclassical but also reflected an awareness of the changing culture, and (5) the neoclassical features of his oratory.

## Everett's Successes and Failures
## in a Changing Oratorical Culture

The successes and failures of Everett's career reflect many of the changes in the nation's oratorical culture, especially the declining sense of community. After earning a Harvard B.A. (1811) and an M.A. in theology (1813), Everett was ordained pastor of Boston's fashionable Brattle Street Church. He was an instant success, but after less than two years in the pulpit, Harvard offered him its new professorship of

Greek language and literature, a post that was part of the emerging system of specialized professorships. Everett accepted on condition that he be allowed to study in Germany, where he had hoped to study ever since being exposed to German theories of biblical criticism during his student days. In 1817, he became the first American to receive a Ph.D. from the famous university at Göttingen. After two more years of European study and travel, Everett began teaching. Once again, he was an instant success as he and George Ticknor (who had also studied at Göttingen) introduced German scholarship to Harvard. Following in the footsteps of his German mentors, Professor Everett did not confine himself to teaching, as did his American colleagues; he also became editor of the nearly defunct *North American Review* and converted it into a financially prosperous quarterly that was read widely by genteel Americans.

Everett was becoming a famous man of letters, but once again he switched fields, this time to enter politics (although he continued to write for literary periodicals). The near-absence of political partisanship in Everett's election to the House of Representatives in 1824 reflected the sense of community that characterized the so-called (albeit somewhat mythical) Era of Good Feeling that had prevailed since the end of the War of 1812. The old Federalist party was so weak, even in Massachusetts, that party politics seemed more like a relic from the past than a present-day reality. When the congressional seat in Everett's district became vacant, the Federalists failed to nominate anyone while the Republican caucus put up a weak candidate. A self-appointed caucus of political unknowns then nominated Everett.

The "nonpartisan" nomination came on the heels of Everett's Phi Beta Kappa oration (1824), which in the ordinary course of events would have had little, if any, political impact; but Everett's speech was given in the presence of the aged Marquis de Lafayette, a Revolutionary hero who was beginning his triumphant tour of the country he had helped to liberate (Loveland 1971). Thousands of ordinary citizens attended the highly publicized event. Adapting brilliantly to an occasion that was partly patriotic and partly academic, Everett spoke on "the circumstances favorable to the progress of literature in the United States in America" (Everett 1878, 1:9–44).[2] Delivered at a time when genteel Americans were sensitive to British charges about their literary inferiority, the tightly organized and clearly developed oration would have been well received under normal circumstances; but

Everett's chauvinism and emotional welcome to Lafayette created a sensation on this unusual occasion. The listening audience went wild. The speech was praised enthusiastically in the newspapers, and it went through several pamphlet editions. After Everett's nomination as an "independent," supporters portrayed him as a "scholar-patriot," not as a partisan politician.

Everett's image was well suited for a nation with a strong sense of community, but the national consensus was breaking down. A "second political party system" was emerging (McCormick 1966). Furious at John Q. Adams's presidential victory in 1824, supporters of Andrew Jackson formed what eventually became the Democratic party, and Jackson's enemies responded with what was first called the National Republican party and later the Whigs. Meanwhile, sectional controversies erupted over the tariff, nullification, and antislavery.

The nation's oratorical culture was profoundly affected. Candidates for public office, who had previously avoided overt campaigning, "took to the stump" with egalitarian appeals (McCormick 1966, 349–50). Political oratory took on a strong partisan cast as speakers argued policy questions less on the merits of the issues than on the basis of party and sectional loyalties. The eighteenth-century ideal of "civic virtue," which precluded open appeals to special "interests" and required politicians to identify their proposals with the "public good," was often replaced with blatant appeals to special interests. In Kloppenberg's words, "Something was gained when the chaotic democracy of Andrew Jackson replaced that more refined concept of what politics ought to be about, but something, namely the republican ideal of civic virtue, was also lost" (1987, 27).

Everett's devotion to the now-declining national consensus made it difficult for him to adapt to the new circumstances. Although joining the Whigs, he admitted privately that he had "neither taste nor talent for the duties of a partizan [sic]" (to J. McLean, August 18, 1828, Everett papers). He publicly pleaded with congressional colleagues to avoid partisanship, but his pleas fell on deaf ears. When he advocated Whig causes such as the protective tariff, he appealed to the old idea of the "public good" by arguing that the entire country, not just the North, benefited from protectionism, but he failed to persuade the South. Equally important is what Everett did not do. He eschewed stump speaking; and despite his antislavery sentiments, he avoided the subject for fear it would ultimately destroy the Union.

Preserving the Union was at the top of his political and oratorical agenda (Reid 1990, 33–47).

For Everett, an important way to rebuild the nation's declining consensus was to remind audiences of the "glorious past" that they all shared. A prominent epideictic orator, he spoke repeatedly on the Fourth of July and commemorated historical events such as the battles of Bloody Brook, Concord, and Bunker Hill. He eulogized many departed American heroes, including Thomas Jefferson and the Marquis de Lafayette. He participated actively in the lecture movement that arose after Josiah Holbrook's founding of a "lyceum" in 1826, but because most of his lectures were on historical subjects, they offered opportunities for him to give what were, in effect, epideictic speeches. His epideictic oratory was filled with ideas that were central to the American consensus: our "great past," our indebtedness to the great Revolutionary heroes, and our mission to serve as a model of freedom to the rest of the world (Reid 1956).

Everett's ceremonial oratory not only helped maintain the nation's sense of community but also kept him before the voters. Appreciative audiences consistently re-elected him to Congress until 1835, when they promoted him to the governorship of Massachusetts. Political success, however, could not last forever. With Jacksonian Democracy on the rise, Everett failed to be re-elected governor in 1839 by the unbelievable margin of one vote. Sick of politics, he took his family on a European vacation. He was in Europe during the Log Cabin campaign of 1840, which would have disgusted him; but log cabins and hard cider put a Whig in the White House (Gunderson 1957), which earned Everett an appointment as Minister to Great Britain. After the Democratic victory in 1844, Everett joined the ranks of the politically unemployed. He accepted the presidency of Harvard College, but he hated the job and soon resigned.

Everett's oratorical output declined during the 1840s, but he again resorted to epideictic oratory to save the Union as he became increasingly alarmed at the sectionalism that followed the Mexican War. Hoping to rebuild a national consensus, he appealed for unity in a highly publicized eulogy of John Quincy Adams (1848), a commemoration of the Battle of Bunker Hill (1850), and an encomium to Washington (1851). Reminding Americans of their great heroes and glorious past was Everett's key rhetorical strategy for preserving the Union. It was a strategy that reflected the old oratorical culture by exploiting the popularity of commemorative oratory and appealing to what remained of the old national consensus.

Meanwhile, controversy over the Compromise of 1850 was destroying the Whig party, which refused to nominate the incumbent president, Millard Fillmore, in 1852. Shortly thereafter, the death of Everett's good friend Daniel Webster left the president without a secretary of state, and Everett accepted the job, serving the last four months in Fillmore's lame-duck administration. When the administration left office in March 1853, Everett entered the U.S. Senate, to which he had been elected by a coalition of Cotton Whigs and conservative Democrats. A year later, the Senate passed the Kansas-Nebraska bill, which Everett opposed on the grounds that it would reignite the slavery controversy and ultimately destroy the Union. Everett, however, was absent for the vote, apparently because of a misunderstanding about when it would be taken; but he was attacked bitterly at home for his failure to vote against the bill. Utterly depressed, Everett resigned from the Senate and went home to brood about the demise of the old national consensus.

Everett decided to withdraw from the world that was falling apart. He planned to write a scholarly magnum opus, an idea he had toyed with for years, but nothing materialized. Instinctively drawn to the oratorical platform, he saw the potentialities of the lyceum movement, which had begun in the 1820s but was now moving beyond its "first phase" (when "local boys" did the speaking) to a second phase that featured professional lecturers who traveled from place to place (Braden 1948). He repeated lectures on "Charities," "Astronomy," and "Franklin, the Boston Boy," but his most famous "lecture" (actually an epideictic oration) was on "The Character of Washington." Still believing that remembrances of America's heroes might save the Union, he delivered "Washington" a total of 137 times between 1856 and 1860, and the tours took him to all sections of the country. He raised $70,000 (plus an additional $10,000 from a series of newspaper articles entitled "Mount Vernon Papers"), all of which he contributed to the Ladies Mount Vernon Association for the purchase of Mount Vernon. Making Washington's home a national memorial, he hoped, would restore the national consensus and save the Union (Reid 1990, 80–85; 1957, 144–56).

Despite Everett's rhetorical efforts to preserve the Union, the nation rushed toward disunion. In 1860, Everett was the vice-presidential candidate for the ill-fated Constitutional Union party; and he joined some other "old line Whigs," as he called them, in urging Congress to enact Crittenden's proposed compromise that, if passed, would allegedly save the Union. Discouraged by his failure, Everett privately told his friends that the South should be allowed to depart in peace; but after the Confederacy attacked Fort Sumter, he vigorously supported Lincoln's war policy. His Fourth of July oration, delivered shortly after the outbreak of hostilities in 1861, was a pro-war speech that circulated widely in several pamphlet editions. He spoke at rallies to raise funds and recruit volunteers for the Union army. He returned to the lecture circuit with an argumentative speech on "The Causes and Conduct of the Civil War," which he delivered sixty times. He is probably best known today for delivering the main oration at Gettysburg in 1863; but today's critics, unlike Everett's contemporaries, usually overlook the fact that his Gettysburg oration was more than an encomium to those who fell in battle. It was also an argumentative speech justifying the Union cause; and the inclusion of argumentation, although criticized bitterly by Copperheads, was much appreciated by Lincoln supporters (and Lincoln himself) because "peace sentiment" was widespread at the time (Reid 1967; 1990, 94–103).

In October 1864, the old orator who had eschewed campaign speaking delivered an electioneering speech for Lincoln. His last oration, delivered a week before his sudden death in January 1865, was to raise funds for war victims. Thus ended the life of the "Cicero of America," a life filled with paradoxes.

## Edward Everett: The Cicero of America?

One paradox is that Everett's political career was furthered by his oratory, but he was unable or unwilling to adapt to many significant changes in the nation's oratorical culture that resulted from the new politics. He had trouble adapting his deliberative oratory to sectionalism and the new party system. Except for the electioneering speech for Lincoln in 1864, he consistently avoided campaign speaking.

This paradox makes us wonder about the appropriateness of calling Everett the "Cicero of America." We remember Cicero primarily for what ancient rhetoricians called deliberative and forensic oratory (i.e., his senatorial and courtroom speaking), not epideictic oratory; but Everett's reputation is the exact opposite. This raises

another paradox. As congressman and senator, Everett spoke on
many controversial issues, including the tariff, nullification, Indian
policy, foreign policy, and the Kansas-Nebraska Act. Yet his oratorical
reputation did not extend to his political speaking. For example, one
contemporary critic was so enthusiastic in praising Everett's epideictic
speaking that even the egocentric Everett was embarrassed; but the
critic dismissed Everett's congressional oratory as unworthy of attention (Parker 1857, 262–326). Contemporary books on American oratory were uniformly enthusiastic about Everett's epideictic oratory
while ignoring his deliberative addresses (Allibone 1858, 569–72;
Loring 1853, 525–46; Magoon 1849, 65–116). When searching for
magazine reviews of Everett's oratory, I found almost no contemporary reviews of his deliberative speeches, but I located over three
dozen items about his lectures and ceremonial addresses, almost all of
which ranged from favorable to ecstatic (Reid 1990, 258–65).

Explaining these paradoxes is not easy; but it is clear that Everett,
in sharp contrast to Cicero, wished to be remembered primarily for
his nonpartisan speaking. Although he published many of his congressional speeches as pamphlets, he deliberately limited his collected *Orations and Speeches on Various Occasions* to nonpartisan addresses. The collection, of course, quickly became the most readily
available source of speech texts for his contemporaries, to say nothing
of later generations. It was first published in one volume in 1836.
Second and third volumes were added in 1850 and 1859, and the set
was reprinted three times during Everett's lifetime. When his son
published a posthumous edition, he added a fourth volume, which
included Everett's argumentative Civil War speeches; but the first
three volumes were merely reprints of earlier editions. Thus the
standard four-volume collection, which reached a twelfth edition by
1895, consisted mostly of lectures and epideictic orations.

Everett's efforts to preserve the Union were reminiscent of Cicero's attempt to save the Roman Republic, but their oratorical methods
were not the same. Cicero relied primarily on deliberative and forensic
oratory whereas Everett relied primarily on epideictic speeches and
argumentative "lectures." Yet Cicero, unlike critics who dismiss Everett's oratory as grandiloquent, would certainly have understood and
probably endorsed Everett's attempt to save the Union by reminding
audiences of their "glorious past." Cicero probably would have also
endorsed Everett's pro-war argumentative speaking during the Civil

War. Whether Cicero would have endorsed Everett's unwillingness to engage in campaign oratory or his reluctance to adapt to the new partisanship is another question. I suspect he would not. In terms of Everett's purpose of saving the Union, therefore, Everett was a Ciceronian; but in terms of rhetorical method, he was only a semi-Ciceronian.

Although Everett's reputation as the "Cicero of America" was not quite on the mark, it is understandable. After all, his fame, like Cicero's, rested heavily on oratory and his goal of saving the Republic.

## Everett the Academician

Everett's semi-Ciceronianism cannot be attributed entirely to his formal education; but a look at his academic career, with emphasis on its rhetorical component, shows that classicism was a major, although not exclusive, influence. After first sketching the neoclassical education he received, I shall examine his educational philosophy, noting especially his attitudes toward rhetorical education and the trends that were moving academe away from the old generalist ideal to the new professionalism.

As the nation's first Ph.D., Everett had an unusually extensive formal education. His doctorate in classics from the world's premier university in classical studies made him well versed in Greco-Roman rhetoric and oratory. Yet we should be wary of attaching too much significance to his doctoral studies. German scholars studied classical rhetoric for the same reason they studied the classics in general: to understand Greco-Roman culture and literature. Living in a monarchical society, the Germans, unlike rhetoricians such as Cicero and Isocrates, had no interest in preparing students to participate in public affairs. Although Everett did not comment explicitly on this difference, his ambivalence about German education suggests that he was aware of it. Scattered throughout his private correspondence are favorable comments about the superior scholarship of the Germans mixed with disparaging remarks about them. They were boorish, irreligious, and more like "tradesmen" than gentlemen. Like good tradesmen, they knew their business very well, but they were tradesmen nonetheless. The Germans studied Cicero, but they gave students no training in the Ciceronian art of adapting oratory to the exigencies of current political life. They exemplified the academic specialization that, as the editors of this book point out in the Introduction, divorced rhetoric from public affairs.

We must turn to Everett's undergraduate education to find evidence of classical training in the practical art of persuading citizens, but even here the evidence is a bit mixed. American colleges during the early nineteenth century had a standard curriculum that was prescribed for all undergraduates. When Everett was a student, the only elective course was Hebrew; but Everett and the other students who took it did so in addition to the prescribed courses, not as a substitute. The curriculum emphasized classical languages and culture, but the curriculum was not exclusively classical. Christian theology was included, and Christian morality permeated courses in ethics, moral philosophy, and the like. Although not felt as intensely at Harvard as it was at John Witherspoon's College of New Jersey, the Scottish Enlightenment also influenced Everett's education. Students imbibed the "new learning" with its moral philosophy, natural philosophy, and political economy.

The college ideal was to produce what even the supposedly egalitarian Thomas Jefferson called a "natural aristocracy," or what today we might call "opinion leaders." Colleges originally concerned themselves with only one type of future opinion leader, the preacher; but long before Everett entered college, a new concept of "civic humanism" had emerged. Colleges were to educate future statesmen, lawyers, and politicians as well as future ministers. The new "civic humanism" was reflected in a moral exhortation that carried over from the old colonial ideal of a society with common interests: Leaders were to promote the public welfare as a whole, not to promote parties, factions, and special interests. This antipartyism, with its emphasis on consensus, was an important aspect of Everett's education because it precluded rhetorical appeals to special interests. Whereas politicians of our generation appeal blatantly to special interests when they take to the stump ("I've done this for the farmer, something else for women, something else for our glorious universities," and so on, ad infinitum, ad nauseam), the gentlemanly Whigs that Harvard produced were expected to eschew such appeals. Nor were they taught how to disguise appeals to special interests under the banner of the "public good." They had to learn it by experience, and Everett never learned it very well.

The new civic humanism was also reflected in what happened to the teaching of rhetoric. In the early colonial period, students gave classroom speeches and argued theses, and they continued to do so for generations thereafter; but by the late eighteenth century, current political issues began to destroy the monopoly that religious topics had formerly enjoyed (Halloran 1982, 251; Potter 1944, 46–47). John Ward's *Lectures on Oratory* became the most popular rhetorical textbook (Guthrie 1947, 44–45). It was organized and developed along classical lines (with lectures on invention, disposition, style, memory, and delivery); but it was studied, not simply to understand ancient culture, as the Germans studied Roman rhetoric, but to teach students the practical art of preparing and presenting persuasive public discourses about public affairs.

A year before Everett entered college, Harvard activated one of its earliest specialized professorships: the Boylston Professorship of Rhetoric and Oratory, the statutes for which were modeled upon Ward's *Lectures*. The first occupant was John Quincy Adams, whose lectures were for the two upper classes; but Everett listened to many of them during his first two years. Adams resigned before Everett's junior year; and Everett then listened to the lectures of Joseph McKean, which were also organized and developed along the lines specified by the statutes (Reid 1959, 240–44; 1960). Both professors supervised Everett while he recited declamations (memorized rhetorical masterpieces), delivered public speeches, and wrote argumentative compositions.

The civic humanism, the classical rhetorical theory, and the exercises in speaking and writing that permeated Everett's undergraduate education obviously prepared him to be a "classical orator." Yet his rhetorical education was not strictly classical. Adams modified the classical concept of invention to meet American legal and legislative standards. Hugh Blair's *Lectures on Rhetoric and Belles Lettres* was a required text, and McKean drew frequently from eighteenth-century Scottish rhetoricians. Perhaps more important, Everett said many years later that "when I was at college, the English authors most read and admired, at least by me, and I believe generally by my contemporaries, were Johnson, Gibbon, and Burke" ([1850] 1878, 2:vii). He mentioned no classical models.

The encroachment of eighteenth-century British rhetoric raises the difficult question of whether it was "classical." On one hand, Blair often referred to ancient authors, talked about the classical rhetorical

genres, and prescribed an organizational pattern for speeches that
was basically Ciceronian. On the other hand, Blair scorned the
classical inventional topoi and used a different typology for classify-
ing style. He broadened his subject to include historical writings and
other types of discourse as well as persuasive public speeches. He also
broadened his subject to include belles lettres, or "polite literature," as
it was often called. As one of the leading "Moderate preachers" of
Scotland, Blair insisted that preachers avoid "barbarisms," employ a
"pure style," and act like "gentlemen." Integral to being a gentleman,
the Moderates claimed, was avoiding "factionalism" and "fanaticism"
(although they promoted their own faction). There is some scholarly
disagreement about the relationship of belletristic rhetoric to Ciceronianism; but I agree with Thomas Miller, who says that "while traces
of the classical interest in political rhetoric can be seen in . . . [Blair],
political discourse is given far less attention than literary issues like
sublimity and genius." Blair was essentially "apolitical" (1990, 9, 24).
To the extent that Blair encouraged young readers such as Everett to be
political, it was a political moderation that reinforced Harvard's antipartyism and its belief that a general liberal arts education best served
society.

Although he learned political moderation, Everett said later that
he was almost totally devoid of political interests during his undergraduate years; however, he was intensely interested in literary topics. While studying for his M.A. in theology, his favorite preacher was
Joseph S. Buckminster, Jr., a Unitarian who fascinated his upper-class
congregation with what the orthodox professor of sacred rhetoric at
Andover Seminary disparagingly called "polite" sermons (Porter
1834, 61). During his brief preaching career, Everett also delivered
"polite" sermons (Reid 1990, 16–19).

Given his early lack of interest in politics, his youthful career as a
"polite preacher," his literary interests, and his disdain of "party
spirit," it is somewhat amazing that Everett went into politics. Yet he
did, and when he did, he brought a rhetorical education that blended
belletristic moderation with classical civic humanism.

The blend of classical and belletristic education both prepared
and failed to prepare Everett for the changing oratorical culture of his
times. His classical education gave him a good grasp of ancient theory,
which his teachers adapted to the practical business of persuading
nineteenth-century Americans, and it gave him plenty of exercises in

writing and speaking. He learned how to organize and develop his orations along classical lines. His education also promoted Everett's dedication to civic humanism, which he interpreted to mean that he should promote the public good by persuading the citizenry to preserve the Union. Yet the schoolboy Everett imbibed too much moderation to allow the future orator to take to the stump. He did not learn how to adapt to the egalitarianism of the Jacksonian era, and all he learned to do about "party spirit," especially the abolitionists' "fanaticism," was to bemoan it. He learned how to give deliberative speeches in Congress, but the plain fact is that they were not very good. Most of them were badly organized and filled with so much historical data that his main points were often obscured (Reid 1990, 33–46). In short, his classical education prepared him to follow Cicero in speaking about public affairs, but his belletristic education encouraged him to do so in a polite and moderate way. His education was a neoclassical one that was well suited for training eighteenth-century statesmen-orators, and Everett's later success shows that eighteenth-century educational ideals were not totally abandoned even as late as the Civil War. The ideals were especially popular among genteel Americans, most notably the conservative Whigs and literati with whom Everett associated in both his private and public life. On the other hand, Everett's failures show that the old educational ideals did not adequately prepare him for the nineteenth century in which he lived.

When the mature Everett looked back on his schoolboy education, he became somewhat ambivalent about the importance of rhetoric, but he never advocated its abolition. Much of his ambivalence, I suspect, resulted from his growing fears that "demogogues" were destroying the national consensus.

The ambivalence was not present during Everett's early political career, when he was still confident about both his and the nation's future. As a young adult, Everett insisted repeatedly on the importance of rhetorical training. "It is astonishing," the newly elected congressman lamented in his diary after listening to a bad sermon, "that those who adopt the profession of public speakers are not taught to speak" (August 28, 1825, Everett papers). He reminded Joseph Cogswell, a German-educated scholar who was then conducting an elementary school modeled on the German gymnasium, of "the importance of early training in the art of speaking" (letter, June

12, 1828, Everett papers). Nor did he keep his views private. For example, as he neared the end of an essay on deliberative oratory, he asserted: "The objects to be promoted, and the duties to be performed by the public speaker, in this country, are as important as they were in ancient Rome. Let us see what pains were thought due by a Roman statesman and orator to the acquisition of the art" (1827b, 448); and he concluded with a three-page translation of Cicero's account of his rhetorical training.

The young Everett's enthusiasm for oratorical training extended to elocution (in the modern sense of delivery). In a favorable review of Ebenezer Porter's elocution manual, Everett again resorted to classical authority: "By the ancients, the art of speaking well was taught with greater application and assuidity, on the part of both master and pupil, than we can now fully realize or believe" (1827a, 334). He filled the essay with citations to show the meticulous attention paid to delivery by Quintilian, Demosthenes, and Cicero.

The first, albeit small, indication of Everett's waning enthusiasm for rhetorical education came in 1835, when Governor Everett reviewed a collection of Daniel Webster's speeches. Pronouncing Webster to be equal to Demosthenes and Cicero, Everett discussed the sources of their eloquence. He said that the ancients were better trained, and he acknowledged that "training, discipline, [and] practice, are good, nay indispensable" (1835, 234). Yet training was not enough, and he implied that the ancients had overdone it. Demosthenes, Cicero, and Webster were eloquent because "they were men of talent, men of sense, men of ambition, men of industry, and they lived in stirring times" (1835, 235). This analysis was consistent with the Ciceronian view that oratorical skill comes from a mixture of nature, training, and experience, but it lacked the enthusiasm for rhetorical education that characterized his earlier writings, and it hinted that the ancients had overemphasized training in rhetorical technique.

We would have a better idea of precisely how much and what kind of rhetorical education the older Everett supported if his presidency of Harvard (1846–1849) had not been so short and if it had not been dominated by controversies that are irrelevant to curricular questions. He became absorbed with disciplinary matters (what to do about students who threw chestnuts at Professor Ware during his lectures, those who entertained females in the dormitory rooms, and those who imbibed alcohol), and he created a huge controversy, especially with alumni, when he insisted on calling the college the University of Cambridge instead of Harvard.

Nevertheless, his four-year presidency provides considerable evidence that he was willing to modify, but not abandon, the Ciceronian tradition. On one hand, he persuaded a prominent industrialist, Abbott Lawrence, to finance a new "Lawrence Scientific School in the University of Cambridge." This was an adjustment to the professionalism that was beginning to affect American education, and Everett believed sincerely that not all students should be required to follow the traditional liberal arts curriculum.

On the other hand, Everett insisted that undergraduates in the old college continue to follow a prescribed curriculum. He set himself against the elective system that was then in its early stages—a system that permits students to substitute specialization for breadth and, as the editors point out in the Introduction, has promoted the decline of rhetorical education. Despite his own Ph.D. from a German university, where the elective system prevailed, he opposed faculty members who tried to institute elective courses, and some private comments reveal that he was thoroughly disgusted with them. For example, after attending "Dr[.] Beck's examination of the Seniors in Cicero's oration for Cluentius," he wrote caustically in his diary: "A few [students] appeared quite well but several did very poorly, shewing the entire futility of the notion, —strenuously urged by Dr[.] Beck himself, —that the Elective system secures a good degree of scholarship for all" (December 23, 1846, Everett papers). Everett did not explicate the prescribed curriculum he favored, but he left the impression that he was satisfied with the one he inherited. It minimized specialization and was not substantially different from the neoclassical one Everett himself had studied a generation before.

The curriculum of President Everett's day had a substantial rhetorical component, although the Boylston Professor, Edward T. Channing, departed from his predecessors' practice of delivering lectures that followed the classical formula. Moreover, Channing broadened the scope of rhetoric so that it included not just persuasive discourse about public affairs but also written and spoken composition generally. He changed textbooks from time to time, but he relied on modern writers, especially George Campbell and Richard Whately. Nonetheless, Channing's approach included a considerable amount of practical instruction in writing and speaking (Anderson 1949; Reid 1959, 246–49). As far as I know, Everett was happy with it.

Additional evidence of Everett's insistence on a broad liberal arts education that included rhetorical study consists of an Everett manuscript, which is undated but was apparently prepared during his college presidency and now resides in the Harvard Archives. Entitled "List of Books recommended to be read by students while at the university," it included many eighteenth-century works such as Adam Smith's *Wealth of Nations*, and it gave heavy emphasis to biography, history, politics, and ethics. The rhetorical-literary works consisted of Quintilian's *Institutes*, George Campbell's *Philosophy of Rhetoric*, Lord Kames's *Elements of Criticism*, Edmund Burke's *On the Sublime and Beautiful*, and Fenelon's *Dialogues Concerning Eloquence* and *Reflections sur le Rhetorique et sur la Poetique*. Many of the rhetorical works were classical in orientation, but despite the somewhat surprising absence of Blair, it made room for the belletristic. Admittedly, the list was not "classical" in the strict sense of meaning only ancient authors, but it was "classical" in the Ciceronian sense of requiring a broad liberal arts education, including rhetorical instruction.

However, within a few years after his departure from Harvard, Everett was privately expressing serious doubts about rhetorical education. For example, after attending some school exercises in declamation and debate, the diarist wrote, "I find that a great deal too much time is given at our schools & at college to declamation & composition" (November 11, 1854, Everett papers).

Unfortunately for us, Everett never explained why his enthusiasm was waning. Yet it seems safe to do a little speculating, and my conjectures are threefold. First, as he matured he became increasingly aware of the importance of audience and occasion, something that Cicero said cannot be taught by rhetorical rules. "The effect of public speaking," Everett once remarked in his diary, "is a curiously complicated result of the action and reaction between speaker & hearer; — to which the latter contributes as much as the former" (August 30, 1846). After reading Pericles' funeral oration, the diarist observed: "It seems scarcely possible that such an address should have stirred the blood of the Athenians: but all depends on times & places and men" (June 1, 1850). Everett's rhetorical practice also shows a keen awareness of audience and occasion. For example, when he started to prepare his oft-repeated "lecture" on "The Character of Washington," he deliberately selected Washington's birthday for the first delivery because he recognized that the date would put the audience in a receptive frame of mind. Whether his sensitivity to audience and occasion helps explain Everett's declining enthusiasm for rhetorical training is, of course, only conjectural, but it certainly shows an awareness of Lady Rhetoric's limitations.

A second conjecture relates to the nation's changing political and oratorical culture and Everett's difficulties in adapting to the changes. In 1850, when disunion appeared imminent and Everett was disgruntled about his political unemployment, he speculated about the sources of political influence. Citing Cicero's observation that success comes from either military or oratorical prowess, the diarist wondered about the success of Franklin, Madison, and Monroe, none of whom he regarded as proficient in either art. His answer: "Upon the whole the acquisition of political influences is an extremely uncertain & capricious affair" (April 29, 1850). On another occasion, the diarist pronounced the electioneering practice of "'stumping the state,' which has been lately introduced," to be "one of the downward tendencies" of the age; and after reiterating his refusal to participate, he sarcastically observed that campaigning should be left to "advertisers" (October 20, 1853). On still another occasion, after he had devoted an evening to reading Aeschines' speech against Demosthenes, he told his diary, "It is instructive to see how little the arts of demogogy have changed in 21 hundred years" (June 14, 1853). Again, we can only speculate, but it seems reasonable to suppose that his enthusiasm for rhetorical education was lessened by the "demogogy" of contemporary politicians and his own political difficulties. The speculation is reinforced by the fact that his reservations were expressed during the late 1840s and early 1850s, when his political career was stymied. They disappeared by the late 1850s, when Everett was enjoying unparalleled success with "Washington" and other lectures.

A third conjecture requires us to proceed indirectly, beginning with Everett's private criticisms of the unnatural manner and lack of passion that characterized many speakers he heard during his later life. For example, within the span of six weeks, the diarist reacted negatively to two preachers (one of whom was a good friend) because of these qualities. One spoke "with great ingenuity, good sense & eloquence; but with a kind of formality in the manner which impairs the effect" (May 10, 1846). A second preached "with great ability & good sense, but apparently with no effect; nor am I sure that any important good effect is to be produced by appeals to reason in a calm and unimpassioned strain" (June 28, 1846).

Everett's emphasis on naturalness and passion is ironic because the lack of these qualities was the major adverse criticism of his oratory even in his own time, to say nothing of ours. For example, a critic of his "Washington" lecture said: "Correct, polished, beautiful as the notes of the Dorian flute, his sentences were *rhythmically*, as harmonious as Art and study could make them, but they lacked that Promethian fire, that energy divine, which can only be imparted to language by the inner workings of the spirit, by the inspiration born of passion, and winged with enthusiasm" ("Editor's Table" 1858, 181). This is not to suggest that Everett was "raked over the coals" by this critic, because he, like most reviewers, was generally favorable towards the orator. Yet the fact remains that artificiality and lack of passion were noted often.

Perhaps even more ironically, Everett agreed with his critics. "I am afraid," he confessed to his diary, that "my manner is too stately:— not sufficiently flowing and natural" (December 22, 1845, Everett papers). Nor did he confine his self-criticism to his diary. In the preface to his second edition of collected orations (1850), he said that "in revising the earlier compositions in this collection for the present edition, I have applied the pruning-knife freely to the style. This operation might have been carried still farther with advantage; for I feel them to be still deficient in that simplicity which is the first merit in writings of this class." Implicitly blaming his education, he observed that his chief rhetorical models had been Johnson, Gibbon, and Burke. Then he added: "I yielded myself with boyish enthusiasm to their irresistible fascination. But the stately antithesis, the unvarying magnificence, and the boundless wealth of diction of these great masters . . . are too apt, on the part of youthful imitators, to degenerate into ambitious wordiness" ([1850] 1878, 1:vii–viii). Everett was even more explicit in a private diary entry. After repeating that "far too much attention is paid at our schools to speaking, and at college to writing," he added, "The style acquired at college is apt to be artificial and has to be unlearned in after life" (February 3, 1855, Everett papers).

Perhaps one of the greatest ironies about Everett is that he was called "classical" by those who criticized his artificiality, but he himself attributed his artificiality not to classical models but to eighteenth-century British models. We cannot help wondering why he did not propose better models. We are also left wondering about the exact place of rhetorical education in the older Everett's view. He never advocated its abolition, only less emphasis. Despite our confusion about details, it is clear that Everett's philosophy of education was heavily classical but that it was modified by his perceptions of changes within American society. The same is true of his theory of discourse, to which we shall now turn.

## Everett's Theory of Discourse

Although Everett never worked out a detailed theory of discourse, we can piece together several basic concepts from miscellaneous comments in his public speeches, private papers (especially diary entries), and reviews he wrote for literary periodicals. His remarks indicate that he was essentially a classicist but that he was also aware of—and usually (although not always) depressed by—the nation's changing oratorical culture. The frequency with which his remarks were amplified with references to Quintilian's *Institutes*, Tacitus's *Dialogue Concerning Oratory*, Cicero's rhetorical works, Greco-Roman orators, English parliamentarians, and contemporary American speakers also show that he had a thorough knowledge of rhetorical theory and practice, both ancient and modern.

Everett's first excursion into theory came in his Phi Beta Kappa oration (1824). It set forth two closely related ideas that were common currency among genteel Americans: Oratory is an essential tool of what our generation usually calls "democracy," but which Everett variously called "free" or "representative" or "republican" government; and freedom breeds eloquence if it does not become too factional and immoderate. He expressed a somewhat limited praise of ancient Greece and Rome, saying that "those tumultuous assemblies of Athens . . . [were] required to be addressed in the profoundly studied and exquisitely wrought orations of Demosthenes" (1878, 1:24); but he also reminded his audience that the Greek city-states and the Roman republic were "factious" at home and tyrannical toward their tributary states (1:12). Their freedom was sufficient to encourage a high level of eloquence, not just of a political nature but of all forms of discourse: "The deep philosophy, the impassioned drama and the grave history, were all produced for the entertainment of the 'fierce democratie' [*sic*] of Athens" (1:24). When freedom died in Greece and Rome, so did eloquence.

The United States, claimed the chauvinistic Phi Beta Kappa orator, was superior to the ancient democracies because it had a federal system that divided political power between the municipal, state, and central governments; and federalism, he asserted optimistically, encouraged universal education and popular participation in government, which, in turn, was encouraging a high quality of political eloquence. Nor was political oratory the only beneficiary: "Statesmen, and warriors, and poets, and orators, and artists, start up under one and the same excitement. They are all branches of one stock" (1:22). Perceiving all forms of eloquence to be "branches of one stock" was not anti-Ciceronian, but it was more reminiscent of Blair's belletristic ideas. In short, the Phi Beta Kappa orator saw republicanism as the cause of both political eloquence in the Ciceronian sense and "polite literature" in the belletristic sense.

The youth of American society made it premature, said Everett in 1824, to predict precisely what new literary genres would emerge, but he was confident that "forms of address wholly new will be devised" as a result of the nation's future progress (1:21–22). We cannot help being disappointed that Everett did not speculate about the new forms of address, but we know of two that he was already helping to bring into being. First, as editor of the *North American Review*, the nation's first successful literary periodical, he had already written dozens of articles that purported to be book reviews but were, in reality, essays on the same subjects as the books. The essay-review was a new genre that originated with the British literary quarterlies, and Everett helped introduce it to America. Second, by 1824, he had delivered popular lectures on classical art; and although it might be going too far to say that they constituted the "inauguration of the Lyceum System," as his admiring nephew once claimed, they predated Josiah Holbrook's founding of the lyceum movement in 1826 ([Hale] 1859, 334). In short, Everett's theory and practice showed an eagerness to adapt to new circumstances in the realm of what we might call "educational" discourse aimed at the general public. However, these innovations were not inconsistent with the old oratorical culture. To the contrary, they reflected a belief in the importance of educating the masses on a wide range of subjects so they could vote intelligently and maintaining a national consensus based on common knowledge and common ideals.

A few years later, Congressman Everett wrote more specifically about the deliberative genre of oratory. The nation's "representative system," he claimed, "is peculiarly adapted to bring the talent of public speaking into exercise" because "the people, as sovereign, seem to sit in audience to hear and judge of the reasons of what is proposed in public service" (1827b, 447). Like the chauvinist he was, he emphasized that the United States was more free than either ancient Rome or modern Britain; but somewhat surprisingly for a chauvinist, he admitted that British parliamentary eloquence was superior to that of the U.S. Congress. Why? The answer involved a chain of reasoning leading to the conclusion, "We may perhaps trace the superiority of the English parliamentary eloquence, in part, to circumstances incompatible with our free institutions" (432). Only a few British parliamentarians—the better ones—spoke, and when they did, it was to persuade their immediate audiences (Parliament and the politically informed populace of London), not their constituents at home; but "with us, the least concern of a member of Congress is how he stands at Washington. His heart is in Carolina, in Maine, or beyond the Alleganies [*sic*]. With these distant regions he communicates through the press. The speaking . . . is only the occasion, the justification, for publishing a speech in a newspaper, and perhaps in a pamphlet, to be sent home to his constituents" (430). Impressing constituents was unnecessary in Britain because re-election was assured by rotten boroughs, wealth, party loyalty, and family connections; but it was essential in America, causing American congressmen to speak often, irrespective of their ability. Much as Everett disliked "special interest" oratory, he was an astute enough theorist to recognize that appeals to the special interests of constituents were becoming the dominant mode of deliberative oratory.

Everett also noted that because there was no necessity of speed in getting a copy of his speech to his constituents and on-the-scene reporting was done haphazardly, a congressman could improve it in the privacy of his study; or "if, like Galba, his *forte* lie not so much in writing as in speaking, he may, as Galba did, get a friend to write it for him. Hence, by a process exceedingly different from that of actually making a handsome speech in his place, it is possible for any member to appear in the report, as the maker of a handsome speech" (439).

Everett's comments about deliberative oratory indicate a clear recognition that congressmen were "speaking" not to their immediate audience but to their constituents via the press, and this in turn showed an awareness of its potential for dividing the country. In contrast, he was a devout believer in the unifying function of epideictic oratory. Although he never discussed this function in detail, he made scores of incidental comments, such as the following from a Fourth of July oration: "It is the natural tendency of celebrating the fourth of July, to strengthen the sentiment of attachment to the Union" (1878, 1:380–81). This point needs emphasis because the tendency of modern critics to dismiss Everett as grandiloquent reflects a view that epideictic oratory is a meaningless genre. However, Everett consciously used it to achieve what he perceived to be the paramount oratorical task of his day: to persuade a divided nation to preserve the Union. His faith in epideictic never waned, as is indicated by his tireless efforts to raise funds for building a memorial to Washington at Mount Vernon in the years immediately preceding the Civil War. His major fund-raising vehicle, the "Washington" lecture, included what Everett privately called "unionist sentiments"—explicit appeals to preserve the Union and restore the national consensus (Reid 1990, 80–85; 1957).

## Neoclassical Features of Everett's Oratory

Despite Everett's self-professed desire to simplify his oratorical style, the plain unvarnished fact is that he did little revising of his early speeches for the second edition (1850) of his collected *Orations* and none for later editions (Reid 1990, 230–34). Nor did his rhetorical method change over time. We shall, therefore, pay little attention to delivery date as we examine the neoclassical features of his oratory.

Although Everett was best known, in his day and ours, as an epideictic orator and lecturer, a few words about his deliberative speaking are in order. After all, he delivered many legislative speeches, even though they apparently were not very effective, and his prowar speeches during the Civil War were highly regarded by Lincoln supporters. The classical formula for deliberative orations was introduced to Everett during his undergraduate days and reinforced in his mind by his subsequent classical studies. Nevertheless, his congressional and senatorial speeches were weakened rhetorically by two bad habits: He documented arguments with so much historical data that main points were often obscured, and he was so obsessed with refuting every conceivable counterargument that he often became disorganized and bogged down in trivia (Reid 1990, 33–46, 71–75). Yet both problems involved going too far with what was essentially sound classical advice. The Romans recommended (1) an attention-gaining and ethos-raising exordium, (2) a narrative of relevant historical facts, (3) a division of points into the agreed and contested, (4) a summary of the speaker's proposition and supporting arguments, (5) a confirmation of those points, (6) a refutation of counterarguments, and (7) a peroration. If Everett had done a little less narrating of history and had managed his refutations more expeditiously, his congressional and senatorial speeches would have exemplified the classical formula.

Unlike his legislative speeches, which were prepared hurriedly and often given in a raucous atmosphere, Everett's Civil War speeches were prepared more leisurely, and they were generally much better than his legislative orations. They followed the classical formula; but they also were dominated by too much history and refutation, as we can see by reviewing his oft-repeated "Causes and Conduct of the Civil War." His exordium was designed to gain the audience's attention and goodwill by praising the audience for its loyalty and commenting on the importance of the war. Then came a long narration of the sectional conflict that constituted approximately two-thirds of the speech. Starting even before the nullification controversy, the narrative included so much historical detail that inattentive or semiattentive listeners might have become confused; but attentive listeners would have realized that Everett was shaping his narration to refute the South's argument that it was a victim of Northern aggression. In Everett's narrative, secession was a long-standing conspiracy of self-serving Southern leaders. Everett then explicated the evils of permitting secession, refuted some Southern grievances, and concluded with an emotional peroration. I doubt if Quintilian would have awarded Everett an "A" on the speech, but it was certainly in the classical tradition. Its effectiveness, I suspect, was due less to what Everett said than to his ethos as a longtime moderate. Whereas some moderates were reluctant to support the war, and many were avidly opposed to Lincoln, Everett's enthusiastic support of Lincoln highlighted the fact that moderation was consistent with pro-war and pro-Lincoln sentiment.

Everett's first exposure to the classical formula for epideictic oratory was probably when he, as an underclassman, listened to John Quincy Adams's lectures; and when Everett arose in Boston's Faneuil Hall in 1848 to eulogize the recently deceased Adams, he followed almost to the letter the rhetorical formula he had learned from his former professor. In his lecture on "Arguments and Demonstrative Oratory," Adams told his students that "in formal panegyric there are two modes of proceeding. . . . The one may be called biographical, the other ethical panegyric. One proceeds from the object, and the other from the qualities. One takes its departure from the person, and the other from the virtue celebrated" (1810, 1:246). Adams also spoke approvingly of combining the two methods, which is what Everett did. The first (and longest) part of the eulogy was a chronologically organized biographical sketch that began with Adams's boyhood and ended with his death. The second enumerated and amplified Adams's virtues (Everett 1878, 2:555–96; see Reid 1990, 61–63 for a discussion of how Everett worked in Unionist appeals).

According to ancient rhetoricians, virtue was not the only topos available for eulogists, as Adams recognized when he mentioned that "a man may be panegyrized for the qualities of his mind, for bodily accomplishments, or for external circumstances," but whereas the *Rhetorica ad Herennium* and similar works gave painstaking attention to all these topoi, Adams emphasized that, for Christians, "the highest praise must be reserved for the first," especially for the mental quality of virtue (Adams 1810, 1:243). Everett followed his mentor, discoursing at length about Adams's honesty, lack of selfishness, habits of hard work, courage, and (in keeping with his Unionist purpose) antipartyism.

Adams also presented three rules for composing eulogies. The first was "a sacred and undeviating regard for truth"; but whereas a "mere biographer is bound . . . to notice the errors and failings, as well as the virtues and achievements of his hero," failings "may be covered [by a eulogist] with the veil of silence" (1:247). Learning this rule very well, Everett said nothing about the alleged deal that Adams made with Clay to gain the presidency or any other such incident.

Adams's second rule was that encomium "be specific. . . . Dwell on all important incidents, exclusively or at least peculiarly applicable to the person, of whom you speak" (1:250). Adams added that "the orator must suit his discourse to the disposition of the audience"

(1:251). Once again, Everett followed his teacher. For example, note the detail included in the following passage about Adams's boyhood, and note too that it recounted events that suited the "disposition" of his chauvinistic listeners and readers to admire Revolutionary heroes:

> In July, 1781, Mr[.] Dana, who, in the preceding October, had received a commission from Congress as minister plenipotentiary to the court of St[.] Petersburg, started for that capital, taking with him John Quincy Adams as private secretary and interpreter, being then just fourteen years of age. . . . But in Mr[.] Adams's career there was no boyhood. The youthful secretary remained at St[.] Petersburg till October, 1782, during which period, the nature of his occupations was such as to perfect his knowledge of the French language, and to give him, young as he was, no small insight into the political system of Europe, of which the American question was, at that time, the leading topic. He also devoted himself with assiduity to his studies, and pursued an extensive course of general reading. The official business of the American minister, who was not publicly received by the Empress Catharine, was mostly transacted with the Marquis de Verac, the French ambassador, between whom and Mr[.] Dana, young Adams acted as interpreter. In October, 1782, Mr[.] Adams senior brought to a close his arduous mission in Holland, by concluding a treaty of amity, navigation, and commerce with the States-General, which remains in force between the two countries to this day. . . . [A]bout the same time, his son left St[.] Petersburg for Holland. The young man, then but a little more than fifteen years of age, made the long journey from the Russian capital alone, passing through Sweden, Denmark, and the Hanse towns, and arriving at the Hague in the spring of 1783. (1878, 2:566–67)

This passage also illustrates Adams's final rule about composing epideictic orations: "The amusement of the audience, and the celebration of some favorite occasion or character, are the immediate purposes of the oration; but the speaker should propose to himself the further and nobler end of urging them to virtuous sentiment and beneficent action. Not by assuming the tone of a teacher . . ." ([1810], 1:251). In the above-cited passage, Everett did not explicitly assume the role of teacher, but the virtues of patriotism, self-reliance, and industry were clearly implied as models for imitation.

The passage also exemplifies a Ciceronian feature of Everett's oratory that is often overlooked by modern critics: stylistic adaptations to the specific end in view. Cicero said that the ultimate end of oratory is persuasion but that persuasion was effected via three subsidiary ends, each of which has its own proper style: the plain style for teaching, the middle style for pleasing, and the grand style for arousing emotions. Thus a good style, said Cicero, was "mixed." In keeping with this advice, which was reinforced by his Ciceronian rhetoric professors, Everett relied primarily on a plain or middle style in his eulogy of Adams. Everett is often condemned by our generation of critics for grandiloquence, but as I have emphasized elsewhere, his use of the grand style was usually limited to introductions and perorations (Reid 1990, 53–54, 97–98).

When Everett commemorated historical events (as distinguished from individuals), he usually employed a chronological arrangement, but he mixed in a considerable amount of praise and dispraise. For example, his Gettysburg Address began with a discussion of the secessionist movement and the Confederate attack on the North, after which he sketched the progress of the war and the military campaign that led to the Battle of Gettysburg. Then he traced in great detail the battle itself. As he proceeded through this historical narrative, he praised Andrew Jackson and condemned John Calhoun for their opposing stands on nullification, praised the heroism of the soldiers, and paid tribute to the nurses, thereby setting the stage for the argumentative portion of the oration that constituted the last half.

Everett's "lectures" were lectures only because they were advertised as such by sponsoring organizations. Almost always on historical topics, they were much like his epideictic orations. When his lectures were about historical events, they were organized chronologically, but he invariably worked in some praise and dispraise. For example, a public lecture, "Anecdotes of Early Local History," began with a historical sketch of the Massachusetts Historical Society (which sponsored the lecture), during which he praised the founder of the society as an "amiable, intelligent, and patriotic writer" (1878, 2:110).

When "lectures" were about individuals, Everett followed the same pattern he used in his eulogy of Adams: He devoted the first section to a chronologically organized biography (telling the truth but ignoring inconvenient facts) and devoted the second to explicating the person's virtues. The most famous such "lecture" was the one on "The Character of Washington," but the mere fact that it was delivered on the circuit does not preclude it from being classified as epideictic.

Indeed, the author of an exceedingly thorough study of epideictic oratory regards "Washington" as "one of the most perfect compositions in the history of . . . the eulogy" (Burgess 1902, 264).

In short, Everett was a "classical" orator. He departed somewhat from the deliberative formula, but he followed the epideictic formula to the letter.

## Conclusion

America's first Ph.D. was well versed in classical rhetorical theory and had the broad liberal arts education that Cicero believed essential for statesmen-orators. Everett's lectures and ceremonial orations were epideictic, and the epideictic orator followed rigorously classical precepts (or more accurately, John Q. Adams's version of the precepts). In keeping with Cicero's advice, Everett relied heavily on a middle style to please his audiences; but much of his teaching was plain, and he indulged occasionally in the grand. All of his orations and writings, whether deliberative or epideictic, exemplified Cicero's injunction to understand the present by understanding history. It is small wonder that Everett was called the "Cicero of America" both by his enemies and his friends; and Everett's popularity as an epideictic orator shows that remnants of the old oratorical culture remained throughout Everett's lifetime.

Yet Everett's political defeats and the posthumous decline of his reputation show that he was anything but an unqualified success. His difficulties resulted from an overcommitment to the moderation and politeness that was glorified by eighteenth-century belletristic rhetoricians. He was psychologically an eighteenth-century gentleman who could not quite come to terms with the changing oratorical culture of the nineteenth century in which he lived. He could, it is true, come to terms with the lecture movement; but this was because he believed strongly that America's representative government required an educated citizenry and that, as a member of the natural aristocracy, he was duty-bound to promote popular education. What the moderate gentleman could not do was to indulge in the raucous political oratory of his day. As a moderate gentleman, he could not bring himself to take to the stump. He could neither adapt to the nation's rising egalitarianism nor engage in blatant appeals to special interests.

Everett's career illustrates what was happening in the schools as well as in the larger society. The old rhetoric departments, which emphasized persuasive public speaking about public affairs, eventually became departments of English, which forgot Ciceronianism as they devoted themselves strictly to literary studies. Everett exemplifies the transition from classicism to polite literature. He was a neoclassical orator, partly Ciceronian and partly belletristic. He was successful primarily with those who appreciated this neoclassicism, that is, the more conservative genteel Americans; but his oratorical popularity extended to the general public. His lifetime popularity and the fact that his collected orations were reprinted frequently until thirty years after his death show that the neoclassical ideal was not dead, but his failures show that it was dying.

## Notes

1. Most of the Edward Everett papers are in the Massachusetts Historical Society. A microfilm edition was published by the society in 1972 along with a *Guide to the Microfilm Edition of the Edward Everett Papers*, ed. Franklin S. Allis, Jr., and Phyllis R. Girouard.

2. The 1878 version (9th edition) of the *Orations* is a reprint of the four-volume 7th edition (1868), the first three volumes of which are reprints of the 3d edition (1859). For convenience, all citations are to the 1878 edition.

# 2

# The Oratorical Poetic of
# Timothy Dwight ✻ *Gregory Clark*

✻Timothy Dwight, always first a minister, came to national prominence twice during his lifetime: Late in the eighteenth century he was
known as a self-consciously American poet, and early in the nineteenth he was known as the influential and innovative president of
Yale. Bringing to both roles the single purpose of establishing in the
new United States his vision of a regenerate nation, Dwight was
persistently a Calvinist committed to the concept of a republic. "The
primary mean[s] of originating and establishing public happiness, in
free communities," he insisted, "is . . . the formation of a good
personal character in their citizens." And by "good personal character" he meant "Virtue . . . in that enlarged and evangelical sense,
which embraces piety to God, Goodwill to mankind, and the effectual Government of ourselves" (1795, 12–13). Those words, preached
in his first year as president of Yale, are from *The True Means of
Establishing Public Happiness*, his widely circulated sermon that articulates his concept of American community. Asserting the proposition
that "as Public Happiness depends, in this country, at least, on the
personal character of its inhabitants . . . , so the promotion of Public
Happiness must, in a great measure, rest on personal exertions" (34–
35), Dwight described those exertions in explicitly evangelical terms
as "the whole energy of the Deity; of every perfect being [that] may
become the whole energy of man." Such "Virtue," he maintained, "of
necessity aims at the happiness of Society" (15).

For Dwight, then, public happiness results from individual citizenship that enacts a regenerate sort of virtue that must come of God's
grace. And he directed his work at Yale during the first two decades of
the nineteenth century toward preparing young men of New England

to promote that sort of citizenship in the new nation. He believed Yale to be "the fountain from which flow the laws of the state and its whole jurisprudence, the rules which form its happy society, and the doctrines and precepts which are inculcated in its churches" (1821, 1:150) and placed himself at its center by functioning as both professor of divinity and professor of rhetoric throughout his presidency.[1] Much of what he taught as divinity and all that he taught as rhetoric directed his students to use public discourse to edify the individual virtue and thus the moral citizenship of those they would address. The theory that guided both courses, however, is not so much a theology or rhetoric as a poetic that the poet Dwight had articulated late in the eighteenth century, before his call to Yale.[2]

My purpose here is to begin with this poetic, pieced together from his early writings about poetry in America and read in terms of both the moral philosophy of the Scottish Enlightenment and the theology of American evangelical Calvinism that appear to be its eighteenth-century sources. With Dwight's poetic explained, I will then examine his teaching of theology and rhetoric at Yale during the first two decades of the nineteenth century in its terms. My point is that Dwight developed and taught a theory of public discourse, both sacred and secular, that is poetic in its focus on the motivating force of the language of sentiment while traditionally oratorical in its commitment to engage those it addresses in the project of shaping and sustaining a common moral and political culture.[3] Finally, though, it is persistently homiletical, treating the language of sentiment as, more or less, a means of grace. In arguing this point, I am suggesting a general observation about the politics of oratorical culture in the early United States. In post-Puritan New England, at least, oratorical culture combined neoclassical and Calvinist political assumptions in a model for community that would authorize in republican America a ruling class.

## Dwight's Poetic and Its Eighteenth-Century Sources

Convinced that "the stability of public happiness is produced by Knowledge and Virtue" (Dwight 1795, 27) — with knowledge developed through "religious education" and virtue through the gift of grace that attends upon "public worship" — Dwight taught and practiced an oratorical poetic that directed public address to sentiment before intellect. In doing that, he drew upon the highly moralized but

increasingly secularized notion of taste learned from the moral philosophers and rhetoricians of the Scottish Enlightenment. But because he was attempting to arrest if not reverse that process of
secularization in America, Dwight addressed sentiment in the language of grace learned from the writings of his grandfather, Jonathan
Edwards. So while he followed the Scots in placing appeal to refined
and refining sentiment at the center of moral persuasion, Dwight's
appeal was inflected by Edwards's use of taste as a metaphor to
describe the effects of grace. This notion of taste functioned as an
evangelical aesthetic that guided his poetry and his preaching as well
as the theology and rhetoric he taught at Yale. Blurring the boundary
between rhetoric and poetic, it did the homiletical work of appealing
to sentiments that would nurture the regenerate virtue that he believed functions as a powerful public bond.

He explained that function in the introduction to his last major
poem, *Greenfield Hill*, by asserting the primacy of poetry as public
discourse that best treats "truth [that] requires little illustration, and
only needs to be set in a strong and affecting light." Poetry, he
maintained, "will be more deeply felt, and more lastingly remembered; and, to say the least, it will . . . be an unusual, and for that
reason, may be a forcible method of treating several subjects, handled
in this poem" ([1794] 1969, 7).[4] Those subjects were the enactments of
public happiness visible to him from the hill that dominated the
parish of Greenfield in Connecticut where he was minister and
schoolmaster for twelve years. Dwight was convinced that he could
best "contribute to the . . . improvement in manners, and in econom-
ical, political, and moral sentiments" by portraying that view in
language addressed directly to the sentiments—the feelings—that
would propel his "countrymen" to individual commitment and action
(6). This conviction that sentiment is the primary motivation follows
Scottish moral philosophers such as Francis Hutcheson (*Essays on the
Nature and Conduct of the Passions and Affections*, 1728) and Adam Smith
(*The Theory of Moral Sentiments*, 1759). For Hutcheson, neither reason
nor passion moves people to action but the felt perception of the
individual moral sense. For Smith, that perception is felt as sympathy—the sense of human "fellow feeling" ([1759] 1976, 3) that enables
individuals to understand and desire what is "right, laudable, and
virtuous" as well as to recognize and reject what is "wrong, blamable,
and vicious" (321).[5]

Addressing the moral sense of his readers in order to refine in them sentiments that would direct their action toward the common good was Dwight's purpose in the portraits of virtue enacted that he presented in *Greenfield Hill*. An instance of that is the final section of the poem, "The Vision," presenting scenes designed to provoke the feelings that would direct individual action toward the common good. Having catalogued the natural wealth of the landscape, he portrayed that public happiness in practice:

> See the wide realm in equal shares possess'd!
> How few the rich, or poor! how many bless'd!
> O happy state! the state, by Heaven design'd
> To rein, protect, employ, and bless mankind;
> Where Competence, in full enjoyment, flows;
> Where man least vice, and highest virtue, knows;
> Where the mind thrives; strong nerves th' invention string;
> And daring Enterprise uplifts his wing;
> Where Splendour spreads, in vain, his peacock hues;
> Where vagrant Sloth, the general hiss pursues;
> Where Business reigns, the universal queen;
> Where none are slaves, or lords; but all are men:
> No nuisant drones purloin the earner's food;
> But each man's labour swells the common good.
>
> ([1794] 1969, 153)

This portrait, Dwight believed, would make the principles assert-ed "more deeply felt, and more lastingly remembered" than any "logical discussion," a belief inherent in the Scots' position that sentiment, not thought, sharpens the moral sense that directs action. The specific principles portrayed here, as well as his concept of the sentiment that would provoke their enactment, were inflected and intensified by his religion. This becomes clear in the final lines of *Greenfield Hill* that envision the new nation as a gathering of the godly in an attempt to constitute that community by addressing in its prospective members sentiments susceptible to perfection by grace:

> From yon blue wave, to that far distant shore,
> Where suns decline, and evening oceans roar,
> Their eyes shall view one free elective sway;
> One blood, one kindred, reach from sea to sea;
> One language spread; one tide of manners run;

> One scheme of science, and of morals one;
> And God's own Word the structure, and the base.
> One faith extend, one worship, and one praise.
> There shall they see, amaz'd; and these convey.
> On rapture's pinions, o'er the distant sea;
> New light, new glory, fire the general mind,
> And peace, and freedom, re-illume mankind.

(526)

These lines from his poetry illustrate the homiletical function that characterizes the oratorical poetic that drove Dwight's practice of public discourse and, perhaps more importantly, his teaching of rhetoric and theology at Yale. I want to examine more closely the roots of this poetic in his concept of taste derived from two disparate eighteenth-century traditions: the moral philosophy and rhetoric of the Scottish Enlightenment, and American evangelical Calvinism. This examination will enable me to explore the socially stratifying function of the theory of public discourse Dwight developed for the new republic. Nan Johnson observes that "the doctrine of taste and the critical rationale for rhetoric it promotes rely on the assumption that principles of taste embody 'natural' inclinations brought to greater conscious awareness" (1991, 86). I want to use this examination of Dwight's version of that doctrine and rationale to suggest that, at least tacitly for him and for those who followed him, taste expressed what amounted to a *super*natural authority that would lend to the discourse of those who claimed it a powerful voice in nineteenth-century Protestant America. It is a suggestion that I hope will contribute to our awareness of the political function of the concept of taste.

Taste in the Scottish Tradition

*Taste* was the Scots' term for the refined moral sentiment that was object and effect of the poetic appeal, and to place taste at the center of rhetorical theory was an important element in the project of the eighteenth-century Scottish Enlightenment. An early contributor to the development of the concept is Hutcheson (1728), who argued that moral and aesthetic perception are not reasoned but felt through an internal counterpart to the five external senses. Taste is the name given this internal sense by subsequent Scot moralists and critics who treated its refinement in individuals as prerequisite to public virtue. According to John Dwyer (1987), this concept of the public function of taste was developed to preserve moral community in the emerging individualistic culture of an increasingly secularized and commercialized Scotland. In 1751, Henry Home, Lord Kames, articulated the moral ground for the public function of taste in his *Essays on the Principles of Morality and Natural Religion* by connecting the moral sentiment of "sympathy" to the refinement of individual judgment and virtue. He described that sentiment emerging naturally from our "participation of the joys and miseries of our fellow creatures" as the "great cement of human society" (16–17). First in 1761, and then in subsequent editions of his *Elements of Criticism*, Kames used the term *taste* to connect this moral sentiment to the aesthetic: "The reasonings employed on the fine arts are of the same kind with those that regulate our conduct" ([1785] 1972, 7); and "no occupation attaches a man more to his duty, than that of cultivating a taste in the fine arts" (176).

Dwight was familiar with Kames's treatment of taste, having used *Elements of Criticism* in 1771 to guide the informal and extracurricular instruction he provided in rhetoric and English literature as a tutor at Yale. But he was more familiar with Hugh Blair's, whose *Lectures on Rhetoric and Belles Lettres* he used throughout his presidency as the textbook to accompany his own lectures on rhetoric to the senior class. Blair's first lecture describes the public function of taste in terms of the practice of criticism: "True criticism . . . is the offspring of good sense and refined taste. . . . It teaches us, in a word, to admire and to blame with judgment" ([1783] 1965, 1:9). This explicit connection of criticism to praise and blame probably derives from the moral philosophy of Blair's teacher, Adam Smith, who explained the public function of private sentiment in *The Theory of Moral Sentiments* by placing the sentiment of sympathy—"our fellow-feeling with any person whatever" ([1759] 1976, 5)—at the center of social morality. Observing that the "correspondence of the sentiments of others with our own appears to be a cause of pleasure, and the want of it a cause of pain" (11), Smith connected pleasure and pain to praise and blame in order to argue that "praise-worthiness and blame-worthiness [express] what naturally ought to be the sentiments of other people with regard to our character and conduct" (183).

Moral people, according to Smith, seek praiseworthiness and avoid blameworthiness. The desire to act in sympathy with other moral people is provoked by an increasingly keen sentiment, or sensibility, of a shared concept of virtue:

> The wise and virtuous man directs his principal attention to . . . the ideas of exact propriety and perfection. There exists in the mind of every man an idea of this kind, gradually formed from his observations upon the character and conduct of both himself and of other people. It is the slow, gradual, and progressive work of the great demigod within the breast, the great judge and arbiter of conduct. (363)

Dwyer observes that Smith's location of the moral arbiter for the community in the sentiment of sympathy engaged the life of the individual with the public good by directing that life toward what Dwyer prefers to call "sociability" (1987, 54). And Blair introduced this moral function of taste in his first lecture by noting that "the elevated sentiments and high examples which poetry, eloquence, and history are often bringing under our view, naturally tend to nourish in our minds publick spirit" ([1783] 1965, 1:13).

However, Blair considered issues of morality best addressed to reason: "Logical and Ethical disquisitions move in a higher sphere; . . . point[ing] out to man the improvement of his nature as an intelligent being; and his duties as the subject of moral obligation" while "Belles Lettres and criticism chiefly consider him as a Being endowed with those powers of taste and imagination, which were intended to embellish his mind, and to supply him with rational and useful entertainment" (1:10). And at the end of that introductory lecture, Blair made that hierarchy clear:

> I will not go so far as to say that the improvement of taste and of virtue is the same; or that they may always be expected to coexist in an equal degree. More powerful correctives than taste can apply, are necessary for reforming the corrupt propensities which too frequently prevail among mankind. . . . At the same time this cannot but be admitted, that the exercise of taste is moral and purifying. From reading the most admired productions of genius, whether in poetry or prose, almost everyone rises with some good impressions left on his mind; and though these may not always be durable, they are at least to be ranked among the means of disposing the heart to virtue. (1:13)

Dwight's own notion of the moral function of taste as developed in a set of magazine essays published in 1786 is closer to that of Hutcheson and Smith than Blair. These essays were written as part of a series entitled "The Friend" that sustains the general argument that the development of an American culture and the progress of an American nation depends upon the improvement of taste in its citizens.[6] In the first essay Dwight acknowledged both the aesthetic and moral function of taste as "the faculty by which we discern propriety and beauty, in the objects with which we are conversant," adding that "as it respects human conduct, it is a ready discernment of propriety, grace, ease, elegance, and dignity." Indeed, he concluded, "the most important application of Taste is undoubtedly to human conduct." Dwight connected the aesthetic and the moral by identifying individual virtue as their common consequence: "There are innumerable ways in which [taste] is the means of improvement, delicacy, propriety, and dignity. All these are natural and necessary means of virtue, as well as of happiness; and of course annex to taste, in the application of it, a most essential importance." Specifically, the refinement of taste produces an "elevation of mind in individuals, [that] will operate with a benevolent hand on the general happiness, and extend a fostering influence to all the inestimable concerns of truth and religion" (1786a).

In his second essay, Dwight described the actual operation of taste by defining it as an "Aptitude of mind, to receive pleasure from the beauties of nature" but focusing his attention on its moral function: "This general definition applies with equal propriety to the moral world," a world that "has a train of objects also . . . producing pleasurable emotions, entirely harmonious with these produced by the natural world." Like Blair, Dwight maintained that the "natural or original taste" is "capable of much improvement" through the "actual inspection" of objects of beauty. With Blair, he located its perceptions outside the realm of the purely rational by describing them as feelings provoked by the immediate experience of beauty that, when attended to, enable ever sharper perception:

> It will, perhaps, be observed, that the mere knowledge of such objects is not taste. It is true, but equally true, that our relish for these objects, or the aptitude of mind to relish them is increased as really, and as extensively, as our knowledge of them by repeated indulgence. Our feeling, or relish, of natural beauties is heightened by every instance of indulging it, and the pleasure becomes more exquisite by every repetition.

And such repetition, he and Blair agreed, produces, in Dwight's words, "a superiority of taste to other persons" that constitutes "a very advantageous standard, with which he may happily compare all imitations and descriptions of them" (1786b). Dwight differs from Blair by treating the refined taste that enables this "relish" of the beautiful as the primary moral sense. And it is his use of this term *relish* to describe the function of a refined taste—a term used persistently by his grandfather, Jonathan Edwards, to describe the refined sensibility enabled by spiritual regeneration—that signals the connection of Dwight's poetic to the moral tradition of American evangelical Calvinism.

### Taste in the Evangelical Calvinist Tradition

The connection of this tradition to Dwight's notion of taste can be traced from Edwards's theological work to Dwight's own. Both located the effects of regeneration by grace in sentiment—or "affection" in Edwards's preferred term—before reason. And both used the refinement of sensory taste as a metaphor to describe the felt effect of grace, relying on the term *relish* to describe the heightened ability to perceive the good that was, for both, a primary consequence of regeneration. In *A Treatise Concerning Religious Affections*, Edwards asserted the primacy of the felt experience of regenerate perception in establishing religious conviction with his initial statement of doctrine that "true religion, in great part, consists in holy affections" ([1746] 1959, 95). He defined these affections as "no other, than the more vigorous and sensible exercises of the inclination and will of the soul" (96)—the will being for Edwards as for the Scots the faculty that directs us in matters of morality. Given that definition, he could then assert that "true religion consists, in great measure, in vigorous and lively actings of the inclination and will of the soul" (99) because "affections are the spring of men's actions" (100).

This doctrine established, Edwards then explained the effects of sin and regeneration on those affections using the metaphor of sensory taste. "Sin," he wrote, "is like some distempers . . . that put the mouth out of taste, so as to disenable from distinguishing good and wholesome food from bad. . . . Men in a corrupt and carnal frame, have their spiritual senses in but poor plight for judging and distinguishing spiritual things" (195). Grace refines those senses, enabling the perception of what was imperceptible before. In Edwards's words:

> There is given to those that are regenerated, a new supernatural sense
> that is as it were a certain divine spiritual taste . . . , and that something

is perceived by a true saint in the exercise of this new sense of mind, in spiritual and divine things, as entirely different from anything that is perceived in them by natural men, as the sweet taste of honey is diverse from the ideas men get of honey by looking on it or feeling of it; . . . the beauty of holiness is that thing in spiritual and divine things, which is perceived by this spiritual sense . . . : this is the sweetness that is the proper object of this spiritual taste. (256)

In terms that parallel the aesthetic language used by his contemporary Scots, Edwards described the evaluative function of this spiritual sense: "A holy person is led by the spirit, as he is instructed and led by his holy taste, and disposition of heart; whereby, in the lively exercise of grace, he easily distinguishes good and evil, and knows at once, what is a suitable amiable behavior towards God, and towards man" (282).

Edwards then made the connection explicit, referring to that secular notion of taste in order to distinguish from it more clearly his spiritual notion:

Now as there is such a kind of taste of the mind . . . which philosophers speak of, whereby persons are guided in their judgments of the natural beauty, gracefulness, propriety, nobleness and sublimity of speeches and actions, whereby they judge as it were by the glance of an eye, or by inward sensation, and the first impression of the object; so there is likewise such a thing as a divine taste, given and maintained by the Spirit of God, in the hearts of the saints, whereby they are in like manner led and guided in discerning and distinguishing the true and holy beauty of actions; and that more easily, readily, and accurately, as they have more or less of the Spirit of God dwelling in them. And thus the sons of God are led by the Spirit of God, in their behavior in the world. (283)

In his later ethical treatise *The Nature of True Virtue* (1765), Edwards restated this connection hierarchically and made grace the bridge between them. Describing the secular and aesthetic sense as an unregenerate version of the spiritual and moral, Edwards defined beauty as the divine will enacted—as "that consent, propensity, and union of heart to Being in general, that is immediately exercised in a general good will," which he termed "virtue" ([1765] 1989, 540). While the secular sentiment of taste perceives an order of beauty he treated as "secondary," it is also the sentiment that grace enables to perceive the higher order of beauty, or virtue, that he identified as divine:

'Tis with regard to this image or resemblance which secondary beauty has of true spiritual beauty that God has so constituted nature that the presenting of this inferior beauty, especially in those kinds of it which have the greatest resemblance of the primary beauty, as the harmony of sounds, and the beauties of nature, have a tendency to assist those whose hearts are under the influence of a truly virtuous temper, to dispose them to the exercises of divine love, and enliven in them a sense of spiritual beauty. (565)

True virtue, for Edwards, begins with this ability to perceive and to relish moral and spiritual beauty. In his terms, virtue is "beauty belonging to beings that have *perception* and *will*" (539), and "it is impossible that anyone should truly *relish* this beauty, consisting in general benevolence, who has not that temper himself" (549). And it is this concept of a regenerate virtue that Dwight drew upon in *The True Means of Establishing Public Happiness*, where he preached to the people of New England of their common need for individual virtue in "that enlarged and evangelical sense, which embraces piety to God, Goodwill to mankind, and the effectual Government of ourselves" (1795, 13). Defining this Calvinist concept of a virtue that encompasses actions in the private and public spheres as "piety," Dwight insisted here that individual piety is the source of public happiness. And genuine piety, as he developed the concept in "Lectures on the Evidences of Divine Revelation: Lecture III" (1810), the central essay of a theological series published in an evangelical magazine late in his life, is accessible through revelation alone—through the revelation of what Edwards had called "primary beauty" perceived through sentiments refined by grace. "Since, then, the duties of piety cannot be understood without the aid of Revelation," Dwight wrote, "the duties of morality will, without that aid, be so far equally unknown" 106–7).[7]

When Dwight needed to illustrate the elevated state of being that follows from grace, he returned to the metaphor of taste. In "The Dignity and Excellence of the Gospel," preached in 1812 at the ordination of a favored former student, Dwight used this metaphor in presenting angels as a paradigm for the regenerate. Angels, in his description, "admit nothing but truth" because they are "*possessed . . . of the most noble and refined taste. Their relish* is as regularly conformed to truth as their *intellect*. Nothing little can engross their attention: nothing debased can give them pleasure" (1828, 2:454). He presented this paradigm as an invitation to those he addressed to aspire to the personal piety that regenerates perception. This invitation took the form of description in order to "illustrate the nature of the doctrine" rather than "prove" it, for "where a doctrine is merely proved, it is loosely regarded, and rarely remembered; but when it is clearly illustrated, and forcibly applied, a hope may justly be entertained, that the impressions, which are made on the minds of an audience, will be permanent, and useful" (2:456). This essentially poetic appeal is required by the primacy of sentiment in the process of regeneration that Dwight learned from Edwards. Indeed, Edwards had articulated this mandate succinctly in *A Treatise Concerning Religious Affections*: "God hath appointed a particular and lively application of his Word, to men, in the preaching of it, as a fit means to affect sinners . . . , and to stir up the pure minds of the saints and quicken their affections, by often bringing the great things of religion to their remembrance, and setting them before them in their proper colors" ([1746] 1959, 117).

In the theological terminology Dwight learned from Edwards, appeal to sentiment was appeal directly to the spiritual faculty susceptible to refinement through regeneration by grace. In the philosophical terminology he learned from the Scots, appeal to sentiment was appeal to the faculty of aesthetic and moral perception that can be sharpened by practice—by repeated perception of beauty in object and action. In both terminologies, taste denotes the individual ability to perceive directly and immediately the beautiful, good, and true, an ability that motivates right action. And, consequently, both traditions placed the poetic appeal to sentiment at the forefront of the discourse that drove the progress of their separate moral projects, projects Dwight combined in his own that he sustained most prominently from the pulpit and podium he occupied as the president of Yale.

## *Teaching an Oratorical Poetic at Yale*

From 1795 until his death in 1817, President Dwight directed an expansion of Yale into a broadly based practical training ground for leaders, religious and civil, who could carry his eighteenth-century vision of a virtuous American community into the nineteenth century. Upon his appointment, Dwight found himself presiding over a faculty of two—himself, functioning as professor of divinity, and a professor of mathematics and natural philosophy. He immediately added to his own responsibilities those of a professor of rhetoric and moral philosophy, though Yale did not establish that professorship until after his death. By 1810 Dwight had established professorships in chemistry, languages and ecclesiastical history, and law and had selected from among his former students men to hold them. By 1814 he had in place a "medical institution" comprising a professor of "materia medica and botany, one of anatomy and surgery, and one of the theory and practice of physic" as well as the professor of chemistry (1821, 1:151). With these professorships, he broadened the curriculum to include courses in geology, mineralogy as well as chemistry, and metaphysics, political science, and modern languages as well as rhetoric and moral philosophy. Under Dwight's leadership the student population of Yale almost doubled, and among the 1,100 to 1,200 men he educated there were Lyman Beecher, John C. Calhoun, James Fenimore Cooper, and Samuel F. B. Morse, as well as most of the faculty, including Benjamin Silliman, Jeremiah Day, and James L. Kingsley, who determined the direction of a Yale education in the nineteenth century (Dexter 1917, 30–35).

At the core of that education was Dwight's vision of an American community unified in the public happiness that follows from the individual virtue of its members, a vision made reality, he believed, by the public discourse of virtuous leaders. The discourse that Dwight both practiced and preached at Yale addressed not only the intellect but also the sentiment that was, for him, the source of both desire and action. Each week of their four years in residence, Yale students heard Dwight lecture in theology, and each day during their senior year they heard his instruction in rhetoric and moral philosophy. Prominent in both courses was the lesson Dwight learned in secular terms from the Scots and in sacred terms from Edwards: that public discourse sustains moral community by refining in those addressed the ability to perceive the beautiful and good from which springs virtuous intention and action. His project in both courses was twofold: first, to provoke his students to embody in themselves the virtue that enables such discourse—virtue accessible only through the spiritual regeneration that comes through the discipline of his religion—and then to initiate them into the practice of that discourse that functions for those addressed, whether it is sacred or secular, as a part of that discipline. Such discourse, rooted theoretically in the belletristic rhetoric of Kames and Blair and practically in the evangelical work of Edwards, was oratorical in its conviction that collective values and actions are established through direct rhetorical address, yet poetic in its insistence that those values and actions spring first from feeling.

Dwight's Course in Theology

Dwight's four-year course in theology, published in 1818 as *Theology; Explained and Defended*, is his institutionalized version of the evangelical Calvinism that became known in the nineteenth century as the New Haven theology. The five volumes of sermons that constitute the course cover the doctrines and duties of "natural religion" in general and "the Christian religion" in particular. Dominating the doctrinal discussions is regeneration, dominating discussions of duties is the means of grace, and prominent in both is the metaphor of taste. Dwight used that term as the Scots did—to locate both the perception of the good and true and the motive force to enact it in sentiment before reason. But he used it for the purpose Edwards did—to invoke in those addressed that refinement of sentiment that enables perception of the divine.

The central doctrinal sermon in his system is "Regeneration: Its Nature," in which Dwight defined that process in terms of a refined and heightened taste, stating that *"this change of heart consists in a Relish of Spiritual objects, communicated to it by the power of the Holy Ghost"* —a "relish" of not only what is immediately associated with the divine but also of "Virtuous men, Virtuous affections, Virtuous conduct, and all kinds of enjoyment found in the contemplation of these objects, the exercise of these affections, and the practice of this conduct" (1818, 3:62). Like the secular notion of taste developed by the Scots, this sacred notion locates the origin of morality in the individual perception and asserts the necessity that native ability be refined to enable one to perceive the good and the true. In Dwight's terms,

> without a *relish* for spiritual objects, I cannot see, that any discoveries concerning them . . . can render them pleasing to the soul. . . . He, who disrelishes the taste of wine, will not relish it the more, the more distinctly and perfectly he perceives the taste. . . . To enable him to relish it, it seems indispensable, that his own taste should be changed, and in this manner fitted to realize the pleasantness of wine. (3:68)

Dwight shifted his attention to the consequences of this refinement by describing the regenerate "change of heart" as a change of "inclination," or the term he preferred, of "disposition" (3:63–64). In a subsequent doctrinal sermon, "Regeneration; Its Evidences: What are real Evidences?," Dwight described the regenerate heart as "the new disposition" manifest in an intense relish of moral attitudes and actions. In doing so, he identified specific evidences of spiritual regeneration in the same terms his public sermons used to describe civic virtue and public happiness: "The new disposition is . . . styled *Disinterestedness; Love; Goodwill; Benevolence*; a spirit inclining him, in whom it exists, to subordinate his own private interest to the general welfare, and find his own happiness in the common prosperity of the divine kingdom" (1818, 3:279). Most prominently, Dwight described the regenerate disposition with the term he had used in *The True Means of Establishing Public Happiness* to describe how one best supports the collective well-being: *"Piety"* (1795, 281). In both sermons, he treated piety as a sentiment of the good and true that directs individual desire toward moral action, and he described that refined moral sense using the metaphorical language of taste: "If a man really relishes the worship of God, he will be apt to be regularly employed in it at all proper seasons. . . . If he relishes the company of religious persons; he will naturally frequent it; seek it; and derive from it when employed; a sensible pleasure" (283).

Corresponding to this doctrinal discussion of regeneration is the discussion of means of grace that is central to the sermons on religious duties that dominate Dwight's course. These focus particularly upon the duty of pious leaders, both religious and civil, to address those they lead in discourse that directs the disposition toward piety. In a sermon titled "The Ordinary Means of Grace. What they are; and what is their influence," Dwight asserted that "the influence of the Means of Grace may . . . be explained under the two general levels of *Instruction*; and *Impression*" (1818, 4:503), of which the *"Impressions, which they make on the heart"* (4:507) is primary. He then explained that primacy in terms similar to those used in the introduction to *Greenfield Hill* to assert the primacy of poetry: "The *Intellect* is not the *motive* faculty of the mind. The *Will*, in which term I include all the affections, gives birth to every effort, which the mind makes" (4:507). Specifically, Dwight argued for the primacy of the appeal to sentiment: "Eloquence, both in speaking and writing, has ever been directed to the Imagination; and to the Passions as well as to the Intellect: and that kind of Eloquence, which has been employed in moving the heart, has been considered as possessing a higher, and more influential, nature than that, which is addressed merely to the understanding" (4:508).

In subsequent sermons in the course, Dwight placed the efficacy of this rhetorical appeal at the center of his discussion of the refining effect of grace, an effect that, in his theology, is open to all. In "Hearing the Word of God," he taught that

> every sinner may . . . feel this truth [that is preached] in a strong and affecting manner. Awakened to a sense of his guilt and danger, he does thus actually feel, antecedently to any change in his moral character, that the scriptures are worthy of all acceptation. But under the conviction, and this sense, all those are sanctified who are sanctified at all. With these very views of divine truth upon their minds, the Spirit of God communicates to them . . . that change of heart which is commonly styled Regeneration. (1818, 4:543–44)

In "The Manner of Preaching," Dwight emphasized the agency of the speaker in this process, asserting that to address the awakening hearer with words that provoke the felt perceptions of divine truth, the speaker "must originally feel them; and must also express his views of them in the native language of feeling" (1818, 5:223–24). When so addressed, Dwight explained in "Hearing the Word of God," the hearer is then responsible "to hear with Evangelical Faith" expressed in "this exercise of the heart" (1818, 4:545). From both perspectives, the speaker's and the hearer's, eloquence is the most significant means of grace in Dwight's theology, functioning in the hearer both poetically and evangelically—terms brought together in the sensory metaphor of taste.

Dwight's Course in Rhetoric

Dwight's lectures in rhetoric have not survived, perhaps because they may never have been written out. He was troubled throughout his adult life by increasingly weak eyesight that forced him, during his years at Yale, to write with the assistance of an amanuensis and to deliver his lectures and sermons from notes. Dwight's senior course on rhetoric seems to have taken the form of a set of extended commentaries on Blair's *Lectures*, comments preserved only in the students' notes. The two student notebooks that are available suggest that he focused much of that commentary on taste and the practical genius that expresses it, developing versions of those notions more evangelical than Blair's.[8] His course thus provided instruction in an oratorical poetic that identified taste as the source of moral and critical judgment and its consequent genius as the source of rhetorical action that had a homiletical function. This emphasis on rhetorical taste and genius seems to be the practical counterpart of his theological emphasis on regeneration and the means of grace. As his theological notion of regeneration describes the refinement of disposition that enables perception of the divine and conception of pious action, his rhetorical notion of taste describes a judgment refined to perception of "moral beauties" as well as of the "natural" (Ravitz 1956, 64). As the practical means of grace are, in his theological discussion, "impressions" made on the heart, genius in his rhetorical discussion is the ability, born of taste, to make such impressions on the hearts of others (66).

This relationship of regeneration and taste is suggested in the first lecture of Dwight's course as recorded in 1803 by John Pierpont. Under the head "Taste," Pierpont noted these statements by Dwight: "Moral beauties are more exquisite than natural. The enjoyment of the mind is higher than sensual enjoyments. Moral enjoyments higher than other mental enjoyments" (64). However, Dwight's discussion immediately shifted to his primary concern with the practical expression of taste: "To communicate good is productive of higher enjoyments than to receive it." He continued in terms that connect his comments on Blair with his theology, asserting that "hence the unprincipled and depraved man cuts himself off from the greatest sources of happiness and enjoyment" (64). In the next lecture, under the head "Genius," Pierpont recorded Dwight saying that genius "is the power of action and is seen in action" (68), action that was, in his mind, clearly rhetorical. Pierpont's notes suggest that in preparing the young men of New England to lead the community he envisioned, Dwight made the refined sentiment that perceives the good and true the source of the ability to evoke that sentiment in others through effective public discourse. In Pierpont's terms, Dwight "proved that the man of taste is the man of Genius" (68).

A somewhat more extensive record of Dwight's lectures is David L. Daggett's notes on the 1807 course. Having briefly noted Dwight's introductory comments on the importance of public discourse and writing, Daggett then summarized Dwight's first lecture under the head "*Taste & Relish.*" Again, Dwight presented the aesthetic notion of taste in moralized, evangelical language, insisting that "they are moral objects which refine the taste" and that "the mind must be elevated before it can acquire a relish for such objects." Consequently, "an immoral man's taste is always corrupted" (Freimarck 1966, 237). Daggett then recorded Dwight's discussion of the relationship of taste and genius. Under the heading of *"Genius,"* defined as "an exercise of the human mind," Dwight defined two kinds: "Logical," which relies upon reason and taste together to examine and evaluate sense impressions, and "Rhetorical," which "is employed in making impressions on the mind." Genius of this second kind—the kind Dwight was preparing his students to exercise—he described as "a relish, or strong sensibility to the beauties of nature, united to a power of compounding, comparing, & abstracting ideas, which is common to all men," terms that echo the Scots (238). But Dwight relied on scripture rather than literature to provide examples of the sublimity and beauty that characterize the discourse of genius.

Later in the notes, having summarized Dwight's comments on such things as the history of the language, the mechanics of style, and tropes, Daggett recorded Dwight's discussions of eloquence, particularly of the pulpit, in terms that echo Edwards as well as Dwight's own course in theology. Advising use of "the language of animated feeling" (245), he instructed his students to "understand the gospel thoroughly, thus feel it thoroughly" and then to express that feeling in "the language of simplicity and that only" (246). He explained the necessity of such expression in a baccalaureate sermon preached to Yale graduates in 1805. "You will find all men substantially alike," he told them, "and all naturally ignorant, and wicked. You will find every man pleased, not merely to be free, but to tyrannize; and to indulge without restraint, and without degree, both appetite and passion." He continued:

> Whatever you find in man, better than I have asserted, is the result of human discipline, or of divine grace. In the Institutions of our own country, this discipline is more perfect, than it has been in any other. . . . Educated in knowledge, in morals, in religion, from the cradle to the grave, our Countrymen *can* enjoy their unexampled freedom, with safety, order, and peace. No nation, not thus educated, can long be free at all. More free than we are, Man, with his present character, cannot be. If we preserve such freedom, we shall do, what has never been done. The only possible means of its preservation, miracles apart, is the preservation of those institutions, from which it has been derived. (303–4)

Dwight charged each of his students with the protection and promotion of those institutions that house the public discourse that he believed enacts this discipline. More specifically, however, he charged those who would practice that discourse with addressing their fellow citizens primarily in the language of sentiment that, refining the perception of the good and true, would enable those citizens to act in ways that would ensure the morality of their community.

## Conclusion

In the closing lectures of his course in rhetoric, Dwight turned to a discussion of poetry. "Poetry," Daggett recorded him saying, "is universally more succinct, elliptical, abrupt, bold, and more intense." Consequently, he added, "it is the proper character of Poetry to enhance everything which is the subject of it" (251). That is, for Dwight, the proper character of rhetoric as well. "The end of the observations, which I have made," he stated at the end of his sermon on the true means of public happiness, "is to impress on the minds of this audience the importance of public and individual exertions to promote knowledge and virtue in this State" (1795, 30). This act of impression was central to his instruction at Yale that was, whether in theology or rhetoric, instruction in a public discourse that addressed first the taste, in both the sacred and the secular senses of that term, from which he believed would spring the sort of citizenship upon which his vision of community depended. As he put it in another public sermon, *The Duty of Americans at the Present Crisis*, preached in 1798 to direct this community into the nineteenth century, "personal obedience and reformation is the foundation, and the sum, of all national wealth and prosperity. If each man conducts himself aright, the community cannot be conducted wrong" (16). His project through the next two decades that took Yale well into the nineteenth century was to teach others to join him in shoring up that foundation with a public discourse directed by an oratorical poetic.

This analysis of his oratorical poetic should expose the politics inherent in a vision of American community that was shared by many public men prominent in the oratorical culture of the United States in the early nineteenth century, a culture whose tendencies toward a neoclassical elitism were intensified by hierarchies seemingly divinely authorized by the prevailing Protestantism. Dwight's theory and practice of public discourse was founded upon his conviction that a few men like himself had the authority to speak for the many in America, a conviction that he articulated and defended in terms of his doctrine of taste. That doctrine, developed in the eighteenth century, influential in the nineteenth, and perhaps still with us residually at the end of the twentieth, worked explicitly against a democratic transformation of public discourse that would enact a politics of equality and diversity. This analysis of Dwight's version of that doctrine can mark a starting point for further study that traces its transformations through the nineteenth century and into the twentieth. Such a study might also contribute to the reconstruction of the discourse of the many American public cultures upon assumptions that reject any residue of an elitist doctrine of taste.

## Notes

1. Soon after his death, Dwight's four-year course in divinity was published as *Theology; Explained and Defended* (1818, 5 vols.). His lectures in rhetoric have not survived but can be partially reconstructed from student notebooks and other writings. See my "Timothy Dwight's Moral Rhetoric at Yale College, 1795–1817" (1987, 149–61).

2. Dwight stopped writing poetry when became president of Yale at the age of 43. Until then, he had directed a significant amount of his energy toward developing an explicitly American and implicitly Calvinist poetry. At Yale, however, he devoted most of his writing time to his *Theology* as well as to a new project, his *Travels; in New-England and New-York* (1821, 4 vols.). He contributed essays and a few short poems to the periodical press, but did not focus his efforts seriously on poetry again.

3. In his specific appeal to sentiment and its connection to his larger purpose of directing individual virtue toward communal action, Dwight presents a similar response in a similar situation to that which John Dwyer observes in eighteenth-century Scotland in *Virtuous Discourse* (1987). Here Dwyer argues that the Scottish "literati" responded to the rise of individualism in a commercialized society and the consequent shift of the moral realm from the rational and collective to the felt and individual by developing an ethics that connected the individual to the community through sentiment. Sentiment, rooted in sympathy, or sociability, was an individual felt sense for the common good that gave morality "its basis in human fellow-feeling rather than abstract reason or utility" (169). Dwight was familiar with the writings of these moral philosophers, and both the situation of his own cultural community and his consequent response were similar. I am indebted to Thomas

Miller for referring me to Dwyer.

4. I am using the facsimile reproduction of the 1794 edition of *Greenfield Hill* included in *The Major Poems of Timothy Dwight* (1969). Page numbers are those of the original edition of the poem, not the facsimile volume.

5. This is the object of Dwight's address throughout *Greenfield Hill*, and what he believed such address could accomplish can be elaborated by following a note appended to his assertion in the introduction that the language of poetry best provokes action: "See Lowth's Lectures on Heb. Po." ([1794] 1969, 7). In *Lectures on the Sacred Poetry of the Hebrews*, Robert Lowth, Bishop of London and Praelector of Poetry at Oxford, asserted the primary motivating power of poetry more directly than Dwight: "It is the part of [the philosopher] so to describe and explain [virtue and truth], that we must necessarily be acquainted with them; it is the part of [the poet] so to dress and adorn them, that of our own accord we must love and embrace them" ([1763] 1815, 7). The portrayal of virtue and truth enacted "allures and interests the mind of the reader, . . . fashions it to habits of virtue, and in a manner informs it with the spirit of integrity" (10). This gives poetry "amazing power . . . in directing the passions, in forming the manners, in maintaining civil life, and particularly in exciting and cherishing that generous level of sentiment, on which the very existence of public virtue seems to depend" (15).

6. These essays, sixteen in all, appeared originally in *The New Haven Gazette, and the Connecticut Magazine* between March 1786 and October 1787 under the pseudonym of James Littlejohn. The two essays that address taste directly are XI (June 22, 1786) and XII (July 6, 1786).

7. This series, "Lectures on the Evidences of Divine Revelation," was published anonymously between June 1810 and December 1813 in *The Panoplist and Missionary Magazine*. There are eighteen essays in all, and all but the first three are devoted to arguing for the historical authenticity of the first five books of the Bible.

8. John Pierpont's notebook of 1803 is described by Abe C. Ravitz (1956). David Lewis Daggett's notebook of 1807 is described by Vincent Freimarck (1966). My citations of these notebooks are designated by the names of the scholars who published them, Ravitz and Freimarck.

# 3

# The Sermon as
# Public Discourse ✳
# Austin Phelps and the
# Conservative Homiletic Tradition
# in Nineteenth-Century
# America ✳ *Russel Hirst*

✳Throughout most of its history, America's pulpits (whether in the chapel or the meadow) have been intense focal points of public discourse. Preaching has been a major factor in forming the minds, hearts, and actions of most Americans, and consciously or unconsciously, every preacher's efforts to influence those minds, hearts, and actions have been guided by some kind of homiletic theory. In this essay I analyze an important dimension of nineteenth-century American homiletic theories through a representative figure: Austin Phelps,[1] Bartlett Professor of Sacred Oratory in Andover Theological Seminary (Andover, Massachusetts) from 1848 to 1879.

Phelps's theory of the social effect of conservative Christian preaching was, in its essence, shared by the majority of Northern, and by many Southern, conservative clergymen in the nineteenth century, and its principles were made particularly clear in debates over social reform, especially concerning slavery. Fundamentally, the theory was that *individual* moral/spiritual and intellectual transformation, initiated and then aided by the right kind of preaching, was the key to social happiness; from the fountain of regenerated individual character would spring the right, unforced, and lasting response to every kind of social ill. Direct confrontation of social problems through rhetoric that attempted to incite mass movements only bred division and (usually) violence, and the changes it effected could only be partial, even when it was directed against real evils such as slavery.

Reid's essay on Edward Everett (this volume) explains Everett's efforts to maintain moral/spiritual/civic unity in America, and thereby save the Union, through nonpartisan, epideictic rhetoric that celebrated national heroes, values, and culture. In this effort, Everett (himself an ordained minister) was in harmony with a large body of clergy who used the sermon, a form of epideictic rhetoric, in their own efforts to preserve and construct society by transforming individual souls. They had faith that individuals truly converted to Christ and growing in virtuous character would, at length, naturally agree on and act virtuously in political/social matters. Clark's essay on Timothy Dwight (this volume) shows Dwight's acceptance of this same principle; Dwight taught an "oratorical poetic" that "did the homiletical work of appealing to sentiments that would nurture the regenerate virtue that he believed functions as a powerful public bond." Phelps's homiletics did not focus on "poetics" in this same way; in fact, Phelps is at pains in *The Theory of Preaching* to explain how preaching is not a poetical but a rhetorical undertaking. However, Dwight's use of poetic is at bottom rhetorical, as Clark explains, and certainly Dwight, Everett, and Phelps shared a great deal in common in terms of their theories of the truths and values to be preached, the sources of those truths and values, and the social goals and effects of preaching/oratory.

Though Everett and Dwight are better known to us than the Andover professor of homiletics, Phelps was, in his day, well known and respected by conservative ministers and educators. During his thirty-one years at Andover, over 1,000 students passed through his course in homiletics, many of them becoming teachers of homiletics or rhetoric themselves. In Congregational/Presbyterian circles during the latter half of the nineteenth century, "The Andover Sermon" became a standard of sermonic excellence. It stood for orthodoxy, literary culture, stability, and intellectual power. It focused on individual salvation and moral/intellectual development, it controlled emotion with the reins of reason, and it generally advocated personal and local improvement over national activity (except missionary

activity, which was simply a spreading and strengthening of autonomous loci).

Phelps offers an elaborately developed theory, complete with
descriptions of the minister's relations and responsibilities to his
congregation and the larger society, the training and character of the
preacher, and of course the sources, structure, style, and delivery of
his materials. He draws significantly on the classical rhetorical traditions and to a lesser degree on various modern rhetoricians such as
George Campbell and Richard Whately, and he is representative of
what I call the conservative homiletic tradition in America, a tradition
that can best be understood as the sacred mode of America's oratorical
culture.

Perhaps the most significant feature of America's oratorical culture is that it conserved the fundamental neoclassical belief in the
process of achieving community consensus at the most general level
of principles through reasoned public discourse. The sacred mode of
that culture shared with the secular mode not only this belief but also
many of the same assumptions about the forms and functions of
public discourse. They differed chiefly in their concepts of the most
powerful sources and formulations of rational argument (the sacred
mode looking primarily to the Bible as a touchstone of invention) and
in their concept of the immediate goals and effects of their respective
kinds of public discourse (Phelps teaching, as I've pointed out, that
the primary goal of preaching was the spiritual transformation and
subsequent intellectual and moral development of the individual
soul). Yet both modes of America's oratorical culture shared the goals
of conserving, improving, and spreading civil safety, harmony, prosperity, and moral/intellectual excellence; both believed that the speaker best equipped to advance these goals was the "elite" orator with a
particular kind of liberal arts education and social standing; and both
assumed a homogeneous population or aspired to create one—a
universal consensus of right principle and mutually accepted authority. This effort, Phelps believed, was the highest calling to which
mortals could aspire, and the successful minister, he maintained, was
the most influential instrument possible, not only of individual but
also of social and political good.

Phelps's theory is a fairly late example of this neoclassical rhetoric
as adapted for sacred oratory. His theory provided a model of public
discourse for a relatively contained community. It was based on the

old Congregational principle of "one flock, one shepherd"—one minister, himself a model of learning and virtue, dedicated to the salvation of a particular community. It was the minister's responsibility to
nurture that community in a steady, systematic, progressive way,
with as little disruption as possible. His chief influence was the public
discourse he engaged in from the pulpit. Among the difficulties in
Phelps's theory (from the general perspective of our modern culture
and from the perspective of various elements of society in Phelps's
own day) were its relation to the larger community—the nation—
when events did threaten disruption; certain cultural infelicities (his
belief that the ministry was for men only, for example); the doctrinal
incompatibility of Calvinism with the practice of sacred oratory that
he advocated;[2] and the idea that those suffering under various social
evils must patiently wait for organic, Christian salvation to overtake
society rather than agitate directly and disruptively for change.

   Phelps's rhetorical doctrines were shared not only in general by
most educated, conservative Protestants but also in many particulars
by an extensive network of colleagues in the conservative homiletic
tradition, men such as John Broadus of Southern Baptist Theological
Seminary, author of the widely used *A Treatise on the Preparation and
Delivery of Sermons*; William G. T. Shedd of Union, Andover, and
Auburn theological seminaries, author/translator of *Eloquence a Virtue*
and author of *Homiletics and Pastoral Theology*; James Hoppin of Yale
Theological Seminary, author of the massive *Homiletics*; and many
others. A survey of homiletic texts and journal articles produced
during the mid- to late nineteenth century at major theological
seminaries in the East and South—mostly Congregational and Presbyterian, but also Baptist and Methodist, since many of them had
made the transition to "respectability" by then—shows a strong
neoclassical influence.[3]

   In this essay, I first make some general observations about nineteenth-century American theories of preaching and their context. I
then examine the goals of Phelps's theory of homiletics and analyze
some specific features of his doctrine of sermonic composition. After
that I consider the nature of the preacher Phelps describes as being
capable of accomplishing the goals of sacred oratory, and I describe
Phelps's opposition to the professionalization of the Christian ministry, a trend that was bringing America's sacred oratorical culture to a
close for many of the same reasons that other kinds of professionaliza-

tion were bringing secular oratorical culture to a close. Finally, I discuss some of the merits, and problems, of Phelps's theory in view of the nineteenth-century transformation of the Christian ministry in America.

## Homiletics in Nineteenth-Century America: Phelps and His Context

This volume's collection of essays analyzes principally the transformation of secular oratorical culture in nineteenth-century America, but it was not only secular rhetoric that underwent a transformation in that period; the sacred dimension of oratorical culture also changed profoundly during that century, and it did so for many of the same reasons secular rhetoric changed. For example, the burgeoning democratic spirit of the new nation, which resulted in so much anti-intellectualism/anti-elitism, brought with it a great deal of prejudice against orthodox, seminary-bred preachers. At the same time, the expanding American frontier called for more and more preachers, which the Eastern (and some Southern) seminaries were not able to produce quickly enough, while many of those they did produce were unwilling to take up pastorates far away from centers of culture. These and other factors resulted in a profusion of preachers not trained in the liberal arts and theological "sciences," unequipped with the essentially neoclassical rhetorical training traditionally provided by most of the orthodox Eastern/Southern colleges and seminaries.

Also, political changes during the century profoundly affected sacred oratorical culture. Traditionally, New England towns had been presided over by civil and ecclesiastical authorities who had, with the full consent of the community, watched over the organic political and theological welfare of the people; civil peace and harmony had been considered to have a natural and necessary relation to spiritual health. The motives of both civil and ecclesiastical authorities were to serve the best interest of the community as a whole, to foster civil harmony and safety along with spiritual/moral/intellectual soundness. Men were chosen for such positions from the spiritual/moral/intellectual elite to protect and prosper the community. Typically, both civil and ecclesiastical authorities spoke on important public occasions (election days, executions, etc.). When public disorder threatened, it was as much (or more) the ecclesiastical authority as it was the secular authority whose discourse called the community back to order, often in the form of a jeremiad.

Though America at the beginning of the nineteenth century was not the New England of the seventeenth and eighteenth centuries, the ideal of the spiritual/civic community was still very much alive as the nineteenth century opened. However, the sociopolitical realities of the new nation were fast changing civil and ecclesiastical relations. In particular, the growing democratic spirit in America brought with it party politics and an emphasis on partisanship, while colleges increasingly emphasized and supported individual/professional success rather than civic service (see Reid, Clark and Halloran, this volume). By mid-century, oratorical culture in America was waning, and, as Bledstein points out, the "culture of professionalism" was waxing; fewer people envisioned their life's accomplishments as "a series of good works or public projects, performed within a familiar and deferential society which heaped respectability on its first citizens" (1976, 173); instead, they saw life as a series of "ascending stages" of personal power, status, wealth, and activity within a narrow, esoteric range.

The orthodox ministry recoiled from these trends for much the same reasons that, according to Reid, Edward Everett recoiled: They threatened the traditional ideals of organic unity, they deposed the ideal of the patriotic/spiritually dedicated civil (or civil/spiritual) servant who used his oratory for the benefit of the whole community or society, and they exalted the ideals of divisive, partisan interests and of the successful individual. This put the clergy in a very difficult position in terms of their sociopolitical activity. On one level was the demand of pro-partisanism that ministers distance themselves from direct political involvement. On another was the spirit of anti-intellectualism and anti-elitism, producing religious reformers and radicals of various kinds and eroding the special status and claims of the orthodox, educated ministry. On yet another level was that manifestation of pro-individualism that was feeding the culture of professionalism. All these things were factors in the increasing professionalization of the conservative Christian ministry itself and its increasing distance from traditional neoclassical rhetorical roots.

There were, however, even into the latter decades of the nineteenth century, important bulwarks of sacred oratorical culture such as Phelps. Phelps saw the various theories of preaching as based upon one of five principles: (1) the "priestly character of the Christian ministry," Catholic/Anglican theories, which subordinate preaching to liturgy, worship, ordinances, architecture, costume, and the like; (2) "poetic sentiment," preaching that "regards poetic feeling as so nearly kindred to a religious experience, and the cultivation of Taste to a religious culture, that it practically subordinates the pulpit to the cause of polite literature"; (3) "social reform," theories that "aim, in their ministrations, at institutions and customs of society, and political systems more earnestly, if not more frequently, than at individual souls"; (4) "emotion," "preaching which addresses itself, directly and mainly, to the sensibilities of men," depending on "the power of exhortation"; and (5) "the argumentative discussion of theology." This last category Phelps regarded as the basis of "the true theory of preaching, in a land where Christianity is nominally established as the ruling element in civilization" (1857, 4–8).

Phelps's ideal orator was the holy man skilled in speaking, the man who had advanced through the Christian equivalent of Quintilian's *Institutio Oratoria*, to emerge with godly character and superb rhetorical powers. Phelps's rhetorical doctrine emphasized lifelong intellectual/moral training in the liberal arts tradition, including training in the classical languages, assimilation of the great works of the past as an essential foundation not only for moral formation but also for rhetorical invention, and training in "scripting for oral performance" (Halloran 1990, 153), which involved the entire canon of classical rhetoric (invention, arrangement, style, memory, and delivery), the centrality of persuasion on the basis of shared values and beliefs, emphasis on audience analysis and on adjusting rhetorical appeals to the condition of the audience, the importance of neoclassical sermonic structure, the art of making powerful rational appeals based on Biblical truth, the necessity of controlling emotion in pulpit oratory, and the vital importance of achieving balance in every dimension of sacred oratory. Only a preacher thus equipped, Phelps believed, could stand as the highest model of virtue and learning in his community, employing his oratorical powers in persuading and educating others toward the highest personal good. In a Christian context, this meant persuasion to Christian conversion and then persuasion to and education in an ever-deepening Christian character. This, in Phelps's theory, would necessarily result in the highest sociopolitical good. In this sense, the goals of the public discourse of conservative preachers embraced—though they would insist that they also transcended—the secular goals of America's oratorical culture.

## The Private and Political Goals of Sacred Oratory

The key to understanding Phelps's rhetorical theory is the idea that the improvement and ultimate perfection of all human societies, the entire race of humankind, depends upon "the moral regeneration of the individual" and that preaching of a certain kind is the foundation for this regeneration.

In this idea of individual moral regeneration, Phelps believed, lay "the rudiment of all that is practiceable [sic] for the amelioration of the race." It was "the germ of the whole tree," the foundation of salvation for all humanity. It was vastly superior as "an organ of political and social movement" to the "flimsy engines of reform" that attempted a misguided, direct approach to solving social problems. In the January 2, 1861, annual election sermon delivered to the legislature of Massachusetts, Phelps declared:

> If the organic corruptions of this world are ever to be purged away, it will be done by the Christian church energized by the grace of God in blessing upon the Christian pulpit. That blessing will go forth to the nations in the channel of *individual regeneration*. Its flow will be like that of subterranean rivers. . . . The moral sense of the world has yet to be trained to the perception of this fundamental principle of Christian progress: that individual regeneration underlies the whole system of the improvement of society, in all its ramifications. And in that specific work of individual regeneration lies the strength of the Pulpit as a power of Reform. (1861, 20–21)

Direct attempts at reform—such as abolitionism—were, in Phelps's view and that of much of the orthodox Northern clergy, entirely the wrong way to approach social problems. Such reforms, they believed, were disruptive and divisive and, when advocated in the pulpit, detracted from its true ministration: "Claims are often made upon preachers, in reference to the advocacy of reforms, which can never be conceded, without a diversion of the pulpit from the main design of its existence" (1861, 28). This was not to say that preachers were never to use the public discourse of preaching to directly engage with their audiences on political topics; there were times, Phelps maintained, when it would be cowardice not to do so. Phelps's election day sermon to the Massachusetts legislature on the eve of the Civil War ends in direct appeals concerning their immediate political decisions. It is very telling, however, that his principal appeal is to their patience and forbearance—to a point—with the errant South: "Up to the limit of national safety, then, we have reason for forbearance. Let the tone of our legislation, and our press, and our pulpits, be generous, until so generous a virtue is silenced by events. If we can yet be heard in debate, let it be in words of temperance and soberness. Let us speak at the height of great argument, as is becoming to Christian states in the discussion of great principles" (1861, 51–52).

In the national crisis of impending civil war, Phelps believed, it was entirely appropriate that sacred oratory should be employed in reasoning about the principles involved in the debate between political factions, in exploring the consequences of various actions, in advocating particular actions, and in urging individuals, organizations, and communities to stand resolutely against sin and error at every level of human interaction. In this sense, in such exigencies, the public discourse of the pulpit was often not greatly different from secular oratory. But the key point for Phelps was that such a usage of the pulpit, though sometimes necessary, was unfortunate; the pulpit's *natural* ministration was part of an organic, God-ordained process by which humanity should be steadily regenerated. It could best accomplish this by basing itself on Biblical thought and addressing itself to human reason: "It is the chief office of a preacher to express [the] correspondences between the written word of God and man's own rational decisions" (1857, 31).

This did not mean, Phelps insisted, an unthinking acceptance of past theological systems; "even a true religious faith, when once established, does not long perpetuate itself uncorrupted, on the mere strength of traditionary evidence" (35). Each age had to interpret the revelations of God for itself, in light of its own questions, discoveries, speculations, problems, and events. But Phelps and his conservative colleagues firmly believed in the correspondence between God's truth, in the Bible and other forms, and man's rational faculty—and in pulpit oratory as the principal public forum in which these truths must be used to persuade and edify individuals and communities to the highest forms of virtue and social happiness. The best way, the safest, deepest, most enduring and fruitful way to do this, they believed, was to keep the pulpit as much as possible to its specific Christian ministration and to minister faithfully to the individual flocks to which God had called them.

Not all Congregational/Presbyterian or other orthodox preachers agreed with this principle, of course. Near the other extreme were abolitionists like Theodore Weld,[4] who endured mob opposition as they traveled about, directly stirring up social action, divisiveness, and trouble of all kinds as they preached against the detestable sinfulness of slavery and demanded that the slaves be freed immediately. I say *near* extreme because although Weld was one of the most important abolitionists, he was not an "extreme abolitionist"; he did not preach that the slaves also should immediately receive full political rights with whites (that would take some years, even by Weld's proposals), nor, before the Civil War began, that their rights should be won by war. But he did advocate immediate freedom from bondage for slaves and the immediate start-up of the machinery that would give them full rights.[5]

A prominent example of a Congregational minister who took a middle position, advocating something between revolution and evolution, was Henry Ward Beecher. After 1846, Beecher often thundered against slavery from the pulpit, but his organic view of the institutionalized church and God's plan for the nation, as well as his comfortable pastorate of a large and fashionable Brooklyn Heights congregation, pulled him up short of joining the abolitionists. Even so, Beecher would sometimes sound off violently against slavery, earning himself the reputation of a fearless antislavery champion. His theatrics, too, magnified this image. For example, on several occasions he brought a slave, in chains, with him into the pulpit and preached a highly emotional sermon in which the slave would be "auctioned off to freedom." And once the Civil War had begun, Beecher was a relentless advocate of the Union cause, so much so that the Union government sent Beecher to England on a speaking tour to garner support for the war effort.

For Beecher and others like him (in practice, if not in notoriety), and certainly for those like Weld, Christian ministers were not only *justified* in direct political activity extending both to their own pastorates and to the world at large, they were also *obliged* to perform it. Preachers who did not take direct political action to address social wrongs were often ridiculed by the slavery reform advocates and

other political activists who called them "aloof," "half-men," and so
on. Phelps was sensitive to these accusations and in his writings and
sermons made it very clear that he believed clergymen should be the
most important political influence in the nation, "manly men, . . .
immersed in the tides of opinion and feeling around them . . . directly, currently, vigorously affecting men's lives" (1882, 68). Phelps firmly
believed that pulpit oratory, far from being aloof or disconnected
from political influence, should be the greatest of all agents of social
change. The orthodox preacher "preaches a system of truth which in
its practical relations is correlative with all forms of human life, and
with history through all time. Its genius is that of practical agitation
and change. It is transforming, it is subversive, it is revolutionary. It
cometh to send a sword on earth. Its destiny is to overturn and
overturn and overturn" (1861, 15). One could imagine that many
abolitionist preachers would heartily agree with this. Yet the method
of "overturning" social wrong in Phelps's theory differs markedly
from that of "immediatists."

   In Phelps's view, preaching should change society organically,
not suddenly, disruptively, violently. The moral force of preaching
should bear upon the human mind like "atmosphere upon the globe's
surface." The moral changes it effects should be general, complete,
solid, lasting. It should be based on a permanent and progressive
moral/intellectual development, engendered in individual souls, "expanding and blooming into the graces of a Christlike character,"
which would then of necessity bring about societal improvement:

> Lifting thus the individual mind, Christianity *sets to work a power which is
> diffusive*. The man is a part of humanity: he begins to move it, as he
> himself is moved. The individual is an elevating force to the family, and
> through the family to the community, and through the community to the
> state, and through the state to the age, and the race. Christianity presup-
> poses what history proves, that individual consciences, thus illuminated,
> intensified, redeemed from the dominion of guilt, will sway the world.
> Dotting the globe over with points of light, they radiate towards each
> other; each reduplicates the illuminating power of another. (1861, 39)

The regenerated consciousness of these communities would then, in a
natural process of development, generate ideas such as "the equality
of the race, the brotherhood of man with man, the nobility of woman,

the inhumanity of war, the odiousness of slavery, the dignity of labor, the worth of education, and the blessedness of charity" (40).

It is important to recognize that in Phelps's theory of preaching, all the themes listed above were proper topics for pulpit oratory, but only in the context of a steady, systematic moral/intellectual development on the part of the congregation. The problem of addressing the social evil of slavery is an excellent example. Like most of the orthodox clergy, and conservatives generally, Phelps abhorred the activity of the abolitionists, especially the more extreme ones: those who traveled about giving highly emotional, disruptive orations, vituperating slaveholders, making demands for immediate action, and so on. He equally abhorred the activity of the extreme *anti*-abolitionists. Phelps's own method involved the "temporary toleration of evil followed by timely efforts for its extinction." Twenty years after the Civil War, in an article for *The Congregationalist* entitled "The New England Clergy and the Anti-Slavery Reform," he wrote:

> We claim that in the forefront of the warfare of antislavery opinion, which this group of states conducted, stood our churches and their ministry. We claim for them more than this. We claim that if they had been let alone they would have been successful. If, starting with even the public sentiment of Virginia a hundred years ago, the great forces of Christian opinion had been left to work in their normal way, unhampered by the inflammatory politics of the extremists on either side, slavery would have succumbed to moral power. To doubt it is to doubt all Christian history. The negro would have come up to the rights of liberty, as he *grew* up to the duties of liberty. He would not have been *exploded* from the cannon's mouth into the miserable fiction of it which he has today, in which he has neither the intelligence to prize, nor the power to use, a freeman's ballot. Every decade adds to the proof that our ministry, and those who thought with them, were right in their faith that liberty *grows*; it never sails into the sulphurous air on the wings of dynamite. (1884, 1)

In Phelps's theory of preaching, then, pulpit oratory is—or should be—the most profound agent of personal and social change. It focuses upon individual spiritual/moral/intellectual development and regards that as the basis for broader political change. Its primary subject matter is Biblical truth, though it does sometimes discuss current political issues in terms of their relation to an overall system of Christian truth and responsibility. Its principal forum is the individual congregation; it insists that the preacher confine himself, for the most part, to administering to his own flock; his public discourse must be primarily dedicated to brightening his own "point of light." This, and not "the strife of parties, the frivolities of politics" (1861, 48), was the key to national and to universal salvation.

However—and this is the second great key to understanding Phelps's theory—the preaching required to bring about the needed "moral regeneration" could be performed only by a particular kind of preacher and a particular kind of preaching. The next section of this essay characterizes the nature of America's sacred oratorical culture by describing Phelps's "argumentative discussion of theology," which he alternately called "the true theory of preaching."

## The True Theory of Preaching

Phelps's writings are full of statements about the intellectual quality of true preaching, the power of sacred rhetoric to influence the human mind, and the importance of drawing on the principles of effective rhetoric from the writings and examples of great orators past and present in order to achieve the same kinds of effects the great ones achieved. At the same time, Phelps, like St. Augustine and Calvin, believed that spiritual conversion was a sovereign act of God. These two principles seem to clash until one looks carefully at Phelps's theory of spiritual regeneration. In *The New Birth*, Phelps writes, "All human instrumentalities and expedients by which truth is intensified, and so made appreciable by human sensibilities, are powerless to change the heart. Authority, sympathy, reasoning, eloquence, the magnetism of person, and whatever else enters the mystery of persuasion, in which mind impels mind by the enginery of speech, may change well-nigh everything in man except his character" (1867, 61–62 ).

At first blush, this would seem to undercut Phelps's entire theory of the role of oratorical art in human persuasion. But Phelps in fact believed that in the realm of sacred oratory, human instrumentalities and expedients were not left alone; if all the proper components were in place, the "suasive working of truth" would be "energized by the Grace of God," because God chose to do it (61). This qualification, it seems, was Phelps's concession to the Calvinistic doctrine that salvation was the free gift of God and came by God's will alone. That concession being made, however, Phelps goes on to articulate a powerful homiletic theory based on human ability to make choices as a result of ethical, emotional, and (predominantly) rational persuasion. Calvinism, he admitted, was "not a rhetorical doctrine," and in the "crisis of the soul," it "flies out the window" and "must fend for itself." Many of its doctrines, he wrote, "if held in the pulpit, must be held in silence" (1881, 479).

This stance would have been considered quite radical by the main contingent of Andover founders, but as Daniel Williams explains in *The Andover Liberals* (1970), modification of Calvinistic doctrine was a continual process at Andover. Even so, Phelps was one of the least liberal of the Andover liberals, and he set his rhetorical theory in opposition to other liberal currents swirling around him. For example, he resisted the idea of "evolution of the soul," or "developmental salvation," a theological analog to Darwin's theory of organic evolution. In the years after the publication of *On the Origin of Species*, many of Phelps's colleagues at Andover (and elsewhere) had begun to redefine salvation as a continual, gradual development of character. This doctrine Phelps stoutly opposed: "The development, then, of an existing germ of holiness is not the scriptural idea of a change of heart. In other words, no process of self-culture can be equivalent in its fruits to the divine act of regeneration" (1867, 52). At the same time, since regeneration of character was absolutely essential to salvation and since God chose to consecrate or energize truth to the work of that regeneration among humanity, and since he had chosen the instrumentality of human preaching to bring his regenerating truth to bear upon the human soul, it was the duty of those he called to this work to master the art of sacred rhetoric and use it in God's service.

Phelps believed, then, that ministers could approach the task of pulpit oratory without the encumbrance of a "mystical" attitude as regarded the operation of the human mind in its response to proper modes of persuasion. This point was essential with Phelps; throughout his writings one finds statements such as, "Ours is a religion of the pulpit, not of the altar" (that is, it operates by the intellectual power of pulpit oratory, not by mystical rites and ordinances), and this:

> The philosophy of its working [that is, Phelps's homiletic theory] is in entire accordance with the laws of the human mind. Not only is success in preaching practicable, not only is it ordained of God, but the *rationale* of the process by which it achieves success contains nothing contradictory

to the laws of the human mind, or suspensive of those laws. Divine decree in the work does not ignore those laws. Decree embraces and energizes the very laws by which mind acts on mind in this work. Preaching therefore has no concern with any miraculous process in its ways of working. Conversion is not a miracle. Persuasion to repentance is not a miracle. Persuasion by preaching is achieved by the very same means and methods of speech by which men are successfully moved by eloquent address on other than religious subjects of human thought. On the evangelical theory the pulpit claims no exemption from dependence on natural laws. We do not expect to escape the consequences of their violation. We entertain no such notion of dependence on the Holy Ghost as to encourage neglect or abuse of the arts of speech. We use those arts, depend upon them, look for success in them, as if we had no other hope of success than that which encourages speech in the senate or at the bar. This again we believe. We come to our work as philosophers as well as preachers. The telescope is not constructed with faith in the operation of natural laws more wisely than the theory of preaching is with faith in the laws of the human mind. (1881, 493–94)

Phelps does not explain at length what he means by "laws of the human mind," apparently because he believed them to be self-evident. *The New Birth* does contain scattered statements about the mind that seem derived from Thomas Reid and the Scottish Common Sense school, whose principles had been widely appropriated by American theologians in defense of rational theology. But Phelps's statements along these lines function primarily to clarify his position that the regenerate human mind operates under precisely the same laws as does the unregenerate mind; it is only the objects of thought and the character of the thinker that are changed at the new birth:

Yet no regenerate man knows anything of a re-creation of his nature, or a multiplication of his powers. No Christian is conscious of new faculties. None exhibits such in common life. A converted man thinks, reasons, remembers, imagines now; and he did all these before conversion. A regenerate heart feels, desires, loves, hates, now; and it did all these before. A new-born soul chooses, resolves, plans, executes; and it did all these before. The chief subjects of thought are changed—they are revolutionized. The prime objects of love and hatred are changed—they are transposed. The supreme inclination of the affections is changed—it is reversed. The *character* of the purposes is changed—it is transformed. (1861, 30–31)[6]

Yet a true preacher did more than bring his flock to an initial conversion or moral transformation; the new child in Christ was not the fully-grown man or woman. A true pastor provided a thorough, lengthy, systematic, intellectual/moral development for his congregation in the form of carefully developed sermons based on the entire range of Biblical text, which text Phelps believed to contain the seeds of the profoundest thought on earth, the stuff out of which the highest kind of oratory could be mined, fit food for the "craving" felt by awakened minds for "stern and strong thought, argument, faultless and vitalized logic" (1857, 34). A systematic treatment, by the way, was an excellent recipe for avoiding various controversies, disproportions, and disruptions; the preacher using a systematic approach was in less danger of being accused of riding any particular "hobby horse," political, theological, or otherwise.

It was vital to find the right Biblical text for each rhetorical occasion, because from the text was derived the proposition, the intellectual backbone of the sermon.[7] In essence, Phelps's whole art of oratory centered around the task of formulating the right scriptural propositions for the needs of a congregation and then finding the right "rhetorical forms" through which to "energize" those propositions to their minds and hearts. Although the proposition derived from a scriptural passage was often a fairly simple one, the rhetorical art needed to actually make it part of the listener's moral/intellectual makeup was complex, or to use Phelps's term, "elaborate." But the proposition itself had to be a direct, crisp, unconcealed address to the intellect, and it constituted the most important piece of intellectual weight in the sermon, the greatest insurance against emotional excess, and the greatest educating component of a sermon. Phelps writes,

> Preaching ought to break up the conglomerate in which thought and feeling, error and truth, spiritual power and animal magnetism, divine suggestion and Satanic temptation lie molten together. Men need to be taught by the pulpit to know what they believe, and why they feel, what emotions are legitimate to one truth, and what to another, and why they differ. Truths need to be individualized by analytic preaching. Only thus can the popular experience of them be deepened by discriminating knowledge. . . . We must generalize less, and analyze more; exhort less, and argue more. We must divide and isolate, and specify and concentrate our most profound conception of elemental truths.[8] That kind of preaching to which a free use of the expedients of logical expression is a

necessity is the only preaching by which the pulpit can accomplish its work as an educating power. . . . Those discourses which commonly produce epileptic and cataleptic phenomena in the audience are rambling discourses. Thought without an aim, emotion without a purpose, stimulation of the sensibilities without intelligent gravitation to an object let loose upon feeble minds [produces] the most unmanageable tendencies to pathological distortion. A center of thought rigidly adhered to, even in the wildest of ranting discourse, would tend to preserve the mental balance of hearers by the mere conservatism of intellect in its control of feeling. Animal sensibilities can scarcely master a mind which is thinking intensely and consecutively to one point. (1881, 289, 301)

This was not to say that emotion was excised from preaching in Phelps's system, only that the emotional force of true preaching must always be heavily counterbalanced by the weight of intellectual preaching that has come before; it is force contained, controlled like a diamond drilling tip into the channel that drives home the intellectual/spiritual matter of the sermon. At that point, the preacher must end his sermon and leave his words "to do their own work silently upon the will" (511).[9]

In Phelps's view, the true art of composing and delivering a sermon was complex and demanding in the highest possible sense.[10] It could not be done by the unlettered preacher, the overemotional revivalist, the self-seeking "professional," the lopsided esthete, the audience-ignoring technical theologian, or the morally weak orator. It required the holy man skilled in speaking, who had received the necessary literary, rhetorical, and moral training. It required a pulpit orator, a man whose Christian *paideia* had developed in him the character, the culture, and the rhetorical power necessary to lead others to permanent spiritual/moral transformation and to nurture them systematically in godly character. The next section of my essay examines Phelps's description of the training, the character, and the rhetorical powers of the true preacher.

## The Nurture and Nature of a Minister

In *The Theory of Preaching*, Phelps writes, "The ideal of a preacher which I have uniformly had in view is that of a Christian scholar using his scholarship with the aim of a Christian orator" (1881, 576). Contrast this with the Methodist revivalist Lorenzo Dow's doctrine:

What I insist, upon my brethren and sisters, is this: larnin isn't religion, and eddication don't give a man the power of the Spirit. It is grace and gifts that furnish the real live coals from off the altar. St. Peter was a fisherman—do you think he ever went to Yale College? No, no, beloved brethren and sisters. When the Lord wanted to blow down the walls of Jericho, he didn't take a brass trumpet, or a polished French horn: no such thing; he took a ram's horn—a plain, natural ram's horn—just as it grew. And so, when he wants to blow down the walls of the spiritual Jericho, my beloved brethren and sisters, he don't take one of your smooth, polite, college larnt gentlemen, but a plain, natural ram's horn sort of man like me. (Hatch 1989, 20)

"Crazy" Lorenzo might just as easily have pointed out St. Peter's lack of attendance at Andover Theological Seminary. The seminary itself had been founded by some of New England's most orthodox Congregationalists and Presbyterians, largely in reaction to the distressing proliferation of "lay preaching," though the appointment of a Unitarian to the Hollis Professorship of Theology at Harvard in 1805 was also a strong motive. However, the deeper concern of the orthodox clergy is clearly evident in the *Sermon Preached at the Opening of the Theological Institution in Andover* by Timothy Dwight. The greatest threats to the orthodox ministry, in his view, were not educated heretics such as the Unitarians (though they were bad enough) but the uneducated pretenders to the ministry:

There are, however, many persons in this and other Christian countries who declare, both in their language and conduct, that the desk ought to be yielded up to the occupancy of Ignorance. While they demand a seven-years apprenticeship, for the purpose of learning to make a shoe, or an axe; they suppose the system of Providence, together with the numerous, and frequently abstruse, doctrines and precepts, contained in the Scriptures, may be all comprehended without learning, labour, or time. . . . Multitudes of them can neither speak, nor write, nor even read English with propriety. They can neither explain, nor understand, the great body of Scriptural passages. . . . Should the Gospel be attacked by an Infidel; they are unable either to answer his objections, or to tell what are the proofs, on which its authority rests as a Revelation from God. Should the translation of a text be called in question; they could neither explain, nor defend it. Should a geographical, or historical fact be mentioned; or a local custom alluded to; it might, so far as they are concerned, as well have been written in *Arabic*, as in *English*. (1808, 7–8)

One finds this same sentiment on the part of the orthodox clergy from the postrevolution era onward. The conservative, university-bred preachers continually warned against the dangers of an uneducated ministry. Such men were incapable, said Lyman Beecher, of exercising "that religious and moral and literary influence which it belongs to the Ministry to exert." They were impostors, greenhorns, incapable of leading humanity to salvation. For its part, the "uneducated ministry" continually lambasted the "learned doctors," the "man-made, devil-sent, place-hunting gentry" (Hatch 1989, 178). As Hatch observes in *The Democratization of American Christianity*, "Instead of revering tradition, learning, solemnity, and decorum, as did Timothy Dwight and Lyman Beecher, a diverse array of populist preachers exalted youth, free expression, and religious ecstasy. They explicitly taught that divine insight was reserved for the poor and humble rather than the proud and learned" (1989, 35). Hatch's book ably demonstrates that the clash of the "dissident religionists" with the orthodox clergy was a class struggle, a forerunner and an outgrowth of America's democratic groundswells as much as an ideological/theological struggle. This is unquestionably true, yet there were profound and legitimate intellectual/theological differences between the two camps.

It was in the context of this kind of popular denigration of the value of liberal arts education, including graduate theological and rhetorical education, that Phelps and his colleagues enunciated their doctrines of the *paideia*, or rather the Christian *doctrina*,[11] that a true Christian orator must undergo if he is to be an instrument in God's hands for converting and nurturing human souls. Phelps's program involved intensive, life-long intellectual and moral formation, much of it through reading great literature,[12] especially literature "steeped in religion."

The objects of reading such authors included "mental discipline . . . the growth of the mind, not mere accumulation of knowledge"; "self reflexivity . . . standards of judgment, and critical taste"; "familiarity with the principles of effective thought and expression"; and "assimilation to the genius of the best authors" (1883, 98–105). This last object was the most telling, for Phelps believed that God used the instrumentality of great books as part of the process of transforming the human mind, and that only those men who had properly assimilated the godly germs of intelligence contained in the world's great literature possessed the proper mental soil for the growth of true sermons. Assimilation of great literature was also a vital component of moral growth. Phelps in fact believed, along with his colleagues, that the inspiration available to humanity in the modern age was unavoidably dependent on this assimilation of the "food" God had provided his ministers; the "plenary inspiration" enjoyed by the original prophets and apostles, and which people like Dow mistakenly assumed to possess, was no longer available to humankind. In its place was now "partial" or "homiletic" inspiration, based on the interaction of God's spirit with the intelligence in the preacher's mind that had been acquired through the process of assimilation just described. In any case, the Christian *paideia* described by Phelps is typical of the conservative brand of American homiletic theory and fundamental to the sacred oratorical culture in which the preacher functioned. It provided not only the rhetorical sensibility necessary to it but also the common ground of intellectual and moral substance that undergirded America's oratorical culture as a whole.

The preacher who acquired the proper Christian *paideia* also acquired, as a natural accompaniment, the proper ethos for preaching, and this, in fact, Phelps regarded as the most important of his persuasive powers. Interestingly, Phelps's discussion of ethos seems to merge with a discussion of logos and pathos in his final lectures on sermonic "application" in *The Theory of Preaching*. In essence, he argues that it is the intellectual solidity of the sermon and the man who preaches it, along with the equally real and perceived moral loftiness of the preacher, that authorize him to employ emotional appeals at this point and that make such appeals genuinely (not ephemerally) effective:

> Eloquence in all its forms is built on, or more significantly is built *in*, intense character in the man. This is as fundamental to secular as to sacred eloquence. No man can be eloquent in any thing, who has not, *quoad hoc* [sic], an intense working of his own character. His personal intelligence, his personal faith, his personal consciousness of an object, the utmost strain of his will-power are the vitalizing forces. Not adroitness in command of language, not zeal in the form of paroxysm, but the character of the man, in an intense unity of purpose, is the soul of speech in those lofty forms of it which we dignify as oratory. (1881, 457)

As I have suggested, Phelps evinces in this belief a strong affinity with Quintilian's *vir bonus* doctrine. He continues to refer to the character of the preacher throughout his discussion of pathetic appeal in the lectures on sermonic application; it is virtually impossible to separate his treatments of pathos and ethos. "The character is the speech, the man is the speech," he writes, and it is the "sanctified character" of the preacher that lends both passion and authority to his words (461). For Phelps, ethos meant the shining through of this sanctified character in both the appeals made in the pulpit and in terms of the preacher's general reputation for piety, compassion, and learning. However, Phelps was careful to distinguish true ethos from its counterfeit. The ethos of the ideal sacred orator was effective precisely because he did not aggrandize himself; he focused attention on God, doctrine, principle, truth, service. His congregation saw him as the embodiment of virtues and learning universally aspired to; it was not anything individualistic or charismatic that made them trust him but the fact that he stood as a covenanted, organic part of the community and had become a good disciple of Christ, just as they were all trying to do. The function of his ethos in the social discourse of pulpit oratory was consistent with the neoclassical ethos of the best kind of orator.

The counterfeit of true ministerial ethos, against which Phelps firmly stood, was the practice of putting *oneself* at the center of one's discourse. Despite his and his colleagues' efforts, however, emotionalized preaching and religious movements that centered on personalities, as well as the increasing professionalization of the Christian ministry, continued to erode the sacred mode of America's oratorical culture.

## Phelps's Stand Against Individualism and Professionalism

Phelps was concerned that the legitimate ethos of the sacred orator not be confused with the tendency to personality cults that began to burgeon after the Civil War (see Clark and Halloran and Antczak and Siemers, this volume). Calhoun notes, for example, that the highly successful evangelical ministries of Henry Ward Beecher and Dwight L. Moody depended largely on "exploiting their own personalities and private lives." Their sermons were full of personal anecdote. Beecher's sermons frequently employed "something involving himself, his own experience or feelings, and his relationship to his hearers," while "Moody iterated stories about the revival process, a large proportion of which afforded what later fan magazines might call 'exciting glimpses' into the life of the celebrity revivalist" (Calhoun 1973, 261–62). However, Phelps was even more deeply concerned about trends towards professionalization in the Christian ministry, which he saw operating right at Andover and all around him in his own tradition.

Before saying more about professionalization in the Christian ministry, however, I must clarify the senses in which conservatives used the term "professional." Timothy Dwight's 1808 *Sermon Preached at the Opening of the Theological Institution in Andover* was based on Matthew 8:52: "Then said he unto them, therefore every scribe, who is instructed unto the Kingdom of heaven, is like unto a man who is an householder, who bringeth forth out of his treasure things new and old." Dwight begins by explaining that "a scribe . . . was a person professionally employed in expounding to the Jewish nation the law of God." The modern equivalent, he declared, was the "minister of the gospel . . . educated to the service of the church," whose treasure was "useful professional knowledge" (1808, 3). Later, he enumerated the "five great divisions" of Theological education — "Natural Theology, Christian Theology, Sacred Literature, Ecclesiastical History, and the Eloquence of the Desk" (1808, 4–29) — and explained the need for and advantages of professional specialization in each of these fields at the new seminary.

It was the specialized, professorial Bartlett Chair of Sacred Oratory that Phelps came to occupy forty years later, at mid-century, just about the time when, according to Bledstein, the "culture of professionalism" was establishing itself in America. In view of Bledstein's time frame, it is interesting to note that for many decades before Phelps came to Andover, the Christian ministry in America had been referred to as a profession. Phelps and his colleagues were aware of the modern meaning that the word was taking on, but it is clear from the contexts in which they use it, and from their comprehensive philosophies, that they saw "profession" and "sacred calling"[13] as synonymous. When Phelps uses the phrases "our great profession" or "our calling" in reference to the Christian ministry, he is using the traditional sense of "profession": to acknowledge or claim, publicly, one's status as an emissary of God's Word and to claim the truth of or acknowledge, in the work of one's life, that Word itself. Profession and professation and confession (of one's status and God's Word) were much the same thing. In medieval Europe, a profession specifically

meant an avowal of faith upon entering a Christian order. This was the
fundamental sense in which Phelps and other traditionalists still
used the word, unless they were criticizing the secular encroachments onto its meaning.

Phelps was acutely aware of those encroachments, of course. He
knew that many young graduates of theological schools saw the
Christian profession as a "career" in the sense just coming into vogue:
a "course of life" that took one from the stage of esoteric education
through successive stages of advancement in social status, power,
wealth, and honor among one's colleagues. It was also coming to
mean, in the ministerial profession as well as in secular professions, a
broad scope of choice among specialities. Many graduates of Andover
Theological Seminary, as well as those from many other seminaries,
were leaving to become agents or board members for various benevolent or moral societies, educators with various fields of specialty,
administrators in missionary organizations, and ecclesiastical administrators of various sorts. One of the principal reasons for this was the
reluctance of many graduates or practicing ministers to accept call-
ings ("calls") from small, poor, or rural churches, especially those in
the rough Western regions (regions that reached much farther east at
that time than presently). It was not simply that they feared hard beds
and backwoods cooking; poor churches or churches far away from
centers of cultural richness did not look promising to young ministerial professionals—that is, to those who expected the Christian
ministry to provide them a career, a ladder of "upward mobility." This
is one of the major reasons why the Methodists and Baptists spread so
rapidly into the West, while the Congregationalist/Presbyterian
churches grew relatively slowly from the late eighteenth century onward. Not only could Methodists and Baptists enter the ministry with
less formal preparation, but they regarded the Christian ministry almost
exclusively as a missionary, preaching, and pastoral ministry—at least
until, later in the nineteenth century, they began to hunger for social
respectability and to suffer their own professionalization.

Phelps's reaction to the professionalization of the ministry in his
own tradition was strong. His personal letters chronicle his grief and
alarm at the trend. The concluding lecture to his Andover students
each year usually dwelt on the evils of self-seeking professionalism
and extolled the traditional virtues of selfless service to one's entire
charge, especially to the uncultured and poor. This certainly did not

mean that the young minister was to let his own culture slip; Phelps reiterated in his final lecture that "the ideal of a preacher which I have uniformly had in view is that of a Christian scholar using his scholarship with the aim of a Christian orator" (1881, 576). That aim was to reach *all* of humanity with Christ's saving Word and to elevate them all into full Christian manhood and womanhood. Phelps referred to the Methodists and their "apostolic adaptation to the lower classes" (580), admitting with "some alarm" the disjunction between theory and practice in conservative homiletics: "A scholarly ministry taken as a whole . . . is working away from the unscholarly masses of the people." Phelps seemed almost to plead with his students to use their training to serve the lower classes; high culture, he insisted, is vital to a preacher's ability to be "made all things to all men, that [they] might by all means save some" (1 Corinthians 9:22). The profession of Christian ministry, Phelps insisted, existed for that reason; its practical function was to save and exalt all humanity. Phelps told his students:

> I wish, therefore, to commit these homiletic discussions to you with the most solemn charge that you receive them with a spirit of practical good sense and of practical piety . . . a preacher had better work in the dark, with nothing but mother-wit, a quickened conscience, and a Saxon Bible to teach him what to do and how to do it, than to vault into an aerial ministry in which only the upper classes shall know or care anything about him. You had better go and *talk* the gospel in the Cornish dialect to those miners who told the witnesses summoned by the committee of the English Parliament, that they had "never heard of Mister Jesus Christ in these mines," than to do the work of the Bishop of London. (1881, 582–83)

This insistence on selflessness and connection with "the masses," to subordination of individuality to community, higher authority, and larger causes, though not a new theme in the history of Christianity, yet had particular significance in Phelps's day, when the Christian ministry was being transformed on many levels. Phelps's position, and that of his orthodox colleagues, was still framed within the traditional oratorical culture. The learning and rhetorical power of the sacred orator was properly engaged in a social discourse dedicated to the welfare of the community, and the orator himself stood "above" the masses only in the sense of his embodiment of knowledge and virtues endorsed and aspired to by the community. His position as leader, shepherd, counselor, was the result of his following a call from

God; his was a response to God's ordering of things, not a self-envisioned, self-advancing career. His relationship with the people was on the basis of their recognition of his call and their covenant with him. His discourse was most successful when it did not stress his individuality but when it reinforced the community's values and their mutual acceptance of an authority to which they all submitted themselves—and when it reasoned with them in what Phelps called the "rhetorical forms"[14] or "adapted forms" of God's truth: forms of social discourse designed to convert and edify the individual soul and create the fundamental consensus upon which the entire community could stand.

## Conclusion

For Phelps and for many of his colleagues in the conservative homiletic tradition, the sermon still functioned as a form of public discourse designed to preserve and create consensus at the most fundamental levels. The ideal orator was conceived to be, as in classical systems of oratory, a man embodying all the very best moral/intellectual virtues and powers—an elite personality using his rhetoric to persuade audiences to correct belief and advantageous social action. As such, Phelps believed ministers and their persuasive discourse stood at the very center of social change, and they functioned at the same time to conserve a system of knowledge and values that made possible the mode of rational persuasion by public discourse that we generally associate with classical rhetoric. Again, the parallel to classicism is seen in the conception of the orator as devoted not to personal advancement or relying on abstruse or exclusionary discourse but fully devoted to the community, a permanent member of that community, and using discourse based on shared values and beliefs, adapted to a popular audience, to promote the safety and development of the entire community. Even in its general forms and in many of its principles, the homiletics of Phelps and his colleagues displayed a clear neoclassical influence; nearly all their treatises on the art of sacred rhetoric are organized around the classical canons and result in a synthesis of classical theories and Christian materials and motives.

Phelps's theory of preaching, then, is representative of what I call conservative homiletic theory in America. It conserved, to a significant degree, various features of classical rhetoric, and it conserved the old Congregational ideal of one flock, one shepherd—the ideal of the holy man skilled in speaking who dedicated himself primarily to the saving and edification of one community. His theory focused on the intellectual dimension of preaching and condemned enthusiastic preaching that did not have sufficient intellectual ballast. At the same time, it allowed for a genuine application of emotional force, as long as the emotion was in proper relation to its intellectual foundation. Preaching in Phelps's system was designed not only to convert but also to edify, to educate, to provide a congregation with a complete diet of moral/intellectual food. Preaching therefore had to be not only Biblically based but also as systematic as possible, though the forms of these systematic sermons had to be carefully adjusted to the needs of the congregations being addressed. The congregation so edified by its pastor would grow up to Christlike character and would spread the fruits of that character in steady, permanent forms, improving not only the local community but also, ultimately, the nation and the world. The ministration of the pulpit, therefore, had to confine itself, for the most part, to the specific Christian enterprise, bringing up sociopolitical issues only within the framework of the congregation's comprehensive moral/intellectual formation and discouraging the various and divisive forms of immediatism. This check on the form of political involvement constituted a modification of the old Congregational ideal, but Phelps believed it was necessary to accommodate the political reality of the nation. It was still consistent in spirit with the old ideal. The public discourse of the true preacher in any age, Phelps was convinced, constituted the most moral and most lastingly effective form of political activity.

Phelps advocated these ideals for over thirty years at Andover Theological Seminary and was an important factor in keeping them alive to the end of the century. However, even during his tenure at Andover, a large percentage of Andover graduates went on not to pastorates but to other professional posts. On this count his own homiletic theory might have worked against him; its stress on the level of culture required for true preaching might have contributed to his students' anxiousness about being isolated on the rough frontier.

It was unquestionably true, however, that the orthodox Protestant ministry, the chief guardian and inculcator of America's sacred oratorical culture, was being transformed, professionalized, throughout the nineteenth century (though with far greater speed in the second half than in the first) and that the Andover students of Phelps's day were only following a well-established trend. One of the impetuses for that trend was that early in the century, the clergy had crossed swords with the divisive influence of party politics and had lost. They had sided with the Federalists, the "Friends of Order," people who resisted democratic and electoral politics and shared the clergy's commitment to the old order of religious nurture, civic and spiritual unity, and rule by a moral/intellectual elite. In time, however, as the Federalists entered more deeply into party politics, the clergy was largely shunted aside as a political liability. The clergy itself, still wanting to promote unity and avoid the accusation of politician partisanship, turned to forming voluntary and various debating and benevolent societies, attempting to hold off public disapproval by distinguishing between these and direct political action. The difference was that voluntary societies were "organized for discussion rather than action" and "did not formally advocate any particular position" (Scott 1978, 106). Scott points out that even in terms of the physical space used for public discourse, there was a distancing: Whereas before the church had been a common gathering place to discuss public issues, now lecture halls and lycea were used even by church-sponsored groups like temperance leagues. Unfortunately, all this contributed to the further diminishing of the clerical ethos as the official guardians of public order. As this dimension shrunk, the clergy was forced more and more into a professional stance. One of the most telling features of this stance, according to Scott, was the fact that clergy became more and more perceived as doctors of a sort: physicians of the soul, specialists in a partitioned and personal dimension of human reality—an essentially apolitical one. Scott also indicates that the subject matter of much orthodox preaching became less "heavy" even theologically; it became more personal, anecdotal, "friendly." This trend toward the trivialization of the pulpit is one that Phelps stoutly resisted; his theory of preaching demanded the spiritual and intellectual content needed to accomplish its ambitious goals.

From the 1850s on, according to Scott, "the role of religion in sustaining the broader public culture consisted of laying out the Christian dimensions of public issues" (151). But whereas Scott sees this as a great reduction in the political power of the clergy, Phelps saw it as one dimension of a comprehensive power wielded by the clergy, a power that, if allowed to function properly, would be more permanently and universally effective than any other agent of social change.

The question is, then, why wasn't Phelps's theory of preaching allowed to function properly—that is, why didn't the orthodox ministry hold to it, why didn't the public discourse of preaching within the sacred oratorical culture gather strength and effect the comprehensive social transformations that Phelps and his colleagues envisioned? My essay has suggested that, fundamentally, America's sacred oratorical culture faded away for the same reasons that its secular counterpart died out: Generally speaking, it suffered a transformation from an oratorical to a professional culture. The spirit of democracy, the exaltation of individual judgment and personality, the rise of specialization, and the new visions of "career" and professional success that Clark and Halloran describe in the Introduction to this volume all had their peculiar effects upon and manifestations in the conservative Protestant ministry, the traditional guardians of sacred oratorical culture. That culture cannot be said to have entirely died out, nor would it be fair to call Phelps's homiletic theory an entire practical failure; many of the preachers Phelps prepared for the ministry in his day did a great deal of good in America and abroad, both personally and politically, and there are still religious seminaries, and some individual preachers and congregations, that have "conserved" many of Phelps's ideals and look to historical figures like Phelps for inspiration. Certainly, religious thought and conviction, often profoundly affected by preaching, still constitute an important groundwork for social discourse and activity of various kinds. However, the personal culture and rhetorical power of the preacher Phelps idealized, the context and connection with the congregation he envisioned, and the organic effects of conservative preaching he anticipated cannot be said to have been realized on the scale he hoped for. America's sacred oratorical culture yielded to the forces of an increasingly professionalized and heterogeneous society, and it lost ground to those denominations and religious movements that exploited emotion, formed personality cults, or simply produced a greater missionary force because their missionaries were not required to pass through a rigorous liberal/theological/rhetorical arts training and were usually more willing to penetrate into and continue to serve in poor, remote, or uncultured territory.

There were other drawbacks to Phelps's theory, as I have suggested. For example, even though he envisioned the day when the educational and political advantages of the few would be spread to the many by the steady growth of regenerated individuals and communities, his system was undeniably elitist. Of course, Phelps and the conservative clergy were not the only class in the nineteenth century to believe that a general, gradual, "evolutionary" development of the human race was taking place—most profoundly in conservative, educated, Protestant New England and perhaps a few adjacent states.[15] The institutions, the laws, the culture, the *people* of Protestant New England were seen as being at the forefront of God's transformation of humanity, and it was vital to support the steady progress of His work; immediatism in any form—anything forced by man's impatience, ignorance, violence, or willfulness—was to be avoided at almost any cost. Not even the individual soul should be pushed towards conversion too quickly or emotionally; it needed proper Christian nurture.

But the most obvious difficulty with Phelps's *modus operandi* for social change, which insisted upon the temporary toleration of evil, was its slowness in changing things for those under the present lash of evil. One can imagine that a slave suffering under this lash might not find comfort in the promise that the true theory of preaching, if allowed to operate without the interference of political extremism, would, within a generation or two, free his children or grandchildren. Yet from Phelps's point of view, and from that of a large body of orthodox clergy and laypeople, this delay was lamentable but necessary. Solid, permanent, lasting peace and improvement can come, they believed, only as individual souls are converted to Christ and built up into Christlike character, and the most powerful agent of this personal and social change is "the argumentative discussion of theology"—social discourse carried on by a true preacher according to the true theory of preaching.

## Notes

1. Phelps, the son of an orthodox Congregational minister, pursued his own development as a pulpit orator deliberately throughout his liberal arts schooling at Geneva College, Amherst, and the University of Pennsylvania, taking classes in classical and modern rhetoric at all three schools. He then

went on for ministerial training at Union Theological Seminary, Yale Theological Seminary, and (briefly) Andover Theological Seminary.

In 1842, he accepted a call to pastor the Pine Street Congregational Church in Boston. Six years later, he resigned to accept the professorship of sacred rhetoric at Andover Theological Seminary. At Andover he wrote, in lecture form, thousands of pages on the art of sacred rhetoric. Much of this material later appeared in book form: *The Theory of Preaching* (1881), *Men and Books* (1882), and *English Style in Public Discourse with Special Reference to the Usages of the Pulpit* (1883). Phelps also published numerous articles on the subject of homiletics as well as a number of theological and devotional books. These theological and devotional works were themselves significant parts of his corpus of homiletical writings, since their themes, such as spiritual regeneration and Christian character, often bore important relationships to preaching.

2. At the same time, we must remember that many of America's preachers, even great evangelists, have been Calvinistic and felt no contradiction between their doctrine and practice, and that during the nineteenth century, the belief that the ministry should be confined to men was nearly universal.

3. Nineteenth-century American homileticians drew upon broad resources in forming their theories of rhetoric: modern British rhetorics, especially those of Campbell and Whately; various Christian homiletic treatises from ancient to modern times; and the rhetorical models provided by the Bible and by famous preachers through the ages. They also drew directly upon major classical theorists, principally Plato, Aristotle, Cicero, Quintilian, and St. Augustine.

4. Weld (1803–1895) had intended to become an ordained minister. Although he attended theological seminary, his reform activities, especially abolitionism, kept him from graduation and ordination (as for abolition activism, it was a matter of crossing the authorities and being expelled from the seminary, but it is also true that he became so absorbed in moral causes that he didn't have time or inclination to earn formal ministerial credentials). Weld had many offers to pastor churches despite his lack of a divinity degree, but he turned them all down, preferring to attack the world's evils through direct and very intense involvement in benevolence and reform movements.

5. As I note Weld's position and even the position of "much of the orthodox Northern clergy" on the "divisive and disruptive" effect of abolition activists, I must acknowledge that there was some profound shifting of sentiment as the nation approached civil war. As animosities between North and South heightened, some who had opposed abolitionists began to tolerate and then even to support them in varying degrees. Weld himself began to sound much more like an immediatist as war approached. When the war actually started, some pulpits that had preached tolerance and forbearance

now sounded the battle cry. My impression is that even Phelps was in favor of ending the war through Union military victory once fighting had begun—but this did not change his convictions about the nature of Christian preaching or its preeminence in bringing about permanent, comprehensive social improvement.

6. Elsewhere in his writings, particularly in *The Theory of Preaching*, Phelps makes it clear that he believes the human mind to be addressable by the three Aristotelian modes of persuasion and that logos is the most important mode. He also discloses his opinion, which he professes to share with Aristotle, of the close relationship of rhetorical art to the science of psychology and to other sciences.

7. Though inventing the proposition was the most important part of sermonic composition, it was yet only one phase of the process. *The Theory of Preaching*, a text 600 pages long, treats at length the art of sermonic invention for each of the many parts of a sermon.

8. Note here the dialectical approach Phelps is advocating as a way of arriving at formulations of elemental truth. Again, he seems to agree with Aristotle—at least with one interpretation of Aristotle—that rhetoric is the "counterpart" of dialectic; that is, he seems to be arguing that a form of dialectical reasoning can and should be used in rhetorical invention, in this case the invention of the proposition of a sermon.

9. The most profound object of preaching, writes Phelps, is simply to bring people into the presence of God, to let the soul feel its "moral loneliness with God": "There is a point in the development of the work of divine grace at which it is expedient that human persuasion should cease. It has done all that it can do. It has tried every thing but silence. Wisdom dictates that now the awakened sinner should be left alone, and for this reason, — that he is alone with *God*" (1881, 549).

This idea of Phelps's shows an interesting parallel with the ancient idea of *kairos*, which has been translated as "the opportune moment," "the right measure," and "balance." This concept is prominent in sophistic rhetoric, and though Phelps and his colleagues never wrote of the sophists except with the standard disapproval (for their time), this is one idea they seemed to share with them. But it is accurate to say that Phelps believed the primary object of preaching was to create a *kairos* for the soul, by providing a careful balance of intellectual, ethical, and emotional appeals, just the right measure to bring the human soul to the verge of decision.

10. I have only touched here on the complexities of Phelps's theory. It is helpful to visualize each component of a sermon in Phelps's system as a level of a pyramid, with application at the apex. Building up to that apex are text, explanation, introduction, partition (division), body (development), and conclusion (consisting of inferences, remarks, and application). Phelps's theory

for handling each of these parts is elaborate.

11. I here use the term *doctrina* in the Augustinian sense explained by Eugene Kervane: "When Augustine uses *doctrina* he means what the Greeks meant by *paideia*, education in the broad sense that constitutes a comprehensive intellectual and moral formation" (1966, 100).

12. However, sermons constructed under the true theory of preaching would not be "esthetic" products; Phelps, though a sophisticated literary scholar, was strongly opposed to bellelettrism in sermons. True sermons could, however, legitimately be called "literary," in this sense: "Let us count that as the most perfect literature, which is most perfectly adjusted to the most perfect ends by the most perfect uses of the materials and the arts of speech" (1881, 8).

13. Bledstein cites in this connection William Perkins's classic definition of a calling, "a certain kind of life, ordained and imposed on man by God for the common good" (1976, 176–77).

14. ". . . those forms in which [theology] is susceptible of presentation to the popular reason, and susceptible of use as motive power upon the popular conscience and heart" (1861, 36).

15. When Darwin's theory of evolution became current, conservatives appropriated his ideas in various ways ("social Darwinism," "social/spiritual Darwinism," etc.), but it is not accurate to say that their ideas about the gradual transformation of humanity through conservative Christian preaching and culture depended on Darwin; those ideas predate him.

# 4

# Margaret Fuller ✳

# A Rhetoric of Citizenship in Nineteenth-Century America ✳

*P. Joy Rouse*

✳The project of positioning Margaret Fuller in transformations of nineteenth-century rhetoric is a slippery one. At best, she is a marginal figure in histories of rhetoric because of their primary focus on institutional rhetorics and rhetorical instruction, and she did not produce any one text that fits easily into the category of rhetorical treatises. She didn't write a textbook or a detailed analysis or theory of her teaching and writing practices. Historians of rhetoric do, however, have access to records of her practices and observations about teaching, her thoughts about women's positions in the nineteenth century, her feminist manifesto, *Woman in the Nineteenth Century*, and a rich collection of articles she wrote for Horace Greeley's *New York Tribune*. Why, then, one might ask, write about Fuller in the context of the history of rhetoric—or more specifically, why Fuller in a consideration of transformations of nineteenth-century rhetoric?

One answer to this question can be gleaned from the range of her practices and her revision of the transcendentalist notion of self-culture. Fuller's understanding of self-culture and her later theory of mutual interpretation, as rhetorics, encouraged individuals, especially women, to participate in civic and communal activity; in addition, her work evoked a standard of public morality addressing the needs of oppressed people. It is paradoxical that during the years I examine here, 1836 to 1846, Fuller's work and commitment to civic virtue were developing alongside the growing emphasis in mainstream society on individualism and economic competition. As the rhetorical instruction and practice of many individuals were adapting to professional and individualistic values, what does it mean that Fuller increasingly resisted these values and opted instead for a model of civic involvement and responsibility? She was certainly not anti-individual; her major writings championed individualism. The paradox is that she claimed the individualist notion of self-culture as a right for marginalized citizens, which ultimately led her to a call for social change. Fuller was certainly a privileged woman, but as her social awareness grew, Chevigny has observed, she learned "that other institutions had to be transformed before the oppressed could really learn, and that the privileged, for all their education, were necessarily oppressors" (1976, 293–94).

Within the context of transformations of nineteenth-century rhetoric, then, Fuller has to be read against the grain. Her value to us today can best be understood not in terms of her standing as an individual figure in rhetoric but in terms of the kinds of developments in the speaking and writing practices of marginalized citizens our histories have yet to account for. I have three primary goals in this essay: to provide a brief introduction to Margaret Fuller, to define what I mean by a "rhetoric of citizenship," and then to position Fuller within the transformations of rhetoric that this collection records through her teaching practices and later writings.

There are numerous studies of Margaret Fuller that describe her pedagogy; her skills as a conversationalist, editor, or journalist; her friendships with the New England circle of transcendentalists; or her feminism. More than any one of these categories, though, Fuller's life and writings demonstrate change, intense personal and political change that occurred as she became involved in each of the activities listed above.[1] Like other marginalized Americans during the nineteenth century, women were struggling to claim their rights as citizens; this struggle, as played out in the life and works of Margaret Fuller, represents the important role that pedagogy and public discourse had in their confronting the social and political barriers imposed on them by the dominant culture. Margaret Fuller provides one example of how marginalized Americans were redefining citizenship through their discursive acts.[2] Although Fuller believed in the power of the individual, as other transcendentalists did, she represents a rhetoric whose aim was to foster community and moral consensus. By tracing her development through her teaching practice, to the conversations she held for women, to her book *Woman in the Nineteenth Century* and her articles in the *New York Daily Tribune*, I hope to establish Fuller's place within the transformations of nineteenth-century American rhetoric as a woman whose self-critical struggle led her to bring other women into the practices of an oratorical culture and whose public discourse can be used to revise notions of citizenship, particularly women's place in it.

Margaret Fuller's father provided her with an education that surpassed the traditional education of young women in early nineteenth-century America. As Chevigny observes, "In his insistence on rigorous classical training, [Timothy Fuller] flew in the face of the fashionable light and sentimental education then offered girls; in his rejection of apology, hesitation, qualification, or circumlocution in her performance, he sought virtually to cut her off from prevalent female speech patterns" (1976, 21). Himself educated at Harvard as a lawyer, Timothy Fuller trained Margaret in Latin and English grammar and sent her to Harvard College tutors and private grammar schools. She received an education more typical of New England's elite young men—immersion in Latin, French, Greek, rhetoric and logic, math, and history. In 1821 her father sent her to Dr. John Parks's school for young women in Boston, which allowed Fuller to continue studying books instead of the domestic skills more typical of women's education. Ann Douglas argues that Timothy Fuller not only kept his daughter from the sentimental and domestic education typical for young women but also "forcibly cut her off from the feminine subculture of etiquette books and sentimental novels" (1977, 319). Margaret Fuller garnered her sense of identity from studying books and facts and endeavored to live a life of thought and action. Timothy Fuller "subjected her to none of the 'bewildering flattery' which makes its recipient dependent on its donor for her sense of identity. . . . [He] fostered in Margaret his own passion for accuracy, a passion which . . . deepened into a profoundly ethical concern for veracity, for reality itself" (320). The last school Margaret Fuller attended was Susan Prescott's Young Ladies Seminary of Groton. Even with this education behind her, though, she was forced to face the contradictory nature of the training she had received when she left Prescott's school in 1826. For a young man of Fuller's time and position, the next step of education was Harvard to begin preparation for a career in law or ministry (Hudspeth 1983, 1: 31–35). As a woman, though, Fuller was forced to confront her position in a culture that simultaneously promised and denied a life of free self-development to women. This restriction, as Fuller both lived and observed it, led her to a commitment to bring women into the social and political activities of a society that, as Barbara Welter asserts, held women "hostage[s] in the home" (1976, 21).

Two well-documented ideals of American womanhood, prevalent in New England, are important to understanding the context of Fuller's life, writings, and the struggle she faced in bringing women into oratorical and political activity: the Republican Mother (Kerber 1980) and True Womanhood (Welter 1976).[3] Republican Motherhood, born out of the American Revolution and based in separate spheres ideology, positioned women as the "custodian[s] of civic morality" (Kerber 1980, 11). While this ideal seems to recognize, or at least allow for, women's agency in training the traditional rhetorical ideal of "the good man skilled in speaking," it also embodied the contradiction in which Fuller and other women of her position lived. Kerber asserts, "Republican political theory called for a sensibly educated female citizenry to educate future generations of sensible republicans," but "domestic tradition condemned highly educated women as perverse threats to family stability" (10). However, Republican Motherhood was subversive in some respects; although women were not legally considered citizens, this ideal led them to revise notions of citizenship that "merged the domestic domain of the preindustrial woman with the new public ideology of individual responsibility and civic virtue" (269). It challenged the public/private dichotomy of the separate spheres ideology that placed men in the public political domain and women in the private domestic space of the home by politicizing motherhood and making it a function of the state. Although it by no means freed women to be active in civic affairs outside of the home, "the notion that a mother can perform a political function represents the recognition that a citizen's political socialization takes place at an early age, that the family is a basic part of the system of political communication, and that patterns of family authority influence the general political culture" (283). While this ideal valorized the work of mothers and wives and young girls in training to be model mothers and wives, it positioned women who resisted these roles as betrayers of the family ideal and, ultimately, of the country.

Republican Motherhood provides the backdrop of cultural values and gendered expectations into which Margaret Fuller was born. After the turn of the century, when Fuller was about ten years old, another and somewhat similar ideal developed—the "cult of True Womanhood." Like Republican Motherhood, supporters of True Womanhood recognized that women had a distinct role to play in society and that it was in the home. Barbara Welter describes the "four cardinal virtues" of True Womanhood as "piety, purity, submissiveness, and domesticity" (1976, 21). Advocates of True Womanhood were critical of any resistence to the ideal; if anyone challenged the virtues of True Womanhood "he was damned immediately as an enemy of God, of civilization and of the Republic" (21). Women who resisted the ideal were even more dangerous; literary and intellectual women were not considered women at all and were used as a warning to other women "not to let their literary or intellectual pursuits take them away from God" (Welter 1976, 21). Sarah Josepha Hale, the editor of *Godey's Lady's Book*, whom Nicole Tonkovich's essay in this volume discusses, used Margaret Fuller as one example of a woman who "threw away the 'One True Book' for others, open to error" (21). Welter observes, "Mrs. Hale used the unfortunate Miss Fuller as a fateful proof that 'the greater the intellectual force, the greater and more fatel [*sic*] the errors into which women fall who wander from the Rock of Salvation, Christ the Saviour'" (23). Within True Womanhood, then, women who assumed an active public role were transgressing their "fearful obligation" and "solemn responsibility" to be redemptive daughters and mothers (21). Margaret Fuller and other women like her, such as Fanny Wright, were committing a crime against the family and womanhood, the women's magazines warned, that would result in "madness or death" (23).

## Self-Culture and Rhetorics of Citizenship

Republican Motherhood and True Womanhood were contributing factors to the restraints that white middle- and upper-class women faced. While many women, such as Hale, embraced these ideals as models for the role women should have in the family, Fuller and a large number of other women used these ideals subversively to bolster their arguments for a philosophy of women's education that would lead to their social and political involvement. They were able to capitalize on the more conservative and accepted arguments for women's education; once an inroad was made into the classroom and schools were made available to young women, for example, Fuller was able to use that space and her position as a teacher to show her students that they had choices that could take them beyond predetermined domestic responsibilities. This early experience as a teacher gave her an opportunity to begin challenging the limitations of self-culture as male privilege.

Before discussing Fuller's practices as a teacher, conversation leader, and writer, some preliminary explanation of my use of "rhetorics of citizenship" as a descriptive category for historiography and Fuller's revision of self-culture will help to demonstrate my rationale for how/why Fuller can be located within transformations of nineteenth-century rhetoric.

### Rhetorics of Citizenship

Classical rhetoric has been used as a barometer of sorts to measure the development of rhetoric in nineteenth-century America. As Clark and Halloran explained the transformations that occurred in the nineteenth century in the Introduction to this collection, early nineteenth-century rhetoric emphasized moral authority formed through public consensus rather than through individual gains and authority. This early practice was closely aligned with classical rhetoric, civic virtue, and responsibility. The strength of the polis was dependent on the civic virtue of individuals who were committed to active citizenship and the public good that they identified or argued for in public discourse. For historians of rhetoric seeking to construct more inclusive histories, it will be helpful to question what "public discourse" means and what its possible roles and sites were. Does it include any topic of social, cultural, and political importance, or is traditionally defined "political debate" its sole concern? As we map transformations of rhetoric, what should or can we take to be our territory? Christine Oravec has written that "the classical or classical-belles lettres tradition described by many scholars resides primarily in the native textbooks, pedagogical practices, and curricula of universities and colleges" (1986, 396). Moving outside of this arena, she observes that "significant rhetorical theory may well have emerged in a much more responsive and politically volatile arena than in the textbooks and the curriculum. Alternatives to what we see now as an established tradition may have resided implicitly in the practical public discourse of the age" (396).

Located within the polis of America, rhetorics of citizenship work toward the common good of the country; within early nineteenth-century university practices, this meant that learning was for public use rather than for individual gain. In this essay I am more concerned with Fuller's pedagogy and writing in relation to the immediate American political context than in trying to determine if her practices engaged with or departed from the classical rhetorical tradition. While I believe we need a full-scale revision of the history of nineteenth-century rhetoric that addresses this argument, my essay here is much more modest. As a way to envision possible directions for this revision, I argue for an understanding of Fuller's public discourse and pedagogy as a rhetoric of citizenship. Moving beyond a notion of public discourse as the political debate generated by elections and engagement in national concerns such as the Constitution, I believe we need to work towards the inclusion of discourse generated in and addressing more local communities. As a way to bring women more adequately into the history of rhetoric, a consideration of their social positioning within the separate spheres ideology will open up many possibilities for recognizing their activity in and contributions to oratorical culture. As men became more engaged in economic competition, women were expected to be the upholders of civic virtue, which many women used in arguments for their education and participation in public discourse. Many women used ideals of womanhood to position themselves as agents of the polis and identified themselves as having a responsibility to work not only for the good of the family unit but for the common good of the community as well.

My focus on alternative sites of and examples of rhetorics of citizenship demands a revised definition of the citizen. I use the term here to denote individuals' relationships to a number of contexts. Although Fuller, her students, and the women she addressed were not legally considered citizens by the United States government, I am more concerned with Fuller's vision of their possible roles as citizens in their immediate communities. I interpret Fuller's practice as a rhetoric of citizenship because she was engaged in issues of immediate concern to local comunities. Using her as a "test case," I hope to indicate enriching possibilities for future work that will attend to the teaching, speaking, and writing practices of marginalized Americans without assimilating them into unchanged, traditional categories, work that will change these categories and create new ones.

### Margaret Fuller's Revision of Self-Culture

> We have to expect suffering when we
> oppose the world. Let this not discourage.
> —William Ellery Channing

Margaret Fuller struggled with her identity as a woman from a very young age. Her early education did not limit her vision of herself or other women to familial relations. Living within a social context that severely limited the options open to women, she committed herself to a life of thought and action through the practice of self-culture. Fuller's use of self-culture was an evolving process as she struggled to negotiate the tensions among her education, her position as a woman, and her desire to bring women into intellectual activity.

Fuller's belief in the potential of self-culture is one characteristic that aligns her with transcendentalism; however, as Charles Capper (1987) observed, her use of the concept in terms of women's positions in the nineteenth century is exactly what sets her apart from this intellectual circle. Providing a convincing argument of the transcendentalist qualities of Fuller's use of self-culture, David Robinson writes, "The idea of self-culture developed by Channing and Emerson satisfied an emotional want formed primarily by religious training, and cultivation of the self assumed major importance to Fuller's generation as traditional Christianity became correspondingly dissatisfying" (1982, 85). Revolting against institutions of all kinds, the transcendentalists focused on the individual and encouraged people to search for what was divine in themselves through nature. Although sympathetic to the causes of reform movements, they maintained a cautious distance. It is unmistakable, however, that Fuller believed individual change, within women as a group, could carry social and political force. Fuller's practice of self-culture, when applied to women, called for a revision of gender relations in society; in short, it required social reform. She was aware that some of her ideas would be at odds with the transcendentalists. A letter she wrote to W. E. Channing in 1840 is worth quoting at length because it demonstrates her impression of transcendentalism, including her reservations. Fuller contextualizes her support of the transcendentalist within a critique of the economic fervor of America that, she writes, is "likely to vulgarize rather than to raise the thought of a nation." She continues:

> The tendency of circumstances has been to make our people superficial, irreverent, and more anxious to get a living than to live mentally and morally. . . .
>
> New England is now old enough, —some there have leisure enough, — to look at all this; and the consequence is a violent reaction, in a small minority, against a mode of culture that rears such fruits. They [the transcendentalists] see that political freedom does not necessarily produce liberality of mind, nor freedom in church institutions—vital religion; and, seeing that these changes cannot be wrought from without inwards, they are trying to quicken the soul, that they may work from within outwards. Disgusted with the vulgarity of a commercial aristocracy, they become radicals; disgusted with the materialistic workings of "rational" religion, they become mystics. . . . [T]hey think that they see evil widening, deepening, —not only debasing life, but corrupting the thought of our people, and they feel that if they know not well what should be done, yet that the duty of every good man is to utter a protest against what is done amiss.
>
> . . . I see in these men promise of a better wisdom than in their opponents. Their hope for man is grounded on his destiny as an immortal soul, and not as a mere comfort-loving inhabitant of earth, or as a subscriber to the social contract. . . . Man is not made for society, but society is made for man. No institution can be good which does not tend to improve the individual. In these principles I have confidence so profound, that I am not afraid to trust those who hold them, despite their partial views, imperfectly developed characters, and frequent want of practical sagacity. I believe, if they have opportunity to state and discuss their opinions, they will gradually sift them, ascertain their grounds and aims with clearness, and do the work this country needs. . . .
>
> Utopia it is impossible to build up. At least my hopes for our race on this one planet are more limited than those of most of my friends. . . . Yet every noble scheme, every poetic manifestation, prophesies to man his eventual destiny. . . . It is on this ground that I sympathize with what is called the "Transcendental party," and that I feel their aim to be the true one. They acknowledge in the nature of man an arbiter for his deeds, —a standard transcending sense and time, —and are, in my view, the true utilitarians. They are but at the beginning of their course, and will, I hope, learn how to make use of the past, as well as to aspire for the future, and to be true in the present moment.

> My position as a woman, and the many private duties which have filled my life, have prevented my thinking deeply on several of the great subjects which these friends have at heart. I suppose, if ever I become capable of judging, I shall differ from most of them on important points. (Hudspeth 1983, 2:108–9)

This letter demonstrates Fuller's enthusiastic endorsement of the movement and her willingness to trust their goals. Although she assumes a distanced critique of an outsider looking in on this intellectual circle, the letter was written two years after she joined the "Transcendental Club" and in the same year that she became editor of the *Dial*, the transcendentalist journal. The letter is ultimately a description of the transcendentalist theory of self-culture, a "version of human perfectibility centered around a metaphor of the soul as a dynamic organism capable of cultivation to ever-increasing harmonious growth" (Robinson 1982, 84). The above text also indicates her struggle to link self-culture with her sense of women's position. Embedded within her endorsement of transcendentalism, this point is easy to miss but carries growing importance as we look to her evolving revision of self-culture. Written after her first series of conversations, Fuller's observation that some in New England "have leisure enough, — to look at all this" is an indictment of the gendered limitations she felt.

Although she shared the transcendentalists' desire to subjugate material life to spiritual life, her attempt to achieve this for women, for herself as a woman, ultimately brought her back to the material life she struggled to transcend. This difference becomes clear in her contemporaries' descriptions of her. Fuller's transcendentalist companions grew increasingly frustrated with her tendency to make connections between intellectual ideas and practices and life—to build the life of thought upon the life of action. James Freeman Clarke wrote that she was "capable of poetic improvisation . . . and clear, complete, philosophic statement" but criticized her for having "a slight overweight of a tendency to the tangible and real . . . and a strong tendency to life which melted down evermore in its lava-current the solid blocks of thought" (Fuller 1852, 1:134). Her need to connect, to recognize the real and tangible, distinguish her from a majority of other transcendentalists. Fuller's experience as a woman led her to recognize the situatedness of individuals. Making a distinction between the widely accepted individualism of the day and Fuller's use of self-culture, her theory of identity—what individuals bring to their discursive acts—is consciously context-bound. Within her historical and cultural context, self-culture (or self-creation, self-determination, or self-knowledge, as it was often called) was a practice in invention that allowed women to challenge essentialist beliefs of what a "woman" is, moving them beyond the notion that they were too delicate for or not intellectually capable of civic involvement and cultural activity.

Imagine the uproar when Fuller claimed for women the same right to self-culture that Emerson and other transcendentalists claimed for themselves. Fuller argued, "Too much is said of women being better educated, that they may become better companions and mothers for men. . . . [A] being of infinite scope must not be treated with an exclusive view to any one relation" (1845c, 95–96). Women needed time to become independent and to develop self-impulse; "an increase of the class contemptuously designated as 'old maids'" is also required, she argued. "Let her put from her the press of other minds, and meditate in virgin loneliness" (121). At once making an individualistic and radical assertion, Fuller's politics are mingled into a theory and practice that can appropriately be called Transcendental Feminism—a paradox that eventually led to her abandonment of transcendentalism.

## Reading Fuller's Practices and Writings as a Rhetoric of Citizenship

Fuller began teaching for Bronson Alcott in 1836 out of economic necessity shortly after her father died (Chevigny 1976). As an experimental primary school, Alcott's Temple School challenged traditional boundaries of education, which led many people to see his project as a societal threat. Alcott's practice of using Socratic conversation to candidly discuss religion and other topics with children and his Wordsworthian belief that children were closer to their "celestial origins" than adults led the Boston community to accuse him of "heresy for treating the children as spiritual authorities, blasphemy for stripping Jesus of any special divinity and obscenity for discussing, however indirectly, the physical aspects of birth" (Chevigny 1976, 151). His conversational approach, which can be located within nineteenth-century reform traditions, emphasized the development of character, formation of confidence, self-understanding, and free-ranging thought. Alcott's philosophy of children's education served as Fuller's orientation into teaching and exposed her to new possibilities and methods for learning that were radically different from the regimen her father had imposed on her.

During her four months at the Temple School, Fuller taught languages and recorded Alcott's conversations with children. Elizabeth Peabody, who recorded the conversations before Fuller, quit because of the notoriety Alcott gained as a result of his progressive pedagogy. The publication of these as *Conversations with Children on the Gospels* in 1836 and 1837 led to the closing of the school after angry parents pulled their children out. Shortly after the Temple School closed, Fuller began working for Hiram Fuller (no relation), a disciple of Alcott, at the Greene Street School in Providence, Rhode Island, in 1837 and stayed there for eighteen months. Most of the surviving details about Fuller as a teacher come from this position; in addition to her letters, several student journals provide some insight into what she was like in the classroom.[4]

At the Greene Street School, Fuller taught languages, composition, elocution, history, ethics, poetry, and natural philosophy; many of her students were eighteen- and nineteen-year-old young women, although there were some young men in her classes (Fergenson 1987). In a letter to Bronson Alcott, Fuller referred to her new setting as "the home of thought" and indicated that she viewed teaching as an act of redemption. "Those who would reform the world," she said, "should begin with the beginning of life." She also recorded in her journal, "I thought I too would be a Redeemer. . . . And, seeing that all other Redeemers had so imperfectly performed their tasks, I sought a new way. . . . They began with men, I will begin with babes" (Hudspeth 1983, 1: 286, 287). Approaching her new "field of action," as she described the Greene Street School to Emerson (288), Fuller placed an emphasis on self-knowledge, whatever the subject matter. It is clear from her letters that this teaching position served Fuller as an experiment in preparation for a series of conversation classes she wanted to hold for women. She wrote to Elizabeth Peabody on July 8, 1837, "As to the school, I believe I do very well there. . . . My plan grows quietly and easily in my mind; this experience here will be useful to me, if not to Providence, for I am bringing my opinions to the test, and thus far have reason to be satisfied" (292).

Fuller combined the love of learning she gained through her educational experience with her father with Alcott's and Hiram Fuller's "Wordsworthian faith in the potential expressive powers of the young" (Shuffelton 1985, 31). As Fergenson has commented, she "inspired her female students with a love of learning and heightened expectations of what they as young women could do in the world and how they might develop their minds" (1987, 131). Fuller wanted to foster independent thinking in her students and also to make them aware of their "deficiencies." Her lessons in rhetoric and moral philosophy provided ample opportunities to challenge their complacency. Using Whately's *Elements of Rhetoric* and Wayland's *Elements of Moral Science*, Fuller took advantage of "Wednesday Rhetoric and Moral Philosophy day" (Fergenson 1987, 135) to encourage her students to be active readers. Anna Gale wrote in her journal, "Miss Fuller said that Dr. Wayland's thoughts would lay upon our minds, like a dry husk, unless they take root sufficiently deep to produce one little thought of our own, something entirely original; then we shall derive advantage from this study" (Hoyt and Brigham 1956, 87). At a later date Evelina Metcalf also recorded, "She wishes to arouse our dormant faculties and break up the film over our mind in order that the rays of the sun might shine upon it" (Fergenson 1987, 135). She insisted on her students thinking for themselves and encouraged them to ask questions about their reading; modeling critical reading skills, Fuller would often disagree with Wayland and then provide her reasons why. On this point Ann Brown commented, "Miss Fuller gave two rules to us . . . which she is very desirous for us to keep. The first is, 'Let nothing pass from you in reading or conversation that you do not understand, without trying to find it out.' Second, 'Let not your age or the shame of being thought ignorant prevent you from asking questions about things and words you do not understand'" (137).

Committed to providing her students with alternatives for their future, Fuller knew that only through recognizing their assumptions and asserting themselves could these young women escape the cult of True Womanhood—or choose it. Self-culture, or the life of free self-development Fuller wanted for all women, prepared women to make choices rather than to accept "fate" and to voice their opinions instead of being subjected to the opinions of others. She worked toward this ideal in her teaching first by encouraging her students to know their thoughts and second by getting them to articulate their ideas effectively. In this second endeavor she met some resistance from Hiram Fuller.

As progressive as the Greene Street School was, girls and boys were not educated equally—a reality that must have grated on the nerves of Margaret Fuller. "In keeping with the feelings of the time about the proper roles of men and women," Fergenson writes, "the boys, but not the girls, would speak, or declaim, once a fortnight. . . . [T]he girls were the audience" (138). However, Fuller did have some control over what happened in her classroom, and she encouraged the girls "to speak aloud and to participate actively in their own education." Mary Ware Allen commented in her journal, "She wished no one to remain in the class . . . unless she was willing to communicate what was in her mind, to make the recitations social and pleasant, that we might make them very pleasant by exerting ourselves, that we should let no false modesty restrain us" (138). In addition to having her students recite from Whately and Wayland, Fuller also expected them to respond orally to their experiences and observations outside of the classroom. After James Silk Buckingham, a British author and traveler, gave a talk that several of the students attended, Fuller asked them to "tell her what we liked in it." Evelina wrote, "As none of us were very communicative she dropped the subject." Aware of her own "deficiency," she returned to the topic several paragraphs later, writing, "I am sorry I did not answer more questions about the lecture last night but as is often the case thoughts flee away from me when most wanted for since I have come from the class I can think of enough to tell her. This is not as it should be and I must try to fasten and confine these airy things in order that I may have them at my disposal" (Shuffelton 1985, 34). This inability "to fasten and confine these airy things" was the general limitation of women's education that Fuller struggled to rectify.

Perhaps more than anything else, Fuller's insistence that these young women articulate their ideas made them aware of women as a social and historical group. Laraine Fergenson remarks that Fuller strived to build up her students' confidence; although she was critical and quick to point out their deficiencies, she openly praised them as well. Possibly trying to counteract Hiram Fuller's rule that girls couldn't speak publicly, one student recorded, "[Miss Fuller] told us that she thought the girls generally recited better than the boys" (Fergenson 1987, 139). She also brought in historical examples of accomplished women to demonstrate possibilities. Ann Brown noted an assignment in which Fuller asked her students "to find out 'what distinguished women' lived in the reigns of Henry II and other English kings" (138). After Fuller told her class of a woman sculptor, Evelina observed in her journal, "It makes me proud when I hear such things as this for it shows what our sex is capable of doing and encourages us to go on improving and doing all we can to show that we are not entirely incapable of intellectual cultivation as some think" (137).

This awareness of women's achievements in history seems to be just what Margaret Fuller hoped to facilitate. Serving as a role model herself, she also wanted her students to realize that they could build a life of action and thought. And it certainly apppears from Evelina's journal that her students were eager to use Fuller as a model. After the last "Wednesday Rhetoric and Moral Philosophy day" with Margaret Fuller as their teacher, Evelina recorded in her journal that the lesson was on "Persuasion" and that it "was very well recited. It spoke of the province of the orator and the requisites of a perfect orator. After we had done [*sic*] reciting our lesson," Evelina continued, "Miss Fuller read to us a description of orators by Lord Brougham high Chancellor of England. She thought it was a 'splendid production and said he was one of the most talented men in modern times'" (Shuffelton 1985, 38). Fuller indicated to her students that Lord Brougham did not quite fulfill the requisites of "the good man skilled in speaking." Evelina responded to her critique, writing, "Miss Fuller said she wished she could speak as well of his conduct in political affairs as of his talents" (39). Taking Fuller as a model for how she could build a life of thought and action, Evelina nostalgically commented,

> This is the last lesson we shall have in Moral Philosophy with Miss Fuller and I never expect to find another such teacher.
>
> Her experience has been great and she is well acquainted with human nature. She has a heart that can sympathize with all, she can rejoice with those that rejoice and weep with those that weep.
>
> Such a heart we do not often see united with so great an intellect and blessed are those who can be taught by her even if it is a short time. Would that there were more like her in this world, how very different the state of society would be if one half the women that composed it had the high, exalted views of Miss Fuller.
>
> May those who have been under her care show that her teachings have not been in vain and though she is no longer to be our teacher in this

school let us remember that she may be an example for us and that we can draw moral lessons from everything around. (39)

Fuller knew that the strategies of self-culture her students learned could help them resist being forced into life options not suited for or desired by them. Her emphasis was equally as strong on self-culture outside of academe. With whatever subject she taught or addressed, Judith Albert asserts, "the message was the same . . . charged with historical fact and conveyed with personal conviction" (1980, 14). Her call to arms was an insistence on active participation in society, which women could do only if they resisted the barriers imposed on them. In reference to Fuller's teaching, Albert continues:

> The volatile, combustive nature of learning seemed exposed through Fuller's need for a greater degree of physical and mental interaction within a classroom. Without this dialogical quality, she felt a static death of ideas and a [loss] of the vital spark of meaning which were so dear and intrinsic to her. With these elements, classrooms were no longer a formal arrangement but a personal involvement, a place where transformation occurs and people are changed. (19)

Even after Fuller quit teaching school she continued to use self-culture as a goal in her other educational projects, such as her "conversations for ladies." When she left the Greene Street School in 1839, Fuller began her long-planned and delayed series of conversations for "well-educated and thinking women" (Fuller 1852, 2:129). Often referred to as the first consciousness-raising groups for women, the conversation classes were set up as study and discussion groups with Fuller as the facilitator. She questioned the use of education without a change in actions. In terms of women's education, she asked, if women didn't apply their thoughts in their language use and actions, what use was their education? This question provided the political underpinning for the conversations, which Fuller held until 1844. She was an eloquent speaker and knew conversation was her strongest talent; she wrote, "Oh, for my dear old Greeks, who talked everything—not to shine as in the Parisian salons, but to learn, to teach, to vent the heart, to clear the mind!" (Fuller 1852, 1:136). She had previously asserted in 1832 that an interactive setting to draw out her ideas was important: "Conversation is my natural element. I need to be called out, and never think alone, without imagining some companion" (1:137).

Fuller was convinced that "women needed a public forum and some practice in thinking together" (Hudspeth 1983, 1:38). So, proposing to organize her circle of "well-educated and thinking women," she wanted to set up conversations "so that what is valuable in the experiences of each might be brought to bear upon all" (Fuller 1852, 2:129). Ann Douglas argues that transcendentalism served as a "bridge" for Fuller "from literary to historical consciousness" and that she wished the transcendentalists would "'learn how to make use of the past'" (1977, 326, 338). She brought this impulse, coupled with her beliefs in the power of conversation, the importance of day-to-day experiences, and the value of independent thinking, to the conversation classes. Douglas writes:

> In her Conversations, Fuller was addressing women who had read too much, listened too much, and thought for themselves too little. She could not teach them . . . to study the natural world, for she herself had little bent that way; but she could at least help them to observe the workings of their own minds, to be critics rather than consumers. And her partly assumed iconoclasm was a way of throwing them back on themselves, of making them take themselves seriously, if only because she allowed them to tap no other resource. (327)

She made the same demands of the women in the conversations that she had required of her students in the Greene Street School. Informed by Sophia Ripley that some women wanted to attend the classes without participating, Fuller responded that she wanted all those who attended to be active: "No one will be forced, but those who do not talk will not derive the same advantage with those who openly state their impressions and consent to learn by blundering" (Hudspeth 1983, 2:88). The self-impulse to take a risk by voicing their thoughts is what Fuller wanted to foster in women's education. Believing the women could find the courage to speak, she used their fear or hesitation to "learn by blundering," to nurture thought (Fuller 1852, 2:130). She resisted a reliance on books in her conversations, perhaps because of her own experience of being subject to hero-worship, a tendency she felt led to self-censure and erasure. This had certainly been the case of her own fascination with Goethe. In 1832 Fuller wrote, "He comprehends every feeling I have ever had so perfectly, expresses it so beautifully; but when I shut the book, it seems as if I had lost my personal identity" (Fuller 1852, 1:194–95 as quoted in Eakin 1976, 53).

Women's education, Fuller began the first conversation, is not typically very useful and is only for display; she then went into a description of how men use what they learn by applying it to their work, by "reproducing" what they know—she intended the conversations to remedy the superficial nature of women's education by proposing the general question, "What were we born to do? and How shall we do it?" (Fuller 1852, 2:130). Outlining her agenda for the conversations, Fuller wrote:

> It is to pass in review the departments of thought and knowledge, and endeavor to place them in due relation to one another in our minds. To systematize thought, and give a precision and clearness in which our sex are so deficient, chiefly, I think, because they have so few inducements to test and classify what they receive. To ascertain what pursuits are best suited to us, in our time and state of society, and how we may make best use of our means of building up the life of thought upon the life of action. (2:130)

Fuller combined writing and speaking practices to get her class "to question, to define, to state, and examine opinions" (2:133). The surviving details of the conversation classes are sketchy; Caroline Healey Dall's *Margaret and Her Friends* provides the most complete record of any of the series.[5] There is evidence, from her letters, the *Memoirs*, and the letters of participants, that she covered a broad range of topics that became increasingly focused on social issues. Although early classes focused on Greek mythology, Capper observes, "Mythology gave way to 'Ethics' and ethics to the family, the School, the Church, Society, and Woman" (1987, 523). Clearly demonstrating her changing ideas that led Fuller from a reliance on the metaphysical aspects of self-culture to an emphasis on the social and political implications of women's self-culture, the conversations suggest that Fuller was gaining a respect for and interest in collective action. "In advocating the collective means of conversation over Emerson's individual ones of lectures and writing," Capper writes, "Fuller, like Alcott . . . , defined culture as at least partly a social phenomenon. . . . Her creation of an independent circle of women organized to address specific needs of women was an inspiration and model, as Elizabeth Cady Stanton and other feminists acknowledged, in their later organization of women's rights groups." Her use of "an analytical and experimental approach to intellectual life helped to nurture, if only locally, an inquiring, critical outlook without which social criticism and reform are hardly possible" (523). While Fuller's experiences in the Greene Street School and the conversations demonstrate her belief in the social power of conversation, *Woman in the Nineteenth Century* and her *New York Daily Tribune* articles indicate that she also came to value writing as a socially powerful act.

*Woman in the Nineteenth Century* unites Fuller's knowledge of literature and history with women's positions in the nineteenth century. She asserts in the preface, "I ask them [women], if interested by these suggestions, to search their own experience and intuitions for better, and fill up with fit materials the trenches that hedge them in" (1845c, 14). In one of the more radical moments of *Woman in the Nineteenth Century*, Fuller argued:

> It may be said that Man does not have his fair play either; his energies are repressed and distorted by the interposition of artificial obstacles. Ay, but he himself has put them there; they have grown out of his own imperfections. If there is a misfortune in Woman's lot, it is in obstacles being interposed by men, which do not mark her state; and, if they express her past ignorance, do not her present needs. (49)

This preliminary argument is important to Fuller's use of self-culture because it serves as a means of motivating women to become active in their own self-culture and showing them how they are connected, as women, to society. With the seductive promises of individualism growing thin, Fuller argues that women live under gendered oppression. Her call for self-culture insists on women being responsible for their lives. She did not write under the pretense that men would liberate women but knew that women would have to liberate women—and she believed women could achieve liberation. Echoing her encouragement in the conversations that the members consent to "learn by blundering," she charges women to take risks. In a patriotic statement of the promise of America, Fuller writes:

> Though the national independence be blurred by the servility of individuals; though freedom and equality have been proclaimed only to leave room for a monstrous display of slave-dealing and slave-keeping; though

the free American so often feels himself free, like the Roman, only to pamper his appetites and his indolence through the misery of his fellow-beings; still it is not in vain that the verbal statement has been made, "All men are born free and equal." . . . It is inevitable that an external freedom, an independence of the encroachments of other men, such as has been achieved for the nation, should be so also for every member of it. That which has once been clearly conceived in the intelligence cannot fail, sooner or later, to be acted out. (26)

Although Fuller had earlier refused to make abolition a topic of her conversations, here she uses it to her advantage to draw a correlation between gender and race oppressions. "Of all its banners, none has been more steadily upheld, . . . than that of the champions of the enslaved African. . . . And this band it is, which, . . . makes, just now, the warmest appeal in behalf of Woman" (28). In discussing the reception of abolitionists and women's rights advocates in society at large, Fuller observes:

"Is it not enough," cries the irritated trader, "that you have done all you could to break up the national union, and thus destroy the prosperity of our country, by now you must be trying to break up family union, to take my wife away from the cradle and the kitchen-hearth to vote at polls, and preach from a pulpit? Of course, if she does such things, she cannot attend to those of her own sphere." (28–29)

Fuller charged women with the responsibility to stand up to this criticism, to determine whether they lived in such relations out of consent or through a "passiveness that precludes the exercise of its natural powers" (29–30). Reiterating the fact that women must liberate women, Fuller writes:

Knowing that there exists in the minds of men a tone of feeling toward women as toward slaves, . . . that the infinite soul can only work through them in already ascertained limits; that the gift of reason . . . is allotted to them in much lower degree; that they must be kept from mischief and melancholy by being constantly engaged in active labor . . . can we wonder that many reformers think that measures are not likely to be taken in behalf of women, *unless their wishes could be publicly represented by women*? (33–34) (emphasis added)

Fuller refers to the drudgery and toil of housework to counter her opponents' notion that women have the highest degree of influence in the home and that the "beauty of the home" and "delicacy of the sex" would be violated if women became involved in civic affairs. People of this opinion, she says, "are by no means those who think it impossible for negresses to endure field-work, even during pregnancy, or for sempstresses to go through their killing labors" (35).

Fuller believed that women's struggle for self-culture would bind them together in loyalty to one another. In emphasizing women's connections to society as oppressed and oppressor, she demonstrates the complexity of what Linda Alcoff (1988) calls positionality by considering how women are simultaneously oppressed as women and complicit in the oppression of other marginalized citizens. For example, in reference to slavery and racism she says,

> Women of my country! . . . have you nothing to do with this? You see the men, how they are willing to sell shamelessly the happiness of countless generations of fellow-creatures, the honor of their country, and their immortal souls, for a money market and political power. . . . Tell these men that you will not accept the glittering baubles, spacious dwellings, and plentiful service, they mean to offer you through these means . . . and that, if they have not purity, have not mercy, they are no longer fathers, lovers, husbands, sons of yours. (1845c, 166–67)

Fuller is asking white women to be aware of the privileges they have and to take responsibility for them. This passage demonstrates how self-culture provides a way for the marginalized to create community unity in a recognition of politically and socially imposed barriers, which is its most radical departure from individualism. It also indicates the powerful role that complicity has as silent approval. Fuller's practice of invention didn't leave women victims but recognized their oppression and their power, making social and political action not only a possibility but also a responsibility.

Taking up the topic of "school instruction for girls," Fuller levels a critique at educational instutions that also indicts her father:

> Just as the tutors of Lady Jane Grey, and other distinguished women of her time, taught them Latin and Greek, because they knew nothing else themselves, so now the improvement in the education of girls is to be made by giving them young men as teachers, who only teach what has been taught themselves at college, while methods and topics need revision for these new subjects, which could better be made by those who had experienced the same wants. (94–95)

Even when girls received "some portion of instruction of a good sort," Fuller continued, "the far greater proportion which is infused from the general atmosphere of society contradicts its purport" (95). Clearly aware of women's socialization, Fuller claims, "'Her mother did so before her' is no longer a sufficient excuse" (95). Arguing that women are more than mothers, wives, or daughters, she writes that "too much is said of women being better educated, that they may become better companions and mothers for men. . . . [A] being of infinite scope must not be treated with an exclusive view to any one relation" (95–96). Fuller's ultimate measure of women living beyond "any one relation" is the single women. In the face of True Womanhood she asserts, "In this regard of self-dependence, and a greater simplicity and fulness [sic] of being, we must hail as a preliminary the increase of the class contemptuously designated as 'old maids'" (96).

Fuller observed the predominant pattern of women's lives that rendered them dependent on other people, usually a man. Instead of passing from father to husband, Fuller claimed that women needed time to become independent, to develop "self-impulse." Returning to the ideals of transcendentalism, she claims, "If any individual live too much in relations, so that he becomes a stranger to the resources of his own nature, he falls, after a while, into a distraction, or imbecility, from which he can only be cured by a time of isolation, which gives the renovating fountains time to rise up" (119). In many ways she is echoing Emerson's assertion in "Self-Reliance": "I shun father and mother and wife and brother when my genius calls me. I would write on the lintels of the door-post, *Whim*. I hope it is somewhat better than whim at last, but we cannot spend the day in explanation. Expect me not to show cause why I seek or why I exclude company" ([1841] 1983, 148). In order to make that freedom available to women, Fuller says, "We shall not decline celibacy as the great fact of time" (Fuller 1845c, 119); women must "retire within themselves and explore the groundwork of life till they find their peculiar secrets" (121). In a critique of the institutions of the family and marriage and simultaneously an application of transcendental ideals to women's position, Fuller asserts:

> I would have Woman lay aside all thought, such as she habitually cherishes, of being taught and led by men. . . . I would have her free from compromise, from complaisance, from helplessness, because I would have her good enough and strong enough to love one and all beings, from the

fulness [sic], not the poverty of being. . . . Let her put from her the press of
other minds, and meditate in virgin loneliness. (120–21)

*Woman in the Nineteenth Century* stands for many things; it is a
history of women as well as a document of the transcendentalist ideals
of harmony and correspondence. However, in my reading I have
focused on how Fuller's adaptation of self-culture called for social
reform. Thick with historical and literary references, her argument is,
at times, hard to follow. In her critique of True Womanhood and other
sociopolitical institutions that depended on it for their strength, there
is no doubt that Fuller was out to broaden women's experiences as she
exclaimed, "Let them be sea-captains, if you will" (174). As she
became more involved in self-critical struggle, Fuller's use of self-
culture transformed into a practice she came to call mutual interpretation. Instead of drawing correlations between oppressions, she grew
to realize that the possibility of self-culture wasn't equally accessible
to all citizens, that poor women or people of color faced barriers that
she, as a white, economically privileged woman, didn't.

Fuller continued her belief in "America's special democratic destiny" (Chevigny 1976, 282) as she wrote for Horace Greeley's *New York
Tribune*. She moved to New York in 1844 after the Greeleys invited her
to live with them and work as a literary critic and social reporter for
the newspaper. As her job as a journalist took Fuller from tours of
prisons, hospitals, asylums, and slums to concerts, lectures, and
schools, her commitments broadened to include the education of the
masses and wide-sweeping social criticism. Her journalism reflects
these new experiences as many of her articles call for reform and
public responsibility for the well-being of the masses. According to
Chevigny, "[As] her job as a reporter gave her access to worlds
hitherto closed to a woman of her class, a deepening concern for other
oppressed groups—immigrants, blacks, the poor, the blind, the in-
sane—followed" (291). As a critic, Fuller claimed social and political
agency by raising public awareness on issues she considered important for public attention and asserted, "I never regarded literature
merely as a collection of exquisite products, but rather as a means of
mutual interpretation. Feeling that many are reached and in some
degree helped, the thoughts of everyday seem worth noting" (292). In
reference to her new writing material and her friends' attitude about
it, Fuller says, "They think I ought to produce something excellent,

while I am satisfied to aid in the great work of popular education" (292).

Chevigny defines mutual interpretation as "the process in which the writer, impatient with static products, joins with the forces of social change" (292). As a social critic Fuller claimed social and political agency by raising public awareness on issues she considered important for public attention. In addition, her notion of citizenship—what it involves and how citizens are connected—becomes clearer in her journalistic writings. Although Fuller wrote over two hundred articles for the *Tribune*, a brief exploration of a few of them will demonstrate her practice of mutual interpretation.

In a 1845 article titled "Prevalent Idea that Politeness is too Great a Luxury to be Given to the Poor," Fuller addressed the rudeness the "purse-proud," a term she uses to refer to wealthy citizens, often inflict on the poor. Like much of her journalistic writing, she begins the article with a story—this one about a little boy taking care of a sibling outside while their mother is at work. Concerned about the health of the baby, a woman approached him with questions, threats, and condemnation. Fuller often used this strategy to play on the emotions and guilt of her readers. She observed:

> The bystanders stared at both; but among them all there was not one with sufficiently clear notions of propriety and moral energy to say to this impudent questioner, "Woman! do you suppose because you wear a handsome shawl, and that boy a patched jacket, that you have any right to speak to him at all, unless he wishes it, far less to prefer against him those rude accusations. Your vulgarity is unendurable; leave the place or alter your manner." (1845b, 3)

Fuller models a way of responding to such rude and assuming behavior while explaining the effects of complicity. She wasn't just criticizing the wealthy woman who had scolded the boy but was also implicating the bystanders for their silence. By writing about this everyday occurrence, Fuller demonstrates that adjustments in individual behavior, a developing of civic virtue, can make a difference. Voicing disagreement provides a means of action to some readers who may otherwise have few opportunities for political action in the public sphere. Fuller indicates the oppressive state of affairs in the city by saying:

In the little instance with which we begun, no help was asked, unless by
the sight of the timid little boy's old jacket. But the license which this
seemed to the well-clothed woman to give to rudeness was so characteristic of a deep fault now existing, that a volume of comments might follow
and a host of anecdotes be drawn from almost any one's experience in
exposition of it. These few words, perhaps, may awaken thought in those
who have drawn fears from others' eyes through an ignorance brutal, but
not hopelessly so, if they are willing to rise above it. (3)

She ends by reinforcing the everyday quality of the incident and tells
her readers that they can choose to change; she joins forces with the
tension between classes in an attempt to persuade the economically
privileged to change their behavior.

Fuller's attendance at an Independence Day celebration led to
another piece of social criticism reminiscent of the passage in *Woman
in the Nineteenth Century* where she evoked the Declaration of Independence. "The audience is putting on its best bib and tucker, and its
blandest expression to listen," she observed. "Yet, no heart, we think,
can beat to-day with one pulse of genuine, noble joy. Those who have
obtained their selfish objects will not take especial pleasure in thinking of them to-day, while to unbiased minds must come sad thoughts
of National Honor soiled in the eyes of other nations, of a great
inheritance, risked, if not forfeited" (1845a, 2). Although many things
have been achieved in the country, she continues, "the noble sentiment which she expressed in her early youth is tarnished." True
patriots cannot rejoice on this day because the promise of the country
had been betrayed:

This year, which declares that the people at large consent to cherish and
extend Slavery as one of our "domestic institutions," takes from the
patriot his home. This year, which attests their insatiate love of wealth and
power, quenches the flame upon the alter [*sic*]. . . . It is not easy, it is very
hard just now to realize the blessings of Independence.
    For what is Independence if it does not lead to Freedom? — Freedom
from fraud and meanness, from selfishness, from public opinion so far as
it does not consent with the still small voice of one's better self? (2)

Fuller's reading of citizenship in this article, as in the previous
one, not only includes the "freedom to" but also the "freedom from."
Calling for individuals "to whom all eyes may turn as an example of

the practicability of virtue," (2) we can see her continued belief that social change relies on individual change. In *Woman in the Nineteenth Century* she had asserted, "Could you clear away all the bad forms of society, it is vain, unless the individual begin to be ready for better. There must be a parallel movement in these two branches of life" (1845c, 76). Her awareness that individual freedom doesn't exist in a vaccuum, that it might and often does come at the expense of another's right to "freedom from fraud and meanness, from selfishness, from public opinion," is not only historically true but also represents one privileged woman calling herself and her country to account for the perpetuation of oppression. Fuller's growing commitment to exposing oppression and naming oppressors is the centerpiece of her rhetoric of citizenship. Her efforts to bring women into oratorical practices and to be active in societal affairs were also an attempt to affect public opinion and foster a public morality that recognized and valued each citizen.

## Notes

1. Shuffelton (1985); Fergenson (1987); Hoyt and Brigham (1956); Johnson ([1910] 1980); Capper (1987); Myerson (1974); Rosenthal (1970); Chevigny (1976). For a more detailed bibiliography see Myerson (1985, 331–85).

2. Fuller's experience of marginalization isn't representative of all disenfranchised Americans. While she did experience oppression as a woman, she was privileged through her race and class and the experience of maturing in New England. The lives of men and women of color and white women in the South and rural settings offer radically different historical narratives. What Fuller shared with these other positions was experiences that compelled her to question her identity, to seek alliances with others who shared her oppression, and to recognize the importance of historical consciousness. In an earlier discussion of Fuller's positions as oppressed and oppressor, I outlined an approach to historiography that accounts for multiple layers of identity and change based on Linda Alcoff's theory of positionality and feminist identity politics; see Rouse (1990). For a discussion of positionality, see Alcoff (1988). Also see Bulkin, Pratt, and Smith (1984).

3. Although the ideals of Republican Motherhood and True Womanhood have been used to describe the general position of women from the Revolution through 1860, it is clear that these ideals were representative of white upper- and middle-class women in New England. Giddings (1984), Sterling (1984), and Lerner (1972) provide not only insightful and important critiques of these

exclusive ideals but also challenge methods of historiography that naturalize exclusion. Also useful for understanding the lives of rural women are Jensen (1986) and Fox-Genovese (1988).

4. Anna Gale's journal is located at the American Antiquarian Society in Worcester, Massachusetts. Ann Brown's journal is located at Brown University. Parts of their journals have been published in Fergenson (1987) and Hoyt and Brigham (1956). One of Evelina Metcalf's journals is located at the University of Rochester, and the other is at the University of South Carolina, Columbia. Parts of her journals have been published in Fergenson (1987) and Shuffelton (1985). Portions of Mary Ware Allen's journal were published in Albert (1980) and Johnson ([1910] 1980). In all cases I quote from these published materials, not the original manuscripts.

5. Using the *Memoirs* and Robert Hudspeth's collections of Fuller's letters, Charles Capper has recorded that over two hundred women eventually attended the conversations (1987, 513). Among other women, he lists Eliza Farrar, Anna Barker, Caroline and Ellen Sturgis, Edna Littlehale, Mary and Sophia Peabody, Lidian Emerson, Elizabeth Hoar, Sophia Ripley, Ann Terry Phillips, Lydia Maria Child, Sarah Alden Ripley, and Elizabeth Peabody. The women in attendance varied in age and interest, some of them former students, such as Jane Tuckerman, and others activists or educators, such as Child and Phillips. In describing the women as a group, Capper writes:

> They were liberal in their religious views and therefore not attracted to the benevolence crusades sponsored by evangelical churches that absorbed many women. And, most importantly, they were brought up in the highly education and culture-conscious families and circles that abounded in Unitarian Boston and, as a consequence, were taught to nourish an interest in literature and thought almost as much as in conventional domestic roles. And these were precisely the sort of women who flocked to the conversation classes of Margaret Fuller, who was herself partly the product of these same influences. . . . Indeed, beyond class, status and education, the most salient feature of the group as a whole was the strong ties many of the women had to various social reform movements. (511–12)

# Part Two ❋ Nineteenth-Century Transformations of Oratorical Culture

# 5

# The Popularization of Nineteenth-Century Rhetoric ❊ Elocution and the Private Learner ❊ Nan Johnson

❊The nineteenth-century academic tradition in rhetoric fostered the view that eloquence in speaking and writing was the mark of the well-educated and thoughtful citizen. Prominent nineteenth-century rhetoricians such as Samuel P. Newman, G. P. Quackenbos, and John Franklin Genung, whose treatises were widely circulated in nineteenth-century colleges and universities, defined rhetoric as the art that contributed the most toward the proper workings of the political process, the disposition of justice, and the maintenance of the public welfare and social conscience. Nineteenth-century rhetoricians equated the moral obligations of the rhetorician with the preservation of democratic culture and promoted the assumption that training in oratory and composition increased a citizen's ability to participate in civil life and thus contribute to the intellectual and spiritual health of a progressive nation. Although the nineteenth-century rhetorical tradition placed the most ideological stress on rhetoric as a form of training for civil life and as a central means of cultivating intellectual and moral taste, academic rhetoricians also promoted the practical uses of rhetoric and increasingly acknowledged the relationship between the study of rhetoric and professionalism as the century advanced.

In the first half of the century, academic training in rhetoric focused on instruction that would benefit young men training in law, the ministry, or politics, all professions in which public speaking was a central and necessary skill. By mid-century, college doors were beginning to open to a more diverse middle class that viewed an advanced education as a final preparation for many walks of professional life. Academic rhetoric was able to offer this group a more encompassing definition of the relevance of rhetorical skills to careerism and social success because the disposition of nineteenth-century theory favored defining rhetoric as a comprehensive art of communication. Strongly influenced by the orientation of the New Rhetoric toward a definition of rhetoric as a general art of discourse, nineteenth-century rhetoricians such as Henry N. Day, Adams Sherman Hill, and Genung defined rhetoric as a general expertise in speaking and writing applicable to a wide range of public and professional uses and settings. For example, Genung defines rhetoric as "the art of adapting discourse, in harmony with its subject and occasion to the requirements of a reader or hearer" and points out that the word "discourse . . . is broad enough to cover all forms of composition, and deep enough to include all its processes" (Johnson 1991, 87–110). Cooperating closely with the expressed ambition of higher education in the latter half of the century to foster a quality of mental discipline applicable to any chosen profession or life of common sense, academic rhetoric placed more and more emphasis on what Genung terms the "broadened field of action" of modern rhetoric. By rationalizing rhetoric as an invaluable skill, Genung and other academic rhetoricians ensured a high status for rhetoric in the face of shifting economic and class distinctions that demanded more of rhetorical education than the training of a comparatively small number of young men for a few highly placed professions. In the service of the presumption that rhetoric should be taught as a general skill of discourse rather than as the art of persuasive oratory alone, academy and college rhetoric courses offered instruction in principles (invention, arrangement, and style) that could be adapted to any text (oral or written) or occasion (public or professional).

Popular rhetorical education in the late nineteenth century garnered credibility and authority by promoting the importance of rhetorical skills for the general citizen and "private learner" along the same lines as the academic tradition—rhetoric was practical and versatile. Although rhetoric manuals were marketed to the general public throughout the late eighteenth century and early nineteenth century, an upsurge in the public's demand for literacy training and interest in rhetorical performance as a social and community event encouraged a burgeoning of popular education in rhetoric between 1850 and 1910.

Relying heavily on the academic discipline's extended definition of the range of rhetoric, popular rhetorical educators designed a program of study tailored to everyday uses of rhetoric by the average individual. One of the most distinctive ambitions of the popular rhetoric movement was its characterization of rhetoric as an indispensable skill in professional and social life. While the importance of rhetorical skills to engaged citizenship was often mentioned in popular rhetoric manuals, more stress was placed on the practical uses of rhetoric in business, community, and private life. Campaigning to make speaking eloquently and correctly every literate person's ambition, the popular rhetoric movement strove to make the cultivation of rhetorical skills a priority in every office and in every parlor. J. W. Shoemaker, author of the popular manual *Practical Elocution*, expresses this creed when he rationalizes the importance of elocution as its benefit "in social life," "in business life," and in "public life" (1886, 21–22). Shoemaker insists that the skills of "practical elocution" apply to every instance in which an individual wants to communicate clearly, whether that be in a social setting, a private conversation, a public discussion, or reading aloud. Although Shoemaker recognized the traditional relationship between elocution and public speaking, his defense of the importance of elocution rested on the general claim of the popular rhetoric movement that the applications of rhetorical skills exceeded the traditional arenas of public address.

Popular rhetoric manuals covered a range of topics, including speech making, composition, letter writing, public readings, and elocutionary entertainment. The most successful and widespread branch of popular rhetorical education in the nineteenth century was the elocution movement, which was supported by the general public's keen interest in oratorical skills and the popularity of the practice of rhetoric in the public forum and the parlor. Interest in oratory and elocution was especially intense, encouraged by numerous and varied occasions for oratory and elocutionary performances serving a variety of political, cultural, and social functions.

> Such speechmaking as has been reported centered chiefly in the courts, the legislature, and the church. Other speechmaking occasions . . . derived from the schools, from business, trade, labor, and from the

multitude of causes that were coming into being. . . . [S]peechmaking
went on in the daily exercise of life in situations and under conditions that
defy classification. And if no situation requiring speechmaking was at
hand, then one was invented. The literary society, the "bee," the debating
society, and the lyceum were largely given over to speechmaking in one
form or another. (Aly and Tanquary 1943, 73, 89)

In addition to supporting a wide range of occasions for public
speaking, the nineteenth-century public showed a self-conscious
interest in promoting high standards for oral performances of all
kinds. It was commonplace for nineteenth-century literary journals
and local newspapers to publish reviews of the addresses of well-
known speakers such as Daniel Webster and Henry Clay and of the
lectures and sermons of distinguished pulpit and platform speakers
such as Ralph Waldo Emerson, Charles Sumner, Wendell Phillips,
Elizabeth Cady Stanton, and Henry Beecher. Local newspapers gave
similar coverage to orations and dramatic readings presented at
community events, church occasions, and college and school ceremo-
nies. Such reviews offered summaries of the speaker's arguments and
typically evaluated the speaker's ideas, style, and elocutionary technique. Herbert A. Wichelns has summarized newspaper reviews of
Emerson's performances that reveal how carefully the popular press
scrutinized the elocutionary skills of platform speakers:

Most observed that the eyes . . . were only occasionally raised from the
manuscript and then in such a way that only those at the side of room met
his glance. None felt that he had the usual platform manner of the
experienced speaker. We read of a "shapeless delivery" without gestures
save nervous twitches and angular movements of the hands and arms—
"curious to see and even smile at" and a slight rocking of the body.
. . . The voice, which James Russell Lowell described to the readers of the
*Nation* in 1868 as a rich baritone, struck on Margaret Fuller's ear as full and
sweet rather than sonorous, yet flexible and haunted by many modula-
tions. But others thought there was little variation . . . report[ing] a
reading without excitement, without energy, scarcely even with emphasis. (1943, 517)

Reviews like this indicate that the literate public was well aware of the
importance of standard elocutionary techniques such as the

modulated voice, timing and emphasis in reading, and control over gesture. By awarding critical attention to elocution, the popular press aided the academy in the enterprise of instilling in the public mind the notion that rhetorical skills, especially delivery, were essential to speech making and dramatic readings, no matter the occasion.

Because the virtues of oratorical and elocutionary performance were so widely regarded in the nineteenth century, Americans were keenly interested in instruction in the rudiments of oratory and elocution for the average citizen rather than for the specialized uses of those preparing to be lawyers, preachers, or public servants. In response to public interest, various forms of popular instruction in elocution developed to provide rudimentary instruction in delivery and multiple selections for practice and performance. These materials supplemented efforts to promote popular instruction in elocution by academic elocutionists such as Alexander Melville Bell, Merritt Caldwell, and J. H. McIlvaine, whose elocution texts were designed for both the student and the private learner.

Popular rhetoric manuals were modeled closely on academic treatises that analyzed the philosophical, aesthetic, epistemological, and physiological elements of elocution. Typically designed for advanced instruction in academies, colleges, and seminaries, texts such as Porter's *Analysis of the Principles of Rhetorical Delivery as Applied to Reading and Speaking* (1827), William Russell's *Orthography* (1846), and Merritt Caldwell's *Practical Manual of Elocution* (1845) were regarded by popular elocutionists as authoritative texts. Nineteenth-century academic elocutionists drew upon a diverse theoretical base to justify their definition of elocution as a practical art and rational science. Major theoretical sources included Cicero's and Quintilian's theories of delivery and the work of British elocutionists Thomas Sheridan (*Lectures on Elocution*, 1762), John Walker (*Elements of Elocution*, 1781), and Gilbert Austin (*Chironomia*, 1806).

The authority of Cicero and Quintilian over academic theories of elocution endured throughout the century, as did the influence of Austin's work on gesture; however, by mid-century, the exclusive theoretical influence of Sheridan's and Walker's theories of the voice had been supplemented by James Rush's *The Philosophy of the Human Voice* (1827). Rush's views shaped the theories of a number of influential American elocutionists including Russell, Caldwell, James E. Murdoch, and Jonathan Barber, who shared Rush's interest in how expressive use of the voice enhances emotional appeals and the clarity of ideas. Rush's theory of the voice was coopted by Silus S. Curry, whose treatises *The Province of Expression* (1891) and *Foundations of Expression* (1907) represent the increasingly eclectic state of elocutionary theory at the end of the century. Curry valued Rush's notions of the natural use of the voice but believed that most other elocutionists of the time relied on an artificial separation between the function of the voice and the body, functions that Curry believed should be unified in a "whole body" approach to delivery.

In taking the "whole body" approach to expression, Curry helped to popularize some elements of the theories of Francois Delsarte, whose theory of expression drew on the assumption that the voice and the body are one with the mind and the soul. Although never exerting measurable influence over the academic tradition in elocution, the "Delsarte system" was promoted by successful popular elocutionists Steele MacKaye, Lewis B. Monroe, and William R. Alger, whose publications and public lectures defined elocution as the development of "physical culture." The Delsarte system was also promoted by elocutionists who applied principles of elocution to the dramatic arts, primarily involving dramatic interpretation, pantomime, and tableaux. Several books addressed to the popular audience advocated this latter program in the last decade of the century, including Genevieve Stebbins's *Delsarte System of Dramatic Expression* (1886) and Anna Morgan's *An Hour with Delsarte:A Study of Expression* (1889), which were both "widely used and sold" (Shaver 1954, 216).

Despite shifting allegiances to theoretical authorities, one of the most characteristic tenets of nineteenth-century academic and popular elocutionary theory was the assumption that the state of mind of the speaker can be inferred from tones and inflections of the voice, movements of the body, and expressions of the face. It is this natural correspondence among mind, voice, and body that allows the speaker to engage the minds and emotions of the audience more completely than the absence of the art of delivery would allow. Like their eighteenth-century predecessors, nineteenth-century academic and popular elocutionists stressed that elocutionary principles should be based on the natural disposition of voice, expression, and gesture. Caldwell explains that the study and practice of elocution provides "a theoretical knowledge . . . of natural language" that leaves "the learner sufficiently in possession of all his natural peculiarities. Their [principles drawn from nature] entire object is to refine and perfect nature; not to pervert it" (1845, viii, 22). Like other prominent elocutionists in this period, Caldwell stresses that the aim of elocutionary technique is to enhance the speaker's or reader's ability to increase the impression ideas and emotions make on others by employing the natural properties of the voice and of action.

Popular elocutionists persistently encouraged the student of elocution to regard conversation as the best source of clues as to how voice and gesture confer individuality on expression. In explaining that "the study of natural speech [is] revealed by Conversation," Shoemaker reiterates the dominant nineteenth-century view that the most effective speakers are those who have studied spoken language in its original and simplest form:

> The conditions of mind and body in ordinary conversation are best adapted for the study of our own individuality. . . . We should study ourselves and seek our examples from that condition where true nature is least modified. This condition we believe to be that of *conversation* with our intimate friends. . . . [W]e will find in it a harmony with our own natures, and constantly recurring lights and shades of natural expression that may serve as models for study and imitation, such as we can find no where else in the whole range of utterance. (1886, ix–x)

While Shoemaker expresses the standard notion that elocutionary abilities are natural and thus potentially in the grasp of any speaker of the language, he also contends that study and practice are required to bring natural skills up to their most effective level. As Shoemaker puts it, "God . . . gives us the plastic material . . . we must develop into mature faculties through the formation of conscious habits" (xii).

Nineteenth-century popular elocutionists confidently proclaimed that the study and practice of principles could allow even the most unpromising initiates to capitalize on their natural expressive inclinations. Practice in elocution helps the speaker become more self-conscious in the use of the voice and body and therefore more skilled. Defending a pedagogy in which the student learns "general principles" and is then "drilled," George L. Raymond, author of the widely used manual *The Orator's Manual* (1879), confides that his years of teaching experience have made him believe that it is only a question of time and patience, and any person, not physically incapacitated, may be made to become an interesting and attractive speaker. By this is meant that he can be cured of indistinct and defective articulation, of unnatural and false tones, and of awkwardness; and be trained to have a clear, resonant voice, an unaffected and forcible way of modulating it so as to have it represent the sense, and a dignity and ease of bearing, all of which together shall enable him to continue to hold the attention of an audience. (7–8)

By promoting a pedagogical model that stresses mastery of principles combined with practice, "time and patience," Raymond and other popular elocutionists reinforce the pedagogical stance of prominent rhetorical theorists of the period such as Newman, Genung, and Alexander Bain who insist that oratorical and composition skills can be acquired through systematic study of theoretical principles and their applications to various types of rhetorical performance (Johnson 1991, 231–40).

One of the most significant gains attributed to the study and practice of elocution is the elimination of speech habits that lower one's standard of expression. Nineteenth-century elocutionists, academic and popular alike, assumed a one-to-one correspondence between natural skills that had been brought up to the level of art and the development of correct habits of speech. Raymond's concern for the elimination of "indistinct and defective articulation" and "false tones" is characteristic of the attitude of other theorists such as Caldwell, Porter, and Russell who regard the preservation of a standard of spoken English as a major goal of elocutionary training. Instruction in elocution promotes "vocal discipline" and the tasteful use of gestures that accompanies a cultivated variant of English. Defending the role of elocutionary training in the eradication of a "low style" of speaking, Russell defines one of the crucial pedagogical commitments of the nineteenth-century elocutionary movement:

It is unnecessary here to enlarge on the intellectual injuries arising from the want of early discipline in this department of education; or to speak of the habits of inattention and inaccuracy, which are thus cherished, and by which the English language is degraded from its native force and dignity of utterance, to a low and slovenly negligence of style, by which it is rendered unfit for the best offices for speech. (1844, 9)

Russell assumes that the study of elocution purifies the speaker of defects and habits that are offenses against nature in the first place. The study of elocution offers the speaker an opportunity to become conscious of those defects and to eradicate them through a program of systematic study and practice. Russell's commitment to the importance of "discipline" indicates the level of confidence in the effects of systematic pedagogy held by elocutionists and rhetoricians alike in this period. Rather than being a type of interference in the development of natural instincts of expression, the formal study of elocution reinforces the most elevated forms of English while it suppresses all forms of the "slovenly." At the foundation of this view is a persistent association between the systematic study of elocution and rhetoric and the development of expression as an art. While art has its origins in the natural, the ways and means of nature can be known through the study of principles, mastered through practice, and applied at will for the greatest effect.

Popular elocutionists also stressed that systematic study of natural expression would eradicate speaking defects that interfered with communication and created negative impressions on others. Addressing more often the practical consequences of poor speaking habits rather than the virtues of acquiring artistic expression, popular elocutionists argued that a working knowledge of the principles of elocution and practice in correct speaking could further professional and social aims and enhance everyday enjoyment of conversation. Emma Griffith Lumm, who introduces her text *The New American Speaker* as an effort to teach "the boy on the farm and the girl in the shop" the art of speech, argues for the everyday importance of elocution: "Not all are public speakers or readers, but everybody talks, and to speak in a well modulated voice is an accomplishment worth effort to obtain (1898, 1, 38). In the introduction to *The American Star Speaker and Model Elocutionist*, Charles Walter Brown similarly points out that it is necessary to speak correctly in order to make "ourselves agreeable in our intercourse with our fellow creatures as our opportunities may permit." Without attention to proper speech, "the consideration and continued high respect of the world" cannot be won (1902, 21).

The social inducement for elocutionary practice promoted by Lumm and Brown is a characteristic of how popular elocutionists created a motive to study elocution for those who had no particular interest in learning the art of oratory but who were invested in getting along with others. Brown conjures a rather unpleasant image to further his argument that no one can afford to be without the skills of proper speech: "The hermit, withdrawing to his forest cabin or mountain cavern, may with impunity lapse into uncouth barbarism and give expression to his aches and pains in rasping pectoral grunts, since no other being is to be attracted or delighted by his words and manners; but woe to him who seeks amid the social hive for human sympathy if he ignores his tones and speech" (21). The contrast implied here between the animal-like utterance of the untutored hermit and the the graceful, clear tones of the skilled speaker is an image often outlined by popular elocutionists as they argued for the improving effects of elocutionary study. One of the most insistent messages of the popular elocution movement was the maxim that the person who speaks correctly wins affection and acceptance; the person who speaks poorly is isolated from social rewards. By equating correct speaking with access to the respect and affection of others, popular elocutionists defined elocution as a necessary study for anyone who hoped to enjoy happiness and success in daily life.

In addition to promoting diligent study of the principles of proper speaking as these apply to conversation and public speaking, popular elocutionists reiterated the claim of academic theorists that elocutionary skills can be acquired through dramatic reading of great works. A prominent claim of nineteenth-century rhetorical theory was the assumption that the critical study of great masterpieces cultivates taste and an appreciation of rhetorical style (Johnson 1991, 75–84). Elocutionists in this period similarly argued that the practice of reading great works aloud sharpens the mind and nurtures elocutionary talent. The dramatic reader benefits intellectually and morally from both the study and the performance of the work, and the audience is similarly improved by experiencing the actual performance and by being exposed to the subject and the rhetorical qualities of the work.

The assumption that the study and practice of elocution has these far-reaching intellectual and moral implications is a pervasive principle in nineteenth-century elocutionary theory and accounts for why popular texts typically combined theoretical discussions of principles with a section of selected works for study and practice. The title pages of popular manuals highlight the importance of the variety and quality of selections for practice: *The Handy Speaker: Comprising Fresh Selections in Poetry and Prose, Humorous, Pathetic, Patriotic* (Baker 1876); *The Peerless Speaker Being a Compilation of the Choicest Recitations, Readings and Dialogues from the Most Celebrated Authors* (Fenno 1900); *The Ideal Speaker and Entertainer: Being a Choice Treasury of New and Popular Recitations, Readings, Original and Adapted Comedies, Recitations with Lesson Talks, Etc. Comprising the Best Selections from the Most Celebrated Authors and Composers* (Northrop 1910). Elocutionists assumed that the oral performance of "choice" works provided ongoing training in the use of the voice and gesture and also exposed the performer to elegant language and moving emotions. While popular elocutionists stressed that one learns most from what is "best," they also made it clear that selections for practice were chosen with the varied needs of the public in mind, especially the need to have appropriate material for performance at social events and in the home. Recognizing dramatic reading as a popular form of entertainment in the way that academics did not, the compilers of elocution readers and speakers stressed the versatility of elocutionary materials as well as their merit. As one compiler explains, selections cover as wide a range of subjects, emotions, and occasions as possible while still offering "excellent specimens":

> Taken as a whole, this work presents an array of choice Poetry and Prose, so comprehensive and varied in style as to offer a responsive chord to every possible mood or phase of human feeling, and call forth every emotion of the heart; presenting a complete Library of Popular Gems. . . . By thus providing intellectual food for all the varying tastes and desires of a reading people, this work must necessarily prove a delightful traveling companion, a welcome visitor at every fireside, and a real household treasure; as no time, occasion or circumstances, but is here furnished suitable and enjoyable material for either reading or speaking. (Garrett 1874, preface)

By characterizing elocutionary material as "intellectual food" suitable for performance and enjoyment in social and private settings, popular elocutionists defend the art of dramatic reading as a skill that enhances private as well as public and professional life. Popular and academic elocutionists alike claimed that the art of dramatic reading ranked with public speaking as an indispensable skill. As Porter argues, "No one is qualified to hold a respectable rank in a well-bred society, who is unable to read in an interesting manner, the works of others" ([1827] 1830, 13–14). Within the nineteenth-century cultural climate, "well-bred" carried with it associations with higher intellectual and moral virtue. Popular elocutionists stressed the relationship between the study and practice of elocution and the development of "well-bred" qualities by pointing out that the practice of correct speaking through dramatic reading and conversation elevates the mind in the same way that the study of great orations enhances the powers of expression. In his introduction to *The Peerless Speaker*, Frank H. Fenno, author of several popular elocution manuals, explains that "an improved style [in conversation] will suggest better thoughts, and as so much of our happiness if not existence itself depends upon a conveyance on our ideas, cultivation in this direction will certainly make us happier, nobler and better (1900, vii). S. S. Curry expresses the same view when he observes that dramatic reading can be used "for the cultivation of taste" and that it provides "a great means for the development of the human being" (1891, xv). Porter, Fenno, and Curry all assume that elocution should be cultivated for the sake of personal development and to ensure full participation in life. Popular elocutionists defined a role for elocution in all spheres of private, professional, and social life by arguing that elocution was just as important in the parlor as in the office, just as crucial to the conversation as to the public lecture, and just as important to the ordinary person as it was to prominent speakers.

Elocutionary texts designed for the private learner typically presented abridged treatments of the theoretical principles treated at length in academic texts. The general public had access to three kinds of instructional materials: cross-over manuals, designed for both the academic student and the home learner that outlined an extensive treatment of the principles and techniques of delivery; popular elocution speakers, which provided rudimentary treatments of theoretical principles of delivery and multiple selections of readings for practice; and elocution reciters, which offered minimal instruction and consisted primarily of anthologized selections for practice and dramatic performances.

Cross-over manuals excised the elaborate philosophical and theoretical justifications typical of the philosophical academic treatises of Porter, Russell, and Curry and treated the principles of the voice and gesture with varying levels of sophistication. Like academic treatises, cross-over manuals were typically organized in two major sections: one devoted to a discussion of the major properties of the voice (articulation, inflection, accent, emphasis, pace, force, time, and pitch) and the second covering action or gesture (stance of the body, gestures of the hands, gestures of the arm, position of the feet and lower limbs, and expression of the face and eyes). Practice readings were usually included as exercises within discussions of the voice, and drawings and diagrams of different gestures, stances, and facial expressions were often included in the discussion of action.

Cross-over manuals combined an account of principles with a compendium of poems, plays, prose, and model speeches for practice, providing both theoretical and practical instruction under one cover. Cross-over manuals announced this double usefulness quite overtly. George L. Raymond and Frank H. Fenno, two of the most successful popularizers of elocutionary theory in the last decades of the century, indicate the range of readers they hope to educate in the subtitles to their manuals. Raymond explains that his text is "designed as a textbook for schools and colleges, and for public speakers and readers who are obliged to study without an instructor" (1897, 1). Fenno's subtitle is even more inclusive in its appeal: "A comprehensive and systematic series of exercises . . . designed to be used as a text book in the class-room and for private study, as well as for the use of readers and speakers generally" (1900, iii). Following the example of academic treatises, Raymond and Fenno provide fairly detailed discussions of principles of the voice and gesture and include readings for exercises and further practice. Other widely circulated cross-over manuals included Alexander Melville Bell's *Principles of Elocution* (1878), J. W. Shoemaker's *Practical Elocution* (1886), and Issac Hinton Brown's *Common School Elocution and Oratory* (1885), later reissued as *Brown's Standard Elocution and Speaker* (in a revised edition by Charles Walter Brown). These texts all incorporate the same organizational framework and cover similar topics: (1) a definition of elocution as the manner or style of speaking; (2) the proposition that good elocution consists of natural expression brought up to its most effective level; (3) the argument that good elocution is necessary in social, business, and public life; (4) the argument that the study of elocution develops the mind and a healthy body; (5) definitions and illustrations of the principles of elocution covering the use of the voice and gestures; and (6) selections for practice, either presented as exercises within discussions of principles or appended as exercises.

Although these elements parallel the contents of academic treatises, cross-over manuals presented this material with what authors claimed as deliberate "conciseness." Charles Walter Brown describes this distinctive theoretical stance of the cross-over text by explaining that the purpose of his text, one directed to "Schools, Colleges, Universities and Private Pupils," is to "present the science of human expression in a manner so simple, so concise and so reasonable that no student with average zeal and ability would experience difficulty in comprehending and applying its principles" (1911, 3). Because he assumed that many of his readers would be studying on their own, Brown shaped his text so that theoretical fundamentals and techniques could be grasped by any individual willing to give the task intelligent attention. What cross-over elocutionists want to avoid is a level of theoretical complexity that might not be self-explanatory.

The concise approach of cross-over manuals is also characteristic of the theoretical style of cross-over readers, texts designed for the use of "advanced pupils" in common schools and academies as well as for the instruction of the home learner and the family. Cross-over readers such as Wilson's *Fifth Reader of the School and Family Series* (1861), *McGuffey's New Sixth Eclectic Reader* (1857), and Parker and Watson's *National Fifth Reader* (1870) offer a more truncated version of elocutionary theory than the cross-over manuals, and they typically treat only principles of the voice, often neglecting gesture altogether. This omission of gesture is largely due to their exclusive focus on the art of reading literature aloud, a type of elocutionary performance in which gesture was considered less important than it would be in public speaking and dramatic performance. The authors of *The National Fifth Reader* represent their text as a "simple, complete, and eminently practical Treatise on Elocution" that provides a "collection of pieces so rich, varied, perspicuous, and attractive, as to suit all classes of minds, all times, and all occasions" (Parker and Watson 1870, iii). Cross-over readers extended an education in elocution and taste to the home learner through the type of selections included for performance and practice. Like other types of cross-over manuals, cross-over readers promote the premise that the student of elocution learns best by practicing the works of the masters:

> The Selections for Reading and Declamation contain what are regarded as the choicest gems of English literature. The work of many authors, ancient

and modern, have been consulted, and more than a hundred standard writers, of the English language, on both sides of the Atlantic, have been laid under contribution to enable the authors to present a collection, rich in all that can inform the understanding, improve the taste, and cultivate the heart, and which, at the same time, shall furnish every variety of style and subject to exemplify the principles of Rhetorical delivery, and form a finished reader and elocutionist. (iii)

The theoretical hallmark of cross-over readers is simplicity, a level of explanation that preserves the theoretical principles of manual-length treatments of elocutionary principles but treats these issues with less sophistication. In his cross-over manual *Elocution: The Sources and Elements*, McIlvaine allots three chapters to an extensive discussion of aspects of correct pronunciation, detailing explanation of articulation, accent, and control over vowels, accent, and word endings (1870, 199–293). In contrast, *The National Fifth Reader* provides a mere fifteen-page summary of the principle of articulation, focusing on a series of sentence-long "definitions" of what articulation must control (Parker and Watson 1870, 21). This type of theoretical simplicity indicates the distillation of theoretical content that accompanied attempts to "popularize" elocutionary theory for a wider readership.

The theoretical distillation of elocutionary theory is at work in cross-over manuals and readers at different stages. This process is revealed in more extreme stages in two types of materials designed exclusively for the popular audience—elocution speakers and reciters. These texts were marketed strictly for use in the home and as a resource for elocutionary performances at social and community events. Efforts on the part of authors to widen the appeal of elocutionary training and performance resulted in the further reduction of theoretical discussion and the inclusion of far more categories of selections for performance in informal settings.

Elocution speakers provided rudimentary theoretical instruction in the form of rules and handy hints; this "how-to" approach represents the popularization of elocutionary theory at its most simplistic. In *The New American Speaker*, Emma Griffith Lumm offers an extremely abbreviated treatment of the principles of elocution in a form of a list of twelve "Practical Suggestions" (1898, 39). For example, Lumm compresses the complex principles of clear pronunciation (articulation), modulation of voice, and time (pace of expression) into two rules: "Finish the sentence, make the pitch of the voice high enough at the beginning of a sentence to keep the last word from dropping back into the throat" and "*Speak slowly*, take time to *think* the words, and the words will express your thought" (40). When compared with the sophistication of discussions of the same issues provided by cross-over manuals, the theoretical distillation characteristic of popular speakers is quite dramatic. In contrast to Lumm's advice that the demands of correct pronunciation are met by the maxim "speak slowly," Fenno explains that articulation (the distinct and correct utterance of elementary sounds) depends on the control of vocal sounds, aspirate sounds, and combined sounds; he also provides a "table of exercises" for the practice of each type of pronunciation (1878, 21–24). Similarly, Fenno offers a far more complex analysis of modulation than does Lumm, who simply implies that correct expression will result from "finishing the sentence," "speaking slowly," or "thinking" the words. Fenno explains that modulation (the use of voice to convey the thought in the best manner) depends upon the control of several qualities of the voice, including melody (effect on the ear of a succession of vocal notes), pitch (elevation or depression of tone), slides (ascending and descending inflection), cadence (tone with which the sentence terminates), and time (rate of speech and use of pause) (25–42). Although not nearly as extensive a treatment of modulation as Porter or Russell offer, Fenno's discussions of articulation and modulation are infinitely more complex than Lumm's, who translates elocutionary theory at the most basic level in order that the principles of elocution can be understood by the greatest diversity of individuals and applied to the greatest range of activities and occasions.

Although simplistic in approach, elocution speakers did successfully popularize a number of standard elocutionary techniques through rudimentary reminders about voice control (pronunciation, rate of speech, tone of voice, force, and stress) and the use of the body and gesture (standing position, head positions, position of the hands, arm movements, and facial expressions) (e.g., Brown 1911, 23–59). Usually organized under attention-getting headings such as "Requirements of Good Elocution" and "The Four Positions," the instructional content of speakers retained distinct theoretical links to the more amplified discussions provided by cross-over manuals. Al-

though providing highly abbreviated treatments of theoretical principles, the "how-to" instructional approach of elocution speakers confirmed the general assumption of the elocution movement that elocution was a skill that required study and practice. The "how-to"
approach to instruction was at its most influential in the 1880s, 1890s,
and the early decades of the twentieth century. Texts like Brown's
*American Star Speaker* (1902), Fenno's *Peerless Speaker* (1900), and John
Coulter's *New Century Perfect Speaker* (1902) combine the how-to instructional mode with the presentation of "appropriate selections
from the masterpieces of thought, sentiment and feeling of great
orators and writers" (Coulter [1901] 1902, preface).

The authors of elocution speakers were often elocutionists who
produced various levels of popular materials, as in the case of Brown
and Fenno, who also authored full-length theoretical manuals. These
authors clearly perceive the simplistic and condensed approach of the
speaker genre to be a direct response to "popular demand for a work
containing information, instruction, an advice regarding elocution . . . with immediate reference to availability in a practical way"
(Coulter [1901] 1902, preface). The "popular" and "practical" appeal of
elocution speakers is confirmed by the fact that these texts include
many more selections for private, social, and community occasions
and fewer selections from the masterpieces of oratory than cross-over
manuals typically offer. Speakers advertise selections for every conceivable occasion: Christmas, New Year's, Easter, Thanksgiving, old
settlers' gatherings, Labor Day, Arbor Day, "dramatic, pathetic, humorous recitals and readings . . . for schools, lodges, public enter-
tainments, anniversaries, sunday-schools;" "selections . . . suitable
for home, school, church, lodge, club, literary societies, . . . and
public and private recitals" (Lumm 1898, 6; Northrop 1920, 1; Brown
1902, 1). The most distinctive characteristic of the popular elocution
speaker as a class of instructional text is this sweeping generalization
of what constitutes everyday rhetorical occasions to which elocutionary skills could apply.

Unlike elocution speakers, elocution reciters provided little to no
instructional content, concentrating on providing anthologized readings for practice and performance. Reciters were published in two
forms, single volume anthologies (often reprinted) and in serials of
monthly, quarterly, or annual issues. Both of these types of texts
present a cross section of selections for practice and performance

geared for the general reader and favoring loose genre categories such as "humorous, pathetic, and patriotic" or simply "prose" and "poetry." The massive number of elocution reciters available in the latter decades of the nineteenth century and early twentieth century testifies to the widespread popularity of elocution as a form of private and public entertainment. Popular reciter series included the two widely circulated series published by Phineas Garrett, *The Speakers Garland and Literary Bouquet* (1870–1926) and *One Hundred Choice Selections for Readings and Recitations* (1866–1914), as well as Werner's *Readings and Recitations* (1890–1915) (published by Edgar S. Werner, founder of the elocutionist magazine *Werner's Magazine*, later *The Voice* [1879–1902]), and George M. Baker's series, *The Reading Club*. Selections from *The Reading Club* were collected in Baker's widely circulated anthology *The Handy Speaker* (1876). Like elocution speakers, reciters fed the public's seemingly inexhaustible interest in elocutionary performance. Baker announces his collection as a response to the general reader's "cry for 'new pieces'" (1870, 2) and Shoemaker introduces his reciter series, *The Elocutionist's Annual*, as a collection that provides eagerly awaited "fresh selections" (1873, 4). Baker's and Shoemaker's perception that the public clamored for "fresh selections" for study and practice indicates that by the 1870s, the popular elocution movement was already responding to the public's conviction that elocution was necessarily applicable to an extensive range of subjects and occasions. The publication of reciters also motivated that interest by continuing to promote the assumption that the application of elocution to everyday professional, social, and private life was nearly unlimited.

Although elocution reciters did not provide the level of theoretical instruction offered by speakers and cross-over manuals, these texts made a distinct contribution to the enterprise of promoting vocal culture, which all popular elocution texts supported. By widening even further the sphere of elocutionary activity to include an extensive list of performance occasions in the community and in the home, compilers of reciters confirmed the general importance of elocution by reminding the average citizen that correct expression was in vogue in all aspects of life. Cross-over manuals and readers recommended the study of elocution for its practical versatility and for the insights into taste, the power of language, and the higher emotions that elocutionary and performance provides. Compilers of widely circulated reciters also stressed the connection between elocutionary performance and the acquisition of "a refined taste and a cultivated judgment" (Werner 1890, iii–iv) and link the practice of elocution with patriotism, culture, and self-improvement: "[This volume is dedicated] to the good and the true of the nation, to the millions of intelligent readers and speakers throughout our country and to all who appreciate Choice Literature, either in the Parlor, School Room, Library or Forum" (Garrett 1885, 6: iii). Like cross-over manuals and elocution speakers, reciters self-consciously affirmed the centrality of elocution by proclaiming its wide applicability and by promoting the cultural norm that correct speaking marked the individual for personal development and a happier life.

By stressing that the dramatic reading of a poem or essay at a backyard picnic was just as likely a means of practicing and acquiring forceful powers of expression as the giving of formal lectures and orations, the popular elocution movement made rhetorical training relevant to a whole group of people for whom formal training in oratory was irrelevant or impractical. The mission of the popular elocution movement to offer "the private learner" the opportunity to develop more dignified and forceful speech drew support not only from the powerful pragmatism of its appeal but also from the commonly held cultural view that improvement in expression contributed in a general way to the improvement of character and the mind. Sharing with their academic counterparts in the academy the notion that rhetorical skills were versatile and essential to good communication of all types, popular elocutionists stressed that self-improvement through better speaking resulted in a life of greater fulfillment, ease, and success.

# 6

# Rhetorical Power in the Victorian Parlor ✳ *Godey's Lady's Book* and the Gendering of Nineteenth-Century Rhetoric ✳ *Nicole Tonkovich*

✳In 1845, amid a heightened national debate over slavery and sectionalism, Sarah Josepha Hale, then editor of the influential *Godey's Magazine and Lady's Book*,[1] outlined in her monthly editorial column a solution to the sectional crisis. American women, Hale averred, could combat sectionalism by maintaining a written correspondence with their children who had left New England for the western territories that were the locus of sectional debate.[2] They should write their scattered children not only of current family news but also of times past, striving to reproduce in their minds the treasured memories of New England. These memories should be based neither in generalities nor in individual experiences but in the common landscape, whose specific locales and sensations all New England youth had shared: "The old elm tree, beneath whose shade was our castle, . . . the rock that was our temple, the stream which poured in music along our path, the bright flowers we could always find; we see them all, enjoy them all, with . . . healthful, unsophisticated relish. . . . These are the feelings that humanize the heart and . . . [impart] the love of country to the patriot" (*Godey's* 1845, 31:82). With those common scenes renewed in the mind, a departed child would be less likely to dwell on how his or her new home differed from the old: "He feels that his happiness is not centered in the spot of his local residence, but . . . his heart is drawn out in aspirations for the prosperity of all that wide country over which his affections range in their journey to his early home" (82). In Hale's formulation, these local memories would function quite literally as *loci communae*, common places, performing the same function as did the rhetorical mnemonic device. That is, the common sensory experiences of locale and landscape would remind wandering children of their heritage, suggest common interests that would unify their hearts and minds, and thus enable them to transcend mere political wrangling. Hale concludes,

> It is this union of hearts and memories which must preserve and perpetuate our political union. When feelings of kindly interest shall be cherished by all . . . there will be no danger of discord between the states. The narrow spirit which sees a rival or enemy in every different section, will yield to the ties of relationship or good feeling. . . . Let ladies sedulously cultivate, through their private friendships and familiar correspondences, that interest in the welfare of families and persons which makes every state in the wide union hallowed as the birth-place or residence of those we love and honour, and not a star will ever disappear from our banner, though its broad folds should in time cover and protect the whole Continent. (82–83)

Hale's appeal for sectional solidarity depended on rhetorical conventions that the editors of this collection have characterized as neoclassic: It depends in large measure on assuming that consensus is the basis for public acts; it is addressed to a readership of like-minded citizens whose function is to judge the reasonableness of a proposal bearing on the civic good of their community. Yet Hale also introduces onto this common ground two new and ultimately revolutionary factors: She proposes that the community-building function traditionally assigned to oratory in a public assembly now take place through writing produced and circulated privately. Furthermore, she assigns the responsibility for such activity to women. Thus potentially divisive public conflicts are brought under the control of a constituency whose gender-related values will ultimately transcend merely political differences of property, location, or party alignment.

Not surprisingly, perhaps, conventional histories of the Civil War do not note Hale's suggested solution for the nation's sectional woes. Likewise, until recently, conventional histories of rhetoric in the United States have overlooked women's roles in the transformation of a neoclassic, communitarian rhetorical culture into a culture of individualized professionalism, as this collection posits. While such histories have derived their understandings from canonical texts, recent revisionist scholars have demonstrated the positive benefit of considering noncanonical textual sources, those that enjoyed a broad, if common, circulation.[3] Close attention to these overlooked sources reveals that conventional understandings of women's political and rhetorical involvement, which usually relegate them to a position of marginal importance, seriously misrepresent the case. In this essay, I will examine how the written practice of one woman, who did not appear bodily in the traditional public arenas of pulpit, court, or senate, contributed to that transformation. I will analyze Sarah Josepha Hale's writing practices in terms of what Susan Miller (1989) has called a "textual rhetoric," one that takes into account how writing differs from oral performance. I will thus argue that even as Hale sought to adapt neoclassic rhetoric's conventions, rules, and proprieties to writing, she and her magazine were a significant factor in its overthrow.

From 1828 to 1833, Hale edited *The Ladies' Magazine*, an early New England periodical; from 1834 to 1872, she edited *Godey's Lady's Book*, one of the most widely circulated magazines of the nineteenth century.[4] That Hale held such a position is not unique—so many women had entered literary production by the mid-nineteenth century, in fact, that she might be considered a representative case.[5] As second-in-command in the *Godey's* enterprise, Hale dictated the terms in which politics, history, and education would be represented. Thus, by extension, she constructed representational norms that assumed hegemonic functions within a constituency of women who, although not yet enfranchised, still could exercise a significant sway over political action.[6] (I am assuming here, of course, that access to representation is a form of power that cannot be overlooked, even or especially if that representation is exercised in such traditionally devalued forms as sentimental novels, conduct books, or ladies' magazines.) This collective opinion Hale orchestrated through the political and social turmoils of the mid-nineteenth century, years that also saw the related transformation of nineteenth-century rhetorical models. When Hale assumed charge of *The Ladies' Magazine* in 1827, the neoclassic rhetorical culture was still apparently the norm, although writing was becoming increasingly available through mass-circulation media, so much so that when Edward T. Channing assumed the Boylston Chair of Rhetoric and Oratory at Harvard in 1819, he could say that "we have now many other and more quiet ways of forming and expressing public sentiment, than public discussion in popular assemblies" ([1856] 1968, 16). When Hale retired from *Godey's* in 1877, however, a culture of individualized professionalism held sway, characterized by autonomous, local, and self-interested acts that claimed significance not for a collective and representative assembly but only for a professional and specialized constituency. In this later moment, a more democratized, heterogeneous, and uncontrollable mass had replaced the community that neoclassic rhetoric had posited. In this essay I will demonstrate that in Hale's early work, as one might expect, given her training and her allegiances, neoclassic assumptions about community consensus predominate. However, because Hale's public work was always already literary—that is, written—we see it simultaneously disturb the consensus those neoclassic oratorical conventions assume. As a woman, Hale stands for a more democratic access to literacy and thus a broadened public participation that characterizes the mid-century. That very democratization, ironically, called forth in Hale's later writing a retrenchment; for as Hale saw the result of such individualism, she reinvoked neoclassic assumptions as a means of maintaining social stability and control within a public arena where those desiderata no longer held force.

Forged in the crucible of the American Revolution and tempered in the political fervor of nationhood, the neoclassic rhetorical culture and its rhetor, "the good man skilled in speaking," was a gendered ideal. As a number of foundational studies in United States women's history have by now established, the Revolution may have made patriots of men, but it left in doubt "the old question of whether a woman could be a patriot— that is, an essentially political person—and it also raised the question of what form female patriotism might take" (Kerber 1986, 9). In the years immediately following the Revolution, an ideological compromise emerged, described by Linda Kerber as "the notion of . . . 'Republican Motherhood.'" Under this rubric, women exemplified the neoclassic virtues of citizenship. Kerber explains: "The Republican Mother integrated political values into her domestic life. . . . [T]he mother, . . . not the masses, came to be seen as the custodian of civic morality" (11). Republican Motherhood assigned women to a private sphere wherein their political duties were subsumed under the responsibilities of raising virtuous, moral, and patriotic sons.[7] Assigning one gender to a sphere labeled private, even metaphorically, necessarily produced a divided polity. Hence, any study of "community values" of neoclassic rhetoric must account for the ideologies of gender governing the community in which those values hold sway. More important, such a split suggests that politics might have a private dimension and anticipates the more general move of fragmentation and specialization that dominates the latter half of nineteenth-century rhetoric. Hale's work, as I have already asserted, invokes neoclassic rhetorical assumptions that writer and readers share a moral consensus; but the consensus that Hale inscribes is frequently a consensus based on gender differentiation: That is, she asserts that women, because of their gender, hold communal values that may be subtly or overtly different from those held by men.

This gendered split in the body politic was widened by the burgeoning of mass-circulation journalism. Historically associated with political concerns, journalism's readership began to broaden early in the nineteenth century as newspapers and magazines addressed themselves to the needs and interests of less entitled readers. At the same time, the physical dictates of print encouraged a more private political participation. Writing, made even more anonymous in print, need not invoke ethos or rhetorical presence. "It could itself be 'logical,' by virtue of articulation, clarification, and citation. It could stand alone," separate from its "author's" authority and from "community traditions" (Miller 1989, 81–82). The gender, race, and authority of the originator of the discourse no longer were evident in the speaker's presence and embodied voice; thus women might construct a public voice in print even while remaining bodily in the "private sphere." What they wrote need no longer depend on public consensus nor on a speaker's ethos, since, as Miller suggests, "the writer, unlike the orator, is working privately in the public, publicly in the private, worlds of texts" (52). The audience was replaced by the reader, absent and necessarily fictionalized, in some sense a function of the text itself. Thus the give and take of oral public debate was increasingly supplemented by silent, individual, and private acts of reading and writing. These concomitants of print communication Hale exploited, delivering to her readership of Republican Mothers information that was public and political but simultaneously ideologically correct in its often anonymous origins and avowedly private uses.

Hale used the anonymity afforded by print to her own personal advantage as she undertook a life of public visibility in an era that preferred to think of its women as privately confined. Like many literate women who were her counterparts, Hale had little formal institutional education but received a good deal of informal training in the neoclassic model at the hand of male mentors. Instructed by her brother and husband (both college-educated lawyers) in the fine points of public discourse, she honed her skills by participating in several informal community literary societies. These clubs, unlike the exclusively male collegiate culture, were less restrictive in their membership. Within their boundaries women like Hale could participate in debate and discussion, write for a familiar but intellectually exacting audience of men and women, and receive friendly criticism on their writing. These early educative experiences prepared Hale to earn her living as a writer after her husband's untimely death. The successful publication of her first novel, *Northwood* (1827), led the Reverend John Lauris Blake to invite her to edit *The Ladies' Magazine*.

The terms in which she justifies accepting his offer have resonance for the subject at hand, since for an early nineteenth-century woman to have moved thus into public life was highly irregular. Hale memorialized the event in writing and repeated the story with little variation in several versions of her autobiography. Even fifty years after the fact, Hale continued to represent her decision as a calling, not unlike a clergyman's. She recalls,

> I had little to depend upon except the promises of God for the fatherless and widow, and my own pen to support my young family of five children, and educate them as their father would have done. I had lived secluded in the dear home where he left me. . . . I must give up this precious home . . . and go out into the world which I so much dreaded. Yet my faith in God was so strong, that this change seemed to me to be the ordering of Divine Providence, and I accepted these new duties and responsibilities as appointed by His will. (*Godey's* 1877, 95:522)

Hale figures herself first as a properly reticent mother, then as an executor of the will of Divine Providence, the details of whose public life had been arranged by a minister and thus presumably also countenanced by God. So sanctioned, she would train other women to assume the responsibilities of Republican Motherhood. Although the immediate terms of her excuse seem personal, when they are so frequently and formulaically repeated, it becomes apparent that they constitute but one component of a textual and institutional persona. During the nine years of her editorial tenure at *The Ladies' Magazine,* her reputation grew to the extent that when Louis Godey hired her in 1837, he proclaimed "Mrs. Hale is too well-known to need eulogies from us" (*Godey's* 1836, 13:90). Over her fifty years at *Godey's,* she and the magazine became as one, much in the same manner Samuel Clemens later "became" Mark Twain. Hale's public image embodied the magazine's unchanging ideal of womanhood. Biographers routinely note Hale's constancy of personal appearance. For fifty years, she wore the same ringletted coiffure. Daguerreotypes taken of her in later life, according to one biographer, "[record] the same firm unwrinkled skin and gentle contours" as the paintings done in her youth (Finley 1932, 89). At the same time, the magazine became so closely identified with her persona that it was generally spoken of as "Mrs. Hale's book."

The standardized forms of print journalism allowed Hale to use her institutional identity to great advantage. Anonymous judicial criticism, practiced by men or by women, found a congenial discursive space within the magazines of the era. Of this early American judicial literary criticism, William Charvat has noted: "Its authority is that of a class or an organization, rather than of an individual. The reader of criticism in those days did not care to know what an individual thought of a book; he wanted the book to be tested by the principles of a journal with which he was familiar. He leaned upon established principle, not upon someone's opinion" (1959, 2).[8] Charvat's claim reminds us of the neoclassic norms that Hale respected but also explains how she could simultaneously function as a cultural arbiter in the public realm and claim to be a private woman. As an editor, Hale did much to construct *Godey's* as an institutional guarantor of morally upright fiction in an era when the ever-increasing amount of writing available from anonymous and/or absent writers called out for evaluation and regulation, an activity best undertaken and authorized by one noted for "her acknowledged good taste" (*Godey's* 1836, 13:144). This guarantee became a hallmark of *Godey's,* assuring readers of a certain degree of literary/moral respectability.[9] In her (unsigned) "Editor's Table" columns, Hale became *Godey's* editress (a title she preferred as gendered, and therefore linguistically more precise). Here she pursued a running commentary on the state of the literary trade, both on specific books, on generic considerations, and even upon other periodicals and their editorial practices.

If the textual rhetor, or writer, is a function of textual inscription, so also is her reader/audience. Assuredly the *Godey's* reader was as careful a construct as was its editor. Well-read, entitled to masculine respect, this reader was a woman who had a right, indeed an obligation, to hold political opinions. The arena for those opinions *Godey's* had brought within its written representation; within this inscribed political world, women were enjoined to act upon their opinions. To these readers Hale brought matters of public interest, enlisting their support in matters whose resolution would benefit them and taking editorial positions on political matters that she knew would affect them. Not surprisingly, she modeled her editorial practice on oral precedent, representing her readership not as private and individual silent readers and writers but as a community of like-minded women. In her inaugural editorial, Hale extended an invitation to readers to join her in "a '*Conversazióne*' of the highest character." This textual assembly was to approximate a literary salon in its form and content. And since *Godey's* was addressed to women, its topics would

> *not* be polemical, political, philological, philosophical, scientific, or critical—but . . . aim to draw forth and form into a pleasant, healthy, and happy combination, the moral uses of all these high sounding pursuits. . . .
>
> We shall not affect the learned, logical, or profound style. . . . Ours will rather imitate that tone of playful vivacity, intelligent observation, and refined taste, which predominates in the social *re-unions* of the good and gifted. (1837, 14:2)

In point of fact Hale did publish material that can only be described as polemical, political, philological, philosophical, scientific, and critical. But she excused her magazine's intrusion into these masculine domains by claiming a womanly perspective on them, emphasizing moral application, a task that might be subsumed under the responsibilities of Republican Motherhood. Further, the form or manner of conversation would not be agonistic but would depend on a common understanding of refined and tasteful discourse presumed to be the particular talent of the ideal *Godey's* reader. The metaphor of conversation was a happy one, for it allowed Hale to claim high purpose without encroaching upon serious political matters. It seems a quintessentially womanly activity, closely aligned with the "visiting" that linked white upper-middle- and middle-class women in the nineteenth century into a closely knit community. It avoids the confrontive overtones of public oratory or debate; its participants were playful, vivacious, even intelligent, but never claimed to dictate public policy. In fact, Hale warranted that in her magazine, "nothing [would] be introduced to undermine those sacred relations of domestic life, in which the Creator has placed the sceptre of woman's empire. We are always at home" (1837, 14:5). All the conversationalists, editor and reader alike, were enclosed in a properly domestic sphere, the public brought within the enclosure of private writing. The important political dimension of that sphere, however, is contained in Hale's characterization of this monthly conversation as a "reunion of the good and gifted." Here she establishes the assumption that she invoked again a decade later as she sought to confront the divisiveness of sectionalism—that the characteristics common to women transcend the divisive wrangling implied in polemics, political debate, and philosophical, scientific, and critical undertakings.

The conversational metaphor also meant that Hale invited her readers to participate with her in constructing the magazine. She invited them to suggest content and to submit written contributions; she made them privy to her editorial processes of acceptance and rejection. Again, her model is based on neoclassic rhetorical assumptions, for the contributions she expected to receive, as evidenced by what she eventually printed or rejected, were in impeccable adherence to the community norms Hale felt she represented: *Godey's* poetry would "[exalt] and [purify] the heart and intellect"; its prose would "communicate . . . the wisdom of the world, which is necessary to be known" (1837, 14:3). The magazine's content was, for the most part, conservatively predictable, demonstrating recognizable maxims of behavior or undertaking to defend some assigned position on a set topic. Acting upon her promise not to undermine communal norms for gendered behavior,[10] Hale handled her editorial selection process publicly, much in the same manner that the neoclassic college classroom conducted its examinations. For some years, rather than write individual letters accepting or rejecting submissions, Hale replied to contributors publicly in her editorial column. Although this procedure's immediate benefit was economic, it also invited readers and the community at large to be assured of the magazine's procedures. Over time, Hale expanded her commentary on submissions into extended essays on writing that became part of the magazine's broader educational undertaking.

Because Hale constructed her readership as conversational partners who held similar social assumptions and concerns, she often orchestrated their communally shared standards into concerted political action, inviting them to join as a group in support of an issue or cause, most frequently gender-related. Readers of *The Ladies' Magazine* were urged to support the Fatherless and Widow's Society of Boston, for example. Between 1867 and 1875, Hale enjoined her readers to undertake an annual letter-writing campaign petitioning Congress to set aside money and land for normal schools where women would be trained as teachers for the West. If it was not gender-specific, women's public activism that threatened to exceed the bounds of gendered appropriateness would be excused as merely exercise of the duties of citizenship appropriate to Republican Motherhood. One such endeavor, the Bunker Hill Monument fund, received Hale's attention over a period of thirteen years. Under the rhetoric of women's exalted patriotic duty she subsumed the potentially threatening fact that women had banded together independently to raise money to complete a project men had abandoned economically.

Addressing the potentially contradictory prescriptions for private domestic refinement and elevated political understanding, Hale asserted that the Republican Mother was to gain the worldly knowledge required to raise her patriot sons by being impeccably and thoroughly educated, either formally through the new seminaries and institutes devoted to women's education or informally at the hand of female mentors. In any case, the education was to be adapted to her gendered identity. Early and late, Hale asserted that a woman's "first right is to education in its widest sense, to such education as will give her the full development of all her personal, [not public or political] mental and moral qualities. Having that, there will be no longer any questions about her rights" (quoted in Woodward 1960, 33). A regular *Godey's* feature, "The Ladies' Mentor," was intended to "give reports of the present state of female education in Europe and America; Sketches of the most celebrated Female Seminaries in the United States; and notices of such literary works as are particularly designed for women, and peculiarly calculated to advance the improvement of our sex, by enlightening public opinion respecting the importance of female influence" (*Godey's* 1837, 14:45). Aware that many of her readers could not enjoy the advantages of specialized institutional instruction, Hale sought to remedy that deficiency through the pages of her magazine. She proposed to publicize institutional education while contributing actively to paracurricular instruction, which she considered an ideal concomitant to proper womanly reticence. Autodidacticism would simultaneously allow a woman to develop her mental faculties and afford her the privacy that Hale felt the womanly nature demanded.

One of her earliest endeavors in this line was to outline a course of reading that could be pursued at home.[11] During 1847, Hale introduced a year-long series of editorials outlining in meticulous detail a curriculum in reading for women that also functioned as a brief introduction to the principles of taste and literary criticism governing the public consumption of mid-nineteenth-century literature. *Godey's* regularly published a monthly book review column noting most, if not all, of the books issuing from American presses in the Northeast with at least a paragraph's summary and evaluation. Aware that its readers were geographically dispersed, the magazine made these books available by shipping to readers upon paid request any book mentioned in the "Literary Notices." Sometimes Hale devoted entire columns to reviewing or reprinting long passages from books she considered to be especially important. Frequently these were dictionaries or handbooks of language use.

Hale supported institutional education as a means of maintaining community values, recognizing that common educational experiences produce solidarity among their beneficiaries. (At the same time, of course, this commonality tends to inscribe a class-based system of domination.) The effect of such solidarity among (masculine) recipients of an upper-class education in the contemporary period chronicled by Pierre Bourdieu is applicable to an earlier period and another gender, as well: "The sharing of a common culture . . . is probably one of the surest foundations of the deep underlying fellow-feeling that unites the members of the governing classes, despite differences of occupation and economic circumstances" (1971, 197).[12] Yet Hale's move to enclose education in domestic privacy had the effect of fostering a dangerous individualism that would eventually help to undermine the homogeneous community upon which her practice of neoclassic rhetoric depended. Because the domestically educated woman was not subject to the powerful normative discipline of the school, she was much more inclined to independent thought and action. Hale's paracurriculum served in many ways to foster that independence. Like her counterparts within formal institutions of education, Hale advocated that women learn to write. Aware that some of her readers would not have easy access to the tools necessary to practice writing, she recommended that women reading at home practice "mental composition." This activity pushes reading beyond mere consumption and asks more of women readers than passive acceptance of a text. Additionally, it is portable, since it

> can be pursued at any time and place, without the requisite paraphernalia of written composition. In reading any work, it greatly conduces to the development of the judgment, to make frequent pauses, and trace out the inference, and the particular bearing and tendency of detached portions of it; and upon its completion, to consider the general scope, its moral tone, the correctness of the sentiments advanced, and the character of the style. Thus, whilst the mind is adding to its stores of knowledge, and the heart is receiving good impressions, these various faculties and affections would be called into vigorous action, and the judgment strengthened and matured, would guide rightly the heart in its decisions. (*Godey's* 1838, 16:191)

This process demanded of women readers more than passive acceptance of a text. Rather, it asked that women enter the reading process in much the same manner as the neoclassic auditor responded to speech, passing judgment on its content. Working from the assumptions of faculty psychology in recommending that the judgment be strengthened by exercise, Hale emphasizes the readers' importance in constructing meaning. The reader (re-)creates context by charting inferences, making connections with other texts, analyzing and evaluating argumentation, noting the felicities of style, and generally evaluating the reading. The dangerous individualism this process would entail is allayed somewhat by Hale's assertion that the thoughtful reader's decisions would be made "rightly." It might also be argued that although mental composition is a step toward producing the individual, it scarcely disturbs a more public consensus because it remains private and undocumented. But Hale does not recommend that mental composition and exercise of judgment mark the end of a reader's engagement with a text. Rather, a woman should strive to supplement mental composition with writing. Hale recommends "the keeping of a *common-place book*, to sketch down one's views, opinions, and sentiments, upon every subject or topic, which may have interested the mind in the perusal of a work. The common-place book, is not designed to serve as an *external* memory to the writer, but rather as a treasury of original thoughts" (1838, 16:191). Again, the surface of Hale's assertion discloses a harmless activity: sketching, not argumentation, criticism, nor any form of active liter-ary production. But the effect of her recommendation exceeds its tenor. For the commonplace book Hale prescribes is not to serve as a repository of others' wisdom but as an intellectual journal, where a woman might in privacy try out her own thoughts—individual opin-ions, and not necessarily reflective of public consensus—about the material she has read.

Thus far I have established that Hale's most easily identifiable neoclassical assumptions were in some degree compromised by threatening technologies of written individualism. I now will exam-ine cases of her practice that even more forcefully document her perhaps unwilling but nevertheless effective contributions to the coming paradigm of individualism. The most irrefutable example of this assertion is Hale's own uses of writing as a technology that both created and maintained the ideology of the private sphere yet made women's confinement there largely a metaphorical construct. Hale turned the ideology of woman's unique needs and sensibilities to comfortable profit, marketing writing that promised a predictable and repeated content to a circumscribed group of readers identified as having particular interests, not to the community at large. She ad-dressed magazines, gift books, cookbooks, etiquette books, novels, and anthologies specifically to bourgeois True Women,[13] often speci-fying by the book's title and physical appearance that its content was for women's private consumption: Titles such as *Flora's Interpreter: or, The American Book of Flowers and Sentiments; Love; or, Woman's Destiny, a Poem*; and *The Lady's Annual Register, and Housewife's Almanac* hailed women readers as having unique interests that could be addressed through books written specifically for and marketed directly to them. The writer's gender could be either emphasized (as it frequently was in pseudonymous circumlocutions such as "a lady of New England" or in the alliterative floral pseudonyms that predominated mid-century) or elided entirely.

When I assert that women's private confinement was largely metaphorical, I am thinking not only of Hale's own biography but also of how she wrote about other women who led (sometimes even more overtly) public lives. Her own struggle to support her family after her husband's death led Hale to take strong journalistic stances about women's work. Even *Godey's Lady's Book*, whose tenor was to advocate women's domestic confinement, stressed that marriage did not necessarily guarantee a woman's financial well-being. In her editorial role, she advocated that women turn their attention to all manner of occupations that, although they might not be dignified with the title of profession, would allow them to earn a decent living while at least giving a nod in the direction of cultural prescriptions for womanly reticence. (She assumed, of course, that these working women were either single or widowed.) As early as 1851, for example, Hale began to publicize Elizabeth Blackwell's medical studies. Blackwell's case could be justified under the logic that women needed expertise in health care in order to execute properly their domestic duties. But Hale's publicity eventually extended to include noticing (and justifying, implicitly and explicitly) all manner of occupations for women. A series entitled "The Employment of Women in Cities" discussed women who worked in shops and in the Philadelphia mint and who attended the Philadelphia School of Design. Later *Godey's* columns featured other occupations deemed appropriate to women and designated with precise and gendered titles: postmistresses, lighthouse-keeperesses, telegraphesses, waitresses, one attorneyess,[14] and women who worked for the publishing house of Harper and Brothers and as colorists for *Godey's* fashion plates.

It might be argued that in noting women's employment, Hale simply was chronicling a phenomenon in the culture at large. Yet two other projects in *Godey's* demonstrate that Hale's advocacy of women's employment contributed to a nascent sense not only of women as a gendered class with gender-specific interests but also of the range of differentiation among women as individuals. First Hale encouraged her readers to adjust their language to acknowledge the reality of women in the work place: "The poetry of women is distinctive and peculiar; their acting is of wholly different parts; their manner of teaching has influences which men cannot reach; their medical practice is required for human preservation; and the language gains greatly in beauty, force, propriety, and power by conveying these differences in a single word" (1867, 75:79). Hale promoted the use of gendered terms—authoress, actress, teacheress, doctress, editress—

as a means of acknowledging women's presence in the occupations. The reasoning behind this move for linguistic precision is complex, and Hale prepared her readers gradually for the change. In 1855 she began to encourage readers to cease using the term "female" (as in "female attorney"), especially in cases where it was not paralleled by a similar use of "male." The designation, she argues, refers primarily to biological differentiation and should properly be used only as an adjective (and then only sparingly). Such awareness also produces a rough grammatical parity: The masculine becomes marked as a gendered construction, not as the norm against which the woman's practice looks aberrant.

As a counter to this locution, Hale next sought to reintroduce into the language archaic gendered nouns or parallel neologisms as a means of making diction more precisely indicate gender. This would allow writers and speakers to avoid the difficulty and impropriety resulting from misusing "female" (*Godey's* 1857, 57:177). More importantly, however, such a practice would mark the recognition that women were an important part of public life. As she publicized Elizabeth Blackwell's struggles to enter legitimate medical practice, she asserted that a woman who practices medicine cannot properly be called "Doctor," a term which "always signifies the masculine person and character. We think it would be more honorable and respectable for such a lady to claim her own title—'*Doctress*'—and ennoble it, as she soon will, in the service of humanity, by her own merits." She printed lists of paired terms to prove that "our language has . . . a rich mine of words for woman and the womanly." One such list included housewife/husbandman; man-milliner and milliner; man-midwife and midwife (as parallels to manservant and maidservant or woman-servant); teacher and teacheress. She entered a special plea for "Americaness" (the parallel to "Britoness," a term favored by Spenser and Tennyson) to be admitted to general use (*Godey's* 1865, 69:279).

Between condemning the improper use of "female" and advocating more specialized and precise terminologies, Hale devoted an inordinate amount of column space to claiming a special vocabulary of designation for women and their occupations. The extent and intensity of her agitation in this regard marks the connection between language and modes of thought and behavior. As Nancy Armstrong establishes in her study of sentimental fiction, such an undertaking has the effect of "[shifting] the entire struggle for political power from the level of physical force to the level of language" (1987, 98). Hale insisted that the language be capable of documenting the fact that women as well as men could pursue honorable occupations. Not incidentally for the purposes of the argument I am making here, such linguistic precision also marked a heightened awareness of gendered individualism.

Still, Hale's agitation for language reform cannot be interpreted as her wholehearted endorsement of women's work. Even as she considers the range of women's occupations, she maintains the distinction between those occupations that could be classified as properly womanly—those subsumed under the notion of domestic duty—as opposed to those that would be pursued merely as work for money. Thus the public exposure she afforded women's employment was tamed by disclaimers, interpretations, and prescriptions:

> *Clerkship, storekeeping, type-setting, factory work*; none of these pursuits can be followed at home, therefore these branches of business do, in some degree, unfit the woman for the wife and mother. *School-keeping*, on the other hand, is one of the best professions for a young woman, because it prepares her for home duties. . . .
> *Needlework*, in all its branches is woman's province. . . .
> In short, we should like to see all pleasant, quiet *home employments* taken up and perfected by American women. (*Godey's* 1855, 50:368)

The second instance of Hale's agitation for women's work was to claim their right to practice *as professions* the several occupations specifically seen to fall within the realm of "woman's sphere." Hale claimed housekeeping, education, and language as areas women could "take up and perfect." She argued for efficient household practice; prescribed and regularized procedures for domestic tasks, codified in writing; and inscribed a scientific/empirical rationale for each home duty. To this end she published articles whose intent was to document the underlying logic that structured cooking, cleaning, sewing, and all the other domestic arts. Beginning in 1840, she published a series of articles entitled "Domestic Economy" that contained hints on household management, recipes, nutritional information, and notes on health and beauty. This department of the magazine continued throughout her entire tenure, eventually expanding to include a column on home medicine. Based on these columns, Hale published a book of domestic practice, *The Way to Live Well and to Be Well While We Live* (1847). *Godey's* also published a semiregular science column that explained elementary astronomy, geology, and chemistry. These topics Hale connected to the professionalization of housework when she could. For example, in a column on cooking, she declares, "Cookery, as every one now understands, is a science. It is in fact a branch of chemistry. No doubt, a person may be a good cook, as another may be a good farmer, without a knowledge of scientific principles. But it is now well understood that those are most successful in any work who not only know how to do it, but the reason why it is so done" (1870, 80:190).

Likewise, she promoted teaching as a profession exclusively for women. In 1868, after having argued for more than thirty years that the education of children ought to be given over to women, Hale called for men to surrender the citadel. Citing statistics that showed that fully two-thirds of teachers in America were women, and presuming a community consensus, Hale proclaimed:

> *By common consent*, in our country, the office of teacher of children is held to be peculiarly proper for woman. It is a noteworthy fact that the older a State becomes, and the more widely education is diffused in it, the more general is the employment of women as teachers. . . . It is easy to see that the time will come when this profession will be almost as entirely surrendered to them as some other professions are and must be appropriated to men. (1868, 77:541; emphasis added)

Hale's campaign to move women into the teaching profession was paralleled by a move to delegitimize classical systems of higher education and to reclaim for women, within the boundaries of the private sphere, even advanced studies. She based her argument on two premises: that an elite education did not answer the needs of an increasingly mercantile and democratic society, and that educated women would be able to provide their sons with an entirely adequate education within the "home circle." By 1853 Hale was tolling the death knell of neoclassic education. I quote from her first editorial on this subject at length so as not to misrepresent her logic:

> The routine of mathematics and the classics, marked out generations ago, has been scarcely altered, while the pursuits for which boys are educated have rapidly progressed. . . .

> Very few men in this country are intended for a life of mental ease and elegant literary effort. Mercantile and mechanical pursuits are considered on a par with professional, yet the planter and the merchant must still pass the curious, active, restless years of boyhood away from home, the genial atmosphere of female society, the busy interests they are to control, or the broad fields it is theirs to cultivate, as they take their place among men.
>
> . . . [I]t is a mother's place to watch over the development of her son's temperament and the natural bent of his mind, as well as the heart; and many a bright boy has been condemned as a blockhead, or obstinate to the last degree, because he turns away in loathing from the dry husks of classical and mathematical lore for the active pursuits of the workshop or the field. Gentlemen, and even elegant scholars, can be found who boast no *alma mater* save the affectionate care and judicious training of the home circle in their boyhood, and every year blots out the old prejudice for that genteel necessity, "a college education." (1853, 47:567)

Hale's first sentences condemn classical education as anachronistic, irrelevant to the broadening categories of professionalism in industrial America. The failure of elite educational institutions to meet the needs of a democratic society has thus created a need best filled by women. A good mother has a special knack for discovering talent in her children ("the natural bent of [their] mind[s]"); thus she should reign as the supreme deity of the child's formative years. In this argument, Hale counters a commonplace assumption of elite education at least as old as Quintilian, who argued that children should be educated in the classroom rather than at home. In the formative adolescent years, the "social and moral" "influence of [feminine] example," is more important than the merely intellectual, whose practical and current value is apparently quickly becoming obsolete (567). This is not to say that Hale would discard the elevation of class that accompanies higher education. Rather, she asserts the ability of home and mother to produce not only better mechanics and farmers but also gentlemen/scholars equal to those trained by the colleges. Thus she can assert that the designation *alma mater* ultimately belongs most properly to the literal mother.

As Hale's writing implies, her call for home education was no trifling matter. To contravene the centuries-old practice of removing young men from the world of home, mother, and vernacular to the agonistic, often physically combative realm of debate, oratory, and academic study (Ong 1971) could have serious consequences: "Men learn their vernacular from their mothers, and that early teaching abides with them through life. Many a man, in some respects thoroughly educated, is unable to free himself from the vulgarisms or the bad grammar learned in the nursery" (*Godey's* 1872, 84:572). If home education is to succeed, it must prove itself equal to that offered in the colleges. Mothers must approach their most serious duty of language instruction in the most professional way and in accord with the most scientific pedagogy. The professional preparation Hale outlines stands as a striking parallel to the professionalization occurring within the elite institutions of higher learning as European-educated philologists established literary study as a legitimate subject for collegiate study.[15] She recommended that all mothers who had not had the chance to study Latin "become familiar with the past history of every word whose meaning they do not thoroughly understand" (*Godey's* 1872, 84:572). (This example offers yet another instance of how written scholarship and mass-production printing made much more democratically available the advantages that once were the property of entitled and restricted classes.)

> The habit of searching out the etymology of all unfamiliar words would be the best substitute for a knowledge of the classics, and afford to the intelligent thinker the proper dress for his or her ideas. . . . [A]s women are the earliest teachers, it follows that they should be thoroughly instructed in their own language. . . . "Webster's Dictionary" . . . will help her task morally as well as intellectually, as right words inspire right thoughts, and right thinking leads to right doing. (*Godey's* 1857, 54:273)

Study based on secondary sources, however, will not produce professional respect. Hale recommends primary research, as well. Linguistic study, the same "science" that was leading college English's move toward professional respectability, she considered to be admirably fitted for women, a fact that is here underscored by her use of dual gendered pronouns, where she usually affected the generic *he*. Unlike the physical sciences, whose study requires both "apparatus" and mobility ("studies in the open air and in outlying districts of the globe" [*Godey's* 1872, 84:572]), language acquisition might be studied empirically by mothers: "They have especial opportunities for observing the language of children and of servants, two important sources and constituents of our common tongue." Women have "the key to much of the primitive history and can make important contributions to that useful and delightful science which has been the growth of this century" (*Godey's* 1875, 91:n.p.). Thus Hale openly claimed philology, like teaching, to be a profession suited to women.

By 1874, Hale more overtly proclaimed the demise of traditional university education. Significantly, that end had been effected by women. Eight years earlier Hale had noted the opening of the Syndicate of Cambridge University examinations to young British women. Annually thereafter she reported the results of those tests. According to Hale, girls generally outperformed the boys, even in mathematics and in Latin, "being especially distinguished for accuracy and good taste in translation." In composition, "the general style of their papers was decidedly better than what the boys produced, and their answers were more to the point, with . . . fewer attempts at fine writing than their boy competitors indulge in" (1866, 73:82). In 1874, she was pleased to note that the American Cambridge planned to adopt the system. Not unexpectedly, she predicted that American women would perform as creditably as their British counterparts in the examinations and pointed to the advantage afforded women who could combine home study with public university certification. Surprisingly, however, she did not link the private study/public examination system with a woman's special need to retire from the world. Rather, she predicted that women who earn the Cambridge certification would be better able to find good employment.

> It is doubted by many whether the present collegiate system is one which should be encouraged either for young men or young women.
>     . . . [A] system of education which withdraws young people from home at the most impressionable age and confines them for three or four years chiefly in the companionship of persons of their own age, is contrary to the social laws designed by nature for their benefit, and cannot be conducive to their . . . improvement or future well-doing. Our colleges, it is argued, are modelled upon the monastic institutions of the middle ages—are, like them, temporary in their nature—and are likely to be swept away, like them, by the advance of society. (1874, 88:378)

All of the above would seem to argue that Hale be seen as a harbinger of—indeed, an active participant in—the decline of public discourse. Yet like other classically trained rhetoricians, Hale bemoaned the democratization, anonymity, and access to public forums that writing allowed. The Civil War and its aftermath, western expansion, and the influx of immigration into the United States made her acutely aware that the communal consensus she had once presumed was seriously eroding. Ironically perhaps, expanded literacy had erased many signifiers of class upon which consensus could be predicated. In an early column on handwriting, Hale had worried that formalized systems of penmanship taught in public schools would blur the surface differences of a handwritten text so that "females of the same class in life, now write, as they dress, nearly alike." She took refuge in the fact that the authority of the absent writer would still be displayed in diction and style, for "the language is a much better criterion of the writer's mental and moral qualities, than the characters in which it is clothed" (*Godey's* 1836, 12:57–58). Forty years later, in a society where print technology had enabled even more anonymity than the handwritten text afforded, where dictionaries extended the privilege of Latin education (theoretically, at least) to anyone who had persistence and access to a public library, the spoken word became transcendentally important for Hale. Near the end of her life, Hale increasingly devoted column space to issues of spoken English. She writes: "In our country, where the fusion of classes is . . . constantly carried on, where men rise from poverty and obscurity to the highest public positions, and finally where so much depends upon the faculty of speech, it is especially necessary that we should learn in the very cradle the grammar and the diction of our native English" (1872, 84:572).

As Raymond Williams points out, spoken language functions as a primary means of class identity: "Our important sense of belonging, to a family, to a group, to a people, will be vitally interwoven with the making and hearing of certain sounds—the making and hearing being a very large part of our social sense" (1961, 214). The apparently natural sound of the voice, the cultivated tone that signals social class, is, of course, as artificial as are the diction and grammatical control that signify class in writing. But if the ultimate signification of class is oral, no amount of written instruction (which, after all, had become generally available) could enable the would-be counterfeiter or social climber to duplicate it. Thus *Godey's* could both offer instruction in oral correctness and take refuge in the fact that that instruction had meaning primarily to those already entitled by class and upbringing to understand its implications. Columns ostensibly offering linguistic advice to would-be bourgeois women functioned simultaneously to mark their linguistic posturing. Thus Hale cautioned readers against elegant diction, an indulgence that implied pretentiousness, and enjoined would-be speakers to avoid the counterfeit: "Be what you say, and, within the rules of prudence, say what you are. . . . When we hear a person use a queer expression, or pronounce a name in reading differently from his neighbor, the habit always goes down, minus sign before: it stands on the side of deficit, not of credit" (*Godey's* 1865, 70:52).

The agitation for correctness in language in the magazine's pages became so great that it was forced occasionally to reassure "cautious writers who have avoided the use of the ordinary forms [of diction] for fear of defacing their style with vulgarisms" (1877, 94:186). (*Vulgarity* had become the operant term signaling the contaminating effect of improper language. It also suggested a debasement of class.)[16] Speakers and writers who cared about their language were instructed in 1871 in the fine points distinguishing euphemism (a necessity of upper-class social interchange) from vulgarity (which was often coupled with imprecision in speech): "There is hardly any reproach which a writer or speaker dreads more than that of vulgarity." The column continues by reassuring readers that incorrect speech does not always constitute vulgarity. "There are many colloquial expressions, used by the best writers and speakers, which do not accord with the strict laws of etymology or grammar, but which it would be highly unjust to term underbred." Among these technically inaccurate terms fall euphemisms: for example, calling a friend's health "delicate," referring to a "mutual" rather than a "common" friend.

> It is hardly fair to attribute the use of such terms either to ignorance or to vulgarity. It often proceeds from a sentiment which is of the very essence of good-breeding — the desire to spare the feelings of others.
> There are, however, genuine vulgarisms, which have their origin in a disregard of the proper distinctions of language, and which cannot be too carefully avoided. (1871, 83:181–82)

Such pronouncements ultimately lead to the question of whom these columns addressed. They clearly were not aimed at Hale's peers, at least not with the purpose of instructing them in correct speech.

Presumably "ladies," the announced readers of *Godey's*, already knew these fine points of grammar. Another, unannounced readership, included newly bourgeois "women." These Hale instructed in do-it-yourself systems of social accommodation. Their choice was clear: They could hold on to their old systems of grammar and pronunciation and be unmistakably separated from the ladies they wished to join; or they could conform, hoping that their counterfeit would not be detected. Hale's discussions about propriety in language use ultimately took refuge in the transcendental vocal signifier — "the good [wo]man skilled in speaking." Thus, her instruction in the fine points of vulgarity and pronunciation may be seen to have functioned both as self-instruction for newly bourgeois women and as a system inscribing the undeniable indicators of social class by which upstart women might be identified and identified against.

The paradox I have just explored is typical of those that confront the student of nineteenth-century writing practices. Hale's importance as an educator, public figure, and arbiter of literary taste and social propriety was freely admitted by her contemporaries.[17] Subsequent literary scholarship, however, whose agenda was to promote the masculine energy of American literature, believed Hale's protestations of domestic retirement and insignificance and failed to recognize that such concessions masked both Hale's power and the contradictions by which she maintained that power. Her means of accomplishing this was simultaneously to expose and hide behind the enablements of writing, promoting it as a means of women's empowerment but always aware of its necessary inseparability from issues of power, propriety, and class. Nor are these paradoxes confined to the life of one nineteenth-century woman. They attend the study of nineteenth-century writing and rhetorical practices generally and demand that such study confront the issues of class, gender, and genre.

Hale's example demonstrates several correctives to the history of nineteenth-century rhetoric as we have thus far understood it. She and scores of literate and public women like her participated in the neoclassic public oratorical culture, invited there by fathers, brothers, and male mentors who had trained them in its norms. Their inclusion, among other factors, hastened its transition into a more individualized and privatized practice. Yet one cannot claim that their presence was simply revolutionary. Many women, Hale among them, respected the norms, both social and intellectual, of the neoclassic practices in which they had been trained and whose practice accrued to them so much respect and profit. Thus, even as they nurtured revolution, they held tenaciously to the old ways of thought, the old patterns of meaning, the old systems of exclusion. To trace the specific details of such women's praxis can complicate our understanding and can demonstrate that, although the transition did take place, it was not a tidy progress. Nor were its major players always publicly present. Masked, hiding behind inscribed and mobile identities, exploring the simultaneously public and private entitlements of writing, Hale and women like her both fueled rhetoric's transformation and impeded it.

## Notes

1. Over the 68 years of its publication, *Godey's* appeared under several different but related and recognizable names. In my citations I will not attempt to give the exact name of the magazine in that particular year but will refer to the magazine simply by *Godey's*, giving the year of the citation followed by volume number and page.

2. Earlier in this column, Hale had established the superiority of writing to face-to-face communication: "Language from the lips may be hasty, inconsiderate or flattering, but written expressions of attachment have a certain evidence of reflection and, consequently, sincerity" (*Godey's* 1845, 31:82). She had long held that letter writing was a skill uniquely fitted to the womanly sensibility. Many of her contemporaries agreed. The popular columnist Fanny Fern, for example, maintained that "no man, since the world began, could pen a letter equal to a woman" (Parton 1873, 424). Shirley Brice Heath uses documents written as early as 1808 and as late as 1867 to document a cultural consensus that women "excelled" in letter writing and conversation (1981, 32–33).

3. See, for example, Nancy Armstrong's *Desire and Domestic Fiction* (1987), Gossett's and Bardes's *Declarations of Independence* (1990), Kelley's *Private Woman, Public Stage* (1984), Ryan's *Women in Public* (1990), and Tompkins's foundational *Sensational Designs* (1985).

4. *Godey's* enjoyed a peak circulation of 500,000 in 1869. The number of actual readers is significantly greater, since subscribers frequently shared copies of the magazine with friends. The *North American Review*, by contrast, reached only a few thousand readers; the *Southern Literary Messenger* had a subscription list of 4,000 in the early 1840s, when *Godeys* claimed 50,000. The magazine has been seriously misrepresented by traditional historians of

literature and journalism who have portrayed it as an apolitical purveyor of sentimental fiction to fainting and crinolined ladies (see, for example, Mott [1930–1968], Satterwhite [1956], and Douglas [1977]).

5. For studies of women who edited and published New England magazines, see Stearns (1929) and Martin (1928).

6. Here I have intentionally refused to call this action of Hale's "influence," a word that Ann Douglas has made a term of opprobrium in her widely read book, *The Feminization of American Culture* (1977). Douglas does link "influence" to the rhetorical shift I am documenting here: "They wished to exert 'influence,' which they eulogized as a religious force. . . . This was the suasion of moral and psychic nurture, and it had a good deal less to do with the faith of the past and a good deal more to do with the advertising industry of the future than its proponents would have liked to believe" (8). Leaving aside the question whether, as Douglas seems to imply, the proponents of "influence" believed they were anticipating advertising, I argue that "influence," moral suasion, was a powerful tool when used by skilled rhetoricians such as Hale. More recent and more carefully theorized studies such as Armstrong's (1987) have established the connections between access to representation, hegemony, and political change while avoiding the trivialization Douglas's work so strongly implies.

7. The literal extent of this metaphoric private sphere is the topic of much current debate among historians. Once uncritically accepted as an apt description of the world of the nineteenth-century woman, the idea of "separate spheres" is currently under revision, its metaphorical force reasserted even as its literal signification is systematically disproven. See Kerber (1988) for a chronological review of scholarship in this area.

8. Although I think Charvat is correct in this matter, the rest of his book demonstrates that for historians of literary criticism of his generation, the individual did matter: As the pronominal rhetoric of this quoted passage indicates, he surveys only criticism produced by the standard institutions representing white, male, New England literary elites.

9. The aura of *Godey's* apparently extended to the writers it published. According to Wright, "To appear in *Godey's Lady's Book* was to be 'made.' Aspiring authors dreamed of the day when they would receive a letter of acceptance signed 'Sarah Josepha Hale.'" (1928, 207).

10. At least one colleague has remarked on the apparent "non-feminist agenda" of my essay. I must emphasize that feminist agendas take many forms, not all of them celebratory, not all of them chronicling a teleological feminist project. The feminism inherent in my work is to insist that women be included in histories of the sort this collection has begun to outline and to argue that when they are included, the history is enriched.

11. Such paracurricula should be seen as part of a longer conduct book

tradition. The function of such reading lists in British conduct books is chronicled by Armstrong (1987, 98–108).

12. This is not to claim that schools did not also contribute to nascent individualism. Horowitz has suggested, for example, that "in opposition to the [family] farm, the seminary took traditional daughters and turned them into nineteenth-century individuals" through monitory and disciplinary procedures such as codified rules, the discipline of bells and schedules, and systems of self-reporting and confession (1984, 15–17).

13. The designation "True Woman," of course, is drawn from Welter's classic essay (1966), which established, among other things, *Godey's* part in constructing and maintaining the "Cult of True Womanhood." But see also McCall, whose content analysis of *Godey's* demonstrates that Welter's formulations are inaccurate.

14. Of the attorneyess, Hale says, "We do not commend this profession for young women, but, if any one enters on it, we advise her to follow this example of retaining always the title that signifies womanhood. Thus only can she preserve her own dignity, and, if she is ambitious and successful, win fame for herself and her sex" (1869, 79:176).

15. Studies by Graff (1987), Graff and Warner (1989), Reid (1959), Parker (1967), and Miller (1989 and 1991) trace this process of academic literary professionalization.

16. Hale had already systematically replaced references to the "vulgar tongue" with the term "mother tongue."

17. The *Dallas Herald* in 1869 called Hale's

a name known wherever literary and moral worth are admitted. . . . Full of years and full of honors, she holds a place in the esteem of every intelligent and true hearted American. . . . The Greeks inscribed the names of Lord Byron, Daniel Webster, Henry Clay, and other illustrious friends of Greece upon the peribolus of their Senate chamber. There is a name inscribed high upon the pillars of the temple of the world, of which every American should be proud—that name is Sarah Josepha Hale. (quoted in *Godey's* 1869, 78:101)

# 7

# Jane Addams and the
# Social Rhetoric of Democracy ✳

*Catherine Peaden*

✳The rhetoric of Jane Addams presents itself as an exemplary site for an examination of resistance to the Burkean "transformation" of oratorical into professional culture as interpreted by Halloran and Clark in the introduction to this volume. Addams, born in 1860 on the threshold of the transformation, forged a powerful rhetoric of social reform by articulating familiar strands of classical oratorical discourse with Enlightenment and contemporary Christian discourses. This late-century synthesis represents a distinctive strand of women's Progressive Era rhetoric.

The daughter of an Illinois pioneer and politician, Addams spoke in the tradition of her father's friend, frontiersman-turned-moral-leader Abraham Lincoln, calling for a new, more moral vision of democracy based not on competitive individualism but on a "social ethic." Appropriating the tradition of Greek democracy, she espoused a higher, democratic ethic in which the social claim would be recognized as superseding the individual and the family claim (Addams [1902] 1907, 77).[1]

In her many speeches, articles, and books, Addams urged women, as the morally superior sex, to be the initiators of this new stage in the "evolution" of democracy. She encouraged them to expand their province from the domestic hearth to "municipal housekeeping," and, in her later texts, extended women's sphere even to the international arena, in particular the global feeding of the hungry. From the 1889 founding of Chicago's Hull-House settlement, Addams and her partner, Ellen Gates Starr, espoused a "feminine cooperative ethic" in a space they had created as a model democracy, "a vital center for the integrated political, economic, social, and cultural life of the city" where even socialists and anarchists could meet to air their differences (Rudnick 1991, 156).

Drawn mostly from her experiences at Hull-House, Jane Addams's many speeches, articles, and books helped persuade a nation to create a new version of society, our modern liberal welfare state. For decades, hers was the most persuasive voice in the country for social reform. Yet scholars disagree on the nature of her reforms, her theories of democracy, whether to characterize her rhetoric as moderate or radical, and even whether her ethic was "essentially" individualist or social.

In her own time, her rhetoric and its reception and translation by the media helped to create a public persona the nation could easily embrace, even worship. So spiritualized and made into a saint and a symbol of American womanhood as she was, the public could usually forget that she was also, as she once said, "sort of a socialist" (Levine 1971, xvii; Addams [1910] 1968, 57–58, 185–88). Biographers Davis and Conway recognize the role that her own autobiographical texts played in constructing her personal image as that of a traditionally nurturing female. This aspect of her persona the public could accept as a feminine version of Sennett's and Antczak's "representative personality" (Sennett 1977, 261; Anctzak 1985, 9–10). But the public's dominant reading of her persona was not all there was to the text of "Jane Addams," and scholars offer varying interpretations of what that persona represented.[2]

The conflicting textual traces of Addams as saintly public legend, powerful institution builder, social theorist, or, more rarely, private woman make her an endlessly complex and intriguing figure. A number of conflicting discourses were available to Jane Addams in the late nineteenth century, discourses that overlap and intersect as they weave her texts. Attention to some of these overlaps and conflicts can help explain some of the rich potential for various readings her texts provide. In focusing on these separate but interwoven discourses or rhetorics, I aim to suggest possibilities and not to represent the origins, scope, or some essential, unchanging character of her discourse. However, I hope such an analysis may contribute to the effort now under way to re-envision Jane Addams as more than the secular feminine saint whose inspirational narratives have been so easily admired and dismissed. Across the spectrum of her liberal and radical modes of discourse, she theorizes a new American democracy, based on a social vision.

It is clear from Addams's college work at Rockford (Illinois) Female Seminary, which she attended from 1877 to 1881, that she even then perceived herself as a speaker and writer. At Hull-House, after an initial decade spent primarily in public speaking, she began to rely more on writing, developing her speeches into articles and books, and she never stopped writing until her death in 1935. As Levine points out, even a rudimentary bibliography would contain more than 200 articles, ten books, introductions to half a dozen other books, and speeches "too numerous to count" (1971, 89).

Her writing process seems familiar to those of us who remember the hands-on production of professional texts before word processors. As with other public figures of her era such as Charlotte Perkins Gilman or William James, her written texts usually began as talks. She often spoke from notes, transcribed those notes into a handwritten manuscript, and refined the manuscript each time she delivered a talk. The initial manuscript went to a typist. Then Addams cut up the clean-typed version with scissors and reordered it, refining transitions and adding more poignant illustrations. Until its next typed version, the discourse-in-progress was sutured together with straight pins (Davis 1973, 152). This image of the pinned scraps and bits of discourse interspersed with the handwritten transitions and emendations serves as a convenient emblem of Jane Addams's discourse itself, the heterogenous rhetorics interrelating and reacting to produce common effects.

As Chantal Mouffe writes of subjectivity, as social agents we are all sites for a plurality of discourses that construct our specific "positionalities, i.e., class, race, generation, nationality, etc." Thus, she argues that "every individual is therefore necessarily multiple, heterogenous, and constructed at the point of intersection of various discourses, variably yet unevenly 'fixed' or sutured at that site" (1983, 142). This very unevenness and the gaps between our discourses create dissonance, space, and opportunities for us to speak and act, in an unending effort to "complete" ourselves. Addams's repeated attempts to justify her life's choices in speech and print demonstrate our common efforts to constitute ourselves as seamless narratives while working with incommensurable, often conflicting narratives and discourses.

Of course, this mélange of discourses varies throughout Addams's life, but some strands have resilience. I have grouped three classes of discourse that Addams used, accepted, and sometimes deflected and discuss them as classical, Christian, and Enlightenment discourses.[3] These often conflicting, intertwined discourses both enabled and constrained not only Addams but also many other of the nation's first college-educated women seeking a purpose in life worthy of their education and powers.

## Classical Discourses and Public Space

I begin with the classical discourses, which Addams internalized from an early age. At the time she graduated from Rockford Female Seminary, her texts would often allude to her Greek and Latin classical learning. For example, in her senior essay, she compares the contemporary state of women with the myth of Cassandra, the intuitive Trojan prophet who predicted the Greek victory and the destruction of her father's city. Woman's tragedy she compared to the Trojan Cassandra's: "always to be in the right, and always to be disbelieved and rejected" (1881, 37). The figure of Cassandra was also used by the classically educated Margaret Fuller (1845). Addams's ideal of democracy began to form with her knowledge of the democracy of the Greek city-states. She may have come to see herself as a prophet who warned individualist Americans when they fell from her utopian social ideal.

At Rockford Female Seminary, she studied Greek and Latin translation and composition, reading both Homer and the New Testament in Greek, becoming so proficient as to deliver a public oration in Greek.[4] Earlier at home in Cedarville, Illinois, her father had paid her to read such classics as *Plutarch's Lives*. She also read Dryden's *Virgil* and Pope's *Iliad* (Davis 1973, 9; Addams [1910] 1968, 13). The classical texts so loved by her father introduced her to the discourses of democracy and republicanism, from the Greeks and Romans to Lincoln and the Italian patriot Guiseppe Mazzini. These discourses stressed the classical virtues of activity, citizenship, and love for community and state. This classical ideal conflicted with the Christian ideal of individual morality, passivity, and domesticity for women, emphasizing public persuasion to action and civic morality over individual virtue. However, this classical discourse also set up a private/public dichotomy organized along the lines of feminine/masculine principles, for women in the classical period had been rigidly confined to private domestic space. Transplanted to the traditionally "masculine" setting of higher education, Addams and her ambitious classmates may have read classical discourse from a subject-position in which they aligned themselves with masculine public space rather than with feminine private space.[5]

Much of Addams's social theory partakes of this classical public space familiar to the oratorical culture of the early nineteenth century. However, by the time she had come to claim this public space, American culture was even then transforming itself around more private concerns, such as professionalism, so that she was moving against the grain. What did she and the many other young women who invested themselves in classical learning at the century's end have to gain? Were they attracted by possibilities for gaining power through discursive knowledge, or were they simply out of step with the times?

Addams's writing provides one plausible answer to these questions: Her texts stress the existence of an alternative social ethic in classical discourse. She embraces this classical ethos, perhaps because it echoes a familiar feminine ethic from the ideal of Republican Motherhood (see Rouse's discussion, this volume), and she employs it to justify women's emancipation from the family claim and an enforced domesticity. Early on in *Democracy and Social Ethics* ([1902] 1907) she constructs her argument that a social ethic should supersede both individual and familial moral claims. She points out that the "collision of interests" among apparently competing claims must be arbitrated and negotiated, for all claims have a "real moral basis and a right to [their] own place in life." This collision, the "struggle between two claims, the destruction of either of which would bring ruin to the ethical life," is, to her, the essence of tragedy.[6] She calls on Greek democratic thought for the solution to modern conflicts between levels of claims:

> Curiously enough, it is almost exactly this contradiction [between competing claims] which is the tragedy set forth by the Greek dramatist, who asserted that the gods who watch over the sanctity of the family bond must yield to the higher claims of the gods of the state. The failure to recognize the social claim as legitimate causes the trouble; the suspicion constantly remains that woman's public efforts are merely selfish and

captious and are not directed to the general good. This suspicion will never be dissipated until parents, as well as daughters, feel the democratic impulse and recognize the social claim. ([1902] 1907, 77)

She further argues that in the interest of progress and evolution, the family "in its entirety must be carried out into the larger life" (79). She also makes a case for historical relativism in ethical codes, implying that a historical rupture with the advent of industrialism has changed conditions that might have once made individualism acceptable. Despite abundant evidence to the contrary, she repeats throughout *Democracy and Social Ethics* that "we are passing from an age of individualism to one of association" and that associated efforts "may represent a finer social quality and have a greater social value" than even a more efficient, effective individual action (137–38). Her argument often relies on authority, the authority of the Greeks, with whom, presumably, her audience will not argue.

Although echoed in the discourses of the Social gospel or Marx, this vocabulary of social ethics and public space recalls classical and Renaissance humanist conceptions. The preferences for the general over special knowledge and the life of action and experience over retirement and reflection parallel the historic conflict of rhetoric and philosophy.[7] Although these preferences overlap with Progressive Era pragmatism, even to their tendency to result in a certain anti-intellectualism, they constitute a resilient strand across her discourses.

Addams's arguments in *Twenty Years at Hull-House* for the "life of action" echo the classical rhetoricians' insistence that a retired, speculative philosophy is less valuable than an active oratory. As Bruce Kimball sums up this rhetoric/philosophy debate:

Beyond expression, the orator also requires that the philosophy make a difference in the world, that is, have an effect—especially that it enhance virtue by persuading others. The philosophers will immediately inquire, But what is virtue? And the orators will make only dogmatic, a priori appeals and not be induced into analysis and speculation. That is the orators' weakness: reliance upon unexamined appeals to a tradition of noble virtue. But just as significant is their epistemological point scored against speculative philosophy: that such philosophy is confirmed to be true only when it is expressed or has an effect.[8] (1986, 35)

Addams makes the epistemological point clearly in *Democracy and Social Ethics*, at the same time revealing a reliance upon an Aristotelian division of theoria and praxis:

> Perhaps the last and greatest difficulty in the paths of those who are attempting to define and attain a social morality, is that which arises from the fact that they cannot adequately test the value of their efforts, cannot indeed be sure of their motives until their efforts are reduced to action and are present in some workable form of social conduct or control. For action is indeed the sole medium of expression for ethics. We continually forget that the sphere of morality is the sphere of action, that speculation in regard to morality is but observation and must remain in the sphere of intellectual comment, that a situation does not really become moral until we are confronted with the question of what shall be done in a concrete case and are obliged to act upon our theory. ([1902] 1907, 273–74)

She here traces two spheres, speculation and action, paralleling Aristotle's separate classifications of philosophical knowledge and political or moral action. Always she comes down on the side of action over contemplation.

Classical discourses weigh heavily in Addams's appeals to the traditions of public action and noble virtue, recalling her heritage from her father and the exemplars Lincoln and the Italian democrat Mazzini (whose violent tactics she seems not to have noticed). In *Twenty Years at Hull-House* and throughout her work, she praises a life of action over a life of study and contemplation. However, she constructs a new association: She rearticulates the active life from its traditional linkage with male political action, reassociating it with women's traditionally active role in opposition to the passive, intellectualized existence of the modern, newly educated—and often neurasthenic—woman. However, as we have seen, this newly activated woman has expanded her sphere into male public space.

In an 1892 lecture on the subjective necessity for social settlements, repeated in part in her autobiography, Addams speaks eloquently of the need young people, especially young women, feel to participate actively in solving social problems. Meanwhile, they have been "cultivated into unnourished, oversensitive lives":

> They have been shut off from the common labor by which they live which is a great source of moral and physical health. They feel a fatal want of

harmony between their theory and their lives, a lack of coordination between thought and action. I think it is hard for us to realize how seriously many of them are taking to the notion of human brotherhood, how eagerly they long to give tangible expression to the democratic ideal. ([1910] 1968, 115–16)

This concern for the thwarting of the "desire for action" on the part of "cultivated young people" — especially women — shows Addams's rejection of a too-confined self-culture movement. She criticizes the dearth of avenues for women's action outside domesticity, arguing that the lack of other alternatives has "all the elements of a tragedy" (120). The enforced passivity and intellectualization of life, associated with "lowered vitality" and "discontent," wastes talent and vigor that could be channeled into solving social problems (121). Enforced passivity and intellectuality associated with the self-culture movement may be one issue here; yet finding suitable action for women in the public sphere takes precedence over any possible exploration of women's uneasiness with or coming to terms with their intellectuality.

At times, Addams's pragmatic orientation, like Dewey's, comes close to anti-intellectualism, although her later texts attempt to harmonize her own speculative intellectual and pragmatic bents. However, her rhetoric here is less anti-intellectual than it is focused on process, on an Aristotelian becoming, and she sees democracy necessarily as a process of "common intercourse" and the bringing-into-being of a common life. This is an action-centered theory and one she never ceases to tie to ethics, specifically to a socialized Christian ethic.

In the 1892 lecture, quoted in her autobiography, Addams links the theme of action not with classical discourse but with Christian discourse — in particular, Christian ideals held at the birth of Christianity by Roman Christians of the catacombs. And yet, the discussion parallels the old debate between philosophers and rhetoricians. As Addams describes this ideal of action: "The [early Roman] Christians looked for the continuous revelation, but believed what Jesus said, that this revelation, to be retained and made manifest, must be put into terms of action; that action is the only medium man has for receiving and appropriating truth; that the doctrine must be known through the will" ([1910] 1968, 122).[9] This epistemological view of social action, at the intersection of two discursive classes — the classical and the Christian—becomes the basis for thought about the settlement life. It represents a repeated strand of Addams's social rhetoric, making a virtual religion of democracy.

## Christian Discourses

Addams's father called himself a Hicksite Quaker; it was a religion he had chosen himself, not one he had been born into (Levine 1971, 6; Addams [1910] 1968, 16). Jane Addams's desire for similar religious independence led her to have a complex and at times conflictual relationship with Christianity, as was apparent from her days at Rockford Female Seminary. Seminary founder Anna Peck Sill intended the institution to train missionaries for the West, and many alumnae heeded the call and pleased her in this regard. However, there was one independent-minded student who miraculously resisted the faculty's intense proselytizing, refusing to be "saved," and that was Jane Addams.

It was not until the dark days after her father's death just after her graduation that she finally joined the local Presbyterian church, but hers was always a searching and never a conventional religious affiliation. In Europe, involved in the "snare of preparation" for her undiscovered life's work, Addams set herself a course of study on the Christians of Rome's catacombs. The collectivist spirit of the early Christians was a great inspiration to her, as was the Christian socialism she encountered in Britain. These vocabularies of cooperation and sociality were more consonant with the discourses of women's culture in which she had been immersed in late Victorian America than was a masculine American individualism.

Thus it is not surprising that Tolstoy's religious philosophy made such an impression on her. She and her life's companion, Mary Rozet Smith, visited Tolstoy in 1895, although Addams soon decided that his theories of agrarian labor were out of place in the city and could not help her Hull-House neighbors. With her beliefs in an action-oriented Christianity, Tolstoy's theories of nonresistance to evil seemed too passive, although they were deeply influential and played a role in her later pacifism. Most immediately, his theories of labor led her to volunteer for bread-making duty at the Hull-House kitchen for a short time after her return.

At Hull-House, the excitement of discussing Florence Kelley's socialist ideas put an end to Addams's nightly reading of the Bible to her settlement residents. Although Addams grew less and less conventionally religious through her lifetime, Christian discourses remained a central feature of her rhetoric, from the morality at the core of all her texts to the use of Christian symbols and parables. However, this Christian strand of her discourse came more and more to rest in an Arnoldian conception of culture as a replacement for religion and more and more intersected romantic rhetoric. Nonetheless, her feminism and moral discourses remain imbricated in the early discourse of her day, especially one discourse that had its grounding in Christianity, the discourse of True Womanhood.

In her book *Disorderly Conduct* Carroll Smith-Rosenberg inquires into the various "languages" of women's culture in the late nineteenth century, focusing on a variation of the discourse of True Womanhood. The discourse of True Womanhood, earlier analyzed by Barbara Welter (see also Rouse's discussion, this volume), existed from about 1820 to 1860 and embodied the cardinal Christian virtues of piety, purity, submissiveness, and domesticity. Welter claims that "the very perfection of True Womanhood, moreover, carried within itself the seeds of its own destruction. For if woman was so very little less than the angels, she should surely take a more active part in running the world, especially since men were making such a hash of things" (1966, 174).

Smith-Rosenberg describes the discourse upon which the New Women of the 1880s and 1890s were raised as a refracted, late version of the discourse of True Womanhood. This was because their mothers' generation had already "transposed the cult's original religious and moral imagery into a female symbolic system that expressed women's attitudes toward family change and justified new roles for women outside the family" as "efficient housekeepers of the nation" (1985, 264).

Jane Addams and her contemporaries—the first New Women— defended the new ways of the first generation of college women in this late discourse of True Womanhood. Addams, always known as a moderate, a negotiator, a compromiser, accepted and extended the late discourse of True Womanhood, and it both contributed to her successes and constrained her. Although this discourse soon came to overlap with Enlightenment rhetoric of rights as well as male "scientific" theories of women's nature, Addams's early use of the discourse of True Womanhood provides a good example of Christian values and their feminine appropriation in discourse. It is probable that Addams's "true woman" discourse reflects in some measure the rhetoric of her stepmother, a figure otherwise absent from her texts.

At Rockford, "Miss Addams" served as president of the class of 1881, who named themselves "breadgivers" after the ideal of the "'Saxon lady' whose mission it was to give bread unto her household" (Addams 1880, 110–11). In her 1880 Junior Exhibition speech to "Friends and Citizens of Rockford," she begins by remarking upon the contemporary change in woman's position that was "gradually claiming the universal attention":

> We mean the change which has taken place during the last fifty years in the ambition and aspirations of woman; we see this change most markedly in her education. It has passed from accomplishments and the arts of pleasing, to the development of her intellectual force, and her capabilities for direct labor. She wishes not to be a man, nor like a man, but she claims the same right to independent thought and action. (110)

She immediately sidesteps the issue of women's suffrage but talks of women's confidence in and hopes for the progress of women. After her initially strong and radical opening, she offers a True Womanhood conciliation: "We, then, the class of 1881, in giving this our Junior Exhibition, are not trying to imitate our brothers in college, we are not restless and anxious for things beyond us, we simply claim the highest privileges of our time, and avail ourselves of its best opportunities" (110). The idea, she explains, is to claim these privileges, to assert woman's independence, while retaining the old ideal of womanhood as breadgiver: "So we have planned to be 'bread-givers' throughout our lives; believing that in labor alone is happiness, and that the only true and honorable life is one filled with good works and honest toil, we will strive to idealize our labor, and thus happily fulfil woman's noblest mission" (110–11). Here, however, she collapses the discourses of domesticity and private, circumscribed service with those of freedom and action in the public sphere.

That she is confident of moving in a wider sphere from the start is signaled in her closing, where she writes of the breadgivers: "And if through some turn of fortune we should be confined to the literal meaning of our words, if our destiny throughout our lives, should be but to give good, sweet, wholesome bread to our loved ones, then perchance we will do that the better, with more of conscious energy and innate power for the memory of our Junior Exhibition" (111). The reverbations of the term "confined" in regard to service in the domestic sphere reveal the shift in the original discourse of True Womanhood, with, perhaps, an interference from the classical discourse in which she was immersed at Rockford. This slippage of discourse, a trope, the turn of fortune that could "confine" the young women to domesticity, was a "turn" to misfortune, signaled in the melancholy tone of the closing. Yet moving from Cassandra to Minerva, throwing in her lot with masculine intellect and values instead of feminine, was never a consideration. In her subsequent creation of Hull-House, Addams opened a social space in which she could harness traditional masculine to feminine values. Thus her model democracy embraces feminine nurturance and cooperation along with masculine individualist development and action. As feminine space expands to civic housekeeping, feminine passivity transmutes into an active civic feminism. Discourses necessary to carry on those ideals and activities come primarily from her Enlightenment heritage.

## Enlightenment Discourses

The third "language group" Addams, as well as most of her contemporaries, accepted and deflected was that of the dominant Enlightenment discourses, including those of Western liberalism. The discourses of both Christianity/True Womanhood and of classicism often intertwined with Enlightenment discourses at the turn of the century, although their epistemologies and ideologies are often at odds. Enlightenment languages provide vocabularies of individualism, liberty, rights, and, perhaps most importantly, evolution and progress, made primarily through rational, scientific thought that privileges observation and quantification of an external reality. This class of discourses served as ground for the cultural transformations leading to professionalism and the cult of the expert as described by Halloran and Clark in the Introduction to this volume.

Enlightenment counterdiscourses include romanticism, from German and British varieties to American transcendentalism, both reactions to and emotional complements of rational, utilitarian Enlightenment rhetoric. At times these discourses rely on social elements in their protest of rational individualism, although their own individual orientation usually dominates. Addams favored romantic discourse as well as a related strain she helped to construct, American pragmatism, which combines both scientific and romantic strains of Enlightenment thinking, incorporating a classical emphasis on process.

Much of Addams's complexity comes from her attempts to blend the optimism of scientific progress with what she saw as the horrors of the industrial age. She attempts to use science to better "picture" the problems around her, all the while rejecting the increasingly atomistic, objectivist epistemology of science. One of her first projects at Hull-House was a pioneering sociological survey of the neighborhood, published as *Hull-House Maps and Papers*. Yet in her speeches and texts, consciously adopting a narrative logic, she presents case after representative case of the failures of individual ethics of the industrial age and the blindness of the objectivist gaze from above. Insisting all the while on a subjectivist, "feminine" stance, she embraces the utopian goals of modern science.

Addams was always on the side of science; a postage stamp issued in her honor in 1940 placed her in a series of famous American scientists (Davis 1973, 293). After all, despite her rejection of academic life, she was considered a founder of the American science of sociology (Deegan 1988). Her initiation into the discourse of science began early. She took not only the classical but also the scientific strands of curriculum at Rockford in preparation for attending medical school after her graduation. Although for health reasons—caused primarily by conflicts over the "family claim"—she completed only the first semester at the Women's Medical School of Philadelphia, her early training had given her a scientific bent. A quasi-religious faith in science never left her, although her youthful trust in Comte and his positivistic religion of humanity would fade.

Comte, Spencer, and Marx all provided her with confirmation of the value of a scientific approach to social relations and their potential for utopian adjustment. She recognized that class conflict existed but refused to believe that a class war was inevitable. Elshtain points to the paradox of Addams's continuing faith that humanity was progressing toward more inclusive, peaceful and just social forms at the same time as she was experiencing at firsthand the crises of industrial society. In Addams's texts, her immigrant neighbors are often described from their own point of view as victims, "from inside their despair, their often stupefied, not-being-at-home in a strange new world that forced many into silence, madness, or self-destruction"

(Elshtain 1990, 7). This recognition of the dualities of "progress" set her apart from less thoughtful progressives.

However, Addams's texts feature another intersecting strand of progressive utopian discourse, a hybrid of nationalism, evolution, feminism, and a distinctive American socialism, that of Bellamy Nationalism. Addams was exposed most directly to this rhetoric when its proponent Charlotte Perkins Gilman stayed at Hull-House in the fall and winter of 1895, a time when Gilman was working on her book *Women and Economics*. Edward Bellamy's novel *Looking Backward: 2000–1887* was one of the three best-selling novels of the nineteenth century.[10] As Lane tells us, the book spawned a movement called Nationalism, inspiring reformers, many of them women, to identify themselves with a particular variety of American socialism calling for a cooperative ethic and peaceful, gradual change in our capitalistic system motivated not by class competition but by a Christian concept of love. Bellamy was the first novelist to identify economic independence with women's freedom, and women played a central role in the classless society of his Cooperative Commonwealth. Not surprisingly, many of the thousands of Bellamites across the country were women, especially in California where the Nationalist movement began. Bellamy's work addressed questions of men's and women's relationships, childrearing, love, and work in a way Marxism did not, despite the flaws that are obvious to us today. The vocabulary of Bellamy Nationalism overlaps with Addams's Christian and the later Enlightenment evolutionist discourses.

Addams's social theory draws heavily on these evolutionary theories of gender shared with Gilman. Conway credits Spencer, Ward, and Geddes as the important sources for Addams's thought. Spencer's 1873 *Study of Sociology* provided an early evolutionary social theory and theory of woman. From him she learned that feminine thought was of special significance in the evolutionary process primarily because women have an innate ability to empathize with the weak (Conway 1971, 171). She met Ward in the 1890s at Hull-House and was receptive to his views that the female was the prototype of the human being and more highly evolved than men (172). Geddes was the author of *The Evolution of Sex*, the major English work in biology on the contribution of gender to evolution, published in 1889. In Conway's characterization, "Geddes believed that from the smallest single-celled organism to man sex differences were ties to differences in cell metabolism which made female organisms passive and nurturing and male organisms warlike and aggressive" (172). Joining forces with Christian discourses including True Womanhood, this "scientific" discourse intensified not only her pacifism but also her maternalism.

While rejecting racism, Addams accepted a scientific view of social evolution that emphasized the evolutionary significance of biologically determined male and female temperaments. In this discourse, the exploiters are men, while those who can see the true vision of a democratic society are women, even if their warnings may sometimes go unheeded, like Cassandra's. Conway has argued that to base social criticism on this essentializing view of gender and human nature is to acquiesce in the traditional stereotypes. Thus she criticizes Addams's maternalist discourse as "unwittingly" preparing the cultural ground for the sexually specialized intellect proposed by the neo-Freudian romantic conservatives (174–75).

With her social-scientific leanings and her insatiable drive to associate with like-minded others in conferences and organizations to bring about change, Jane Addams might have taken on the discourse of "expert" or "professional" had not her gender and moral theories prevented her. Many other women gravitated to early forms of professionalism, attracted by the gender-neutral roles professionalism seemed to offer. Although Addams sometimes appears in the professional role, the rhetoric remains that of woman reformer and not sexually neutral expert. She was the first woman president of the National Conference of Charities and Corrections, a post she finally gained in 1909 (Davis 1973, 198). Yet her reaction to the professionalization of social work was mixed, becoming even more negative as she began to see its fruits.

Speaking to the National Conference of Social Work in 1926, she attacked psychiatric social workers for their "carefully established professional neutrality" (Conway 1968, 410). She criticized social work's objective, individualized stance and the absence of political and moral commitment to do away with poverty and social ills. Moreover, she spoke approvingly of a previous reference to herself as the leader of "pre-efficiency social work" and blasted the narrow professionalism of succeeding generations of social workers (410–11).

Nonetheless, her resistance to professionalism came primarily from the social democratic rhetoric of the engaged, generalist citizen opposing that of the socially detached specialist. She had an Aristotelian faith that humans possess a common ability to discern truth. In *Democracy and Social Ethics*, she repeatedly articulates her view that knowledge and goodness cannot be imposed from above to solve problems. For example, in the matter of education and culture, she argues, "We have learned to say that the good must be extended to all of society before it can be held securely by any one person or any one class; but we have not yet learned to add that unless all men and all classes contribute to a good, we cannot even be sure that it is worth having" ([1902] 1907, 220). Her rhetoric here is based on democratic, constructivist thinking and constitutes no less than a social epistemic rhetoric. The "good" here is a process as much as a product, and the democratic means and process of its production is the determinant as well as the assurance that it is "good." As Elshtain stresses, the distance is great between Addams's "participant-interpreter and the bureaucratic case worker; between a social science that views the world through the lens of functionalist givens and an interpretive approach alive to the sights, sounds, and smells of everyday human existence" (1990, 11–12).

Jane Addams's texts have more in common with those of the Victorian prophet or sage—or even the postmodern social critic—than with the sexually neutral professional wielding science as an objective tool. Conway and Davis both refer to Addams as a feminine Victorian sage or prophet who "claimed access to hidden wisdom by virtue of feminine insights" (Conway 1971, 167). Based on the classical figure of the sybil, the role was constructed earlier by romantic writers such as Carlyle, Coleridge, and Emerson, writers in whom she immersed herself early at Rockford and during the "snare of preparation" just afterward. What Addams adds to deflect their theories was a more positive view of science and a foregrounding of the repressed social aspects of their aesthetics. For example, she reinterprets Ruskin's dictum that labor without art brutalizes, protesting that the sense of joy to be found in art is not pure individual ecstacy, such as might function as a compensation for the brutalities of labor, but a commingling—"the solace of collective art inherent in collective labor" ([1902] 1907, 219).

Perhaps the most important element gleaned from romantic discourse was a Rousseauian concept of the primitive—at times conflated with the immigrant—whose essential goodness she never doubted. This belief in essential human goodness fed her growing belief in environmentalism so at odds with the Horatio Alger myth of individual self-sufficiency. People would be good, she maintained, if their civic life provided the proper channels for their naturally moral instincts. Yet if the urban and industrial environment in which she lived was malignant, in it she also saw and imagined broader opportunities and stimuli for women. If women's abilities to provide nurturant domestic spaces could only be expanded to "municipal housekeeping" (a phrase from her socialist coworker Florence Kelley), that environment could be improved.

But women's abilities were also seen as higher and less mundane; woman's soul participated in a kind of transcendental oversoul in which the memories of all women resided and could be tapped (as in Addams's *The Long Road of Woman's Memory*, 1916). This notion is perfectly in the Platonic register of the Victorian sage. In the same quasi-mystical vein, individual vignettes from Addams's everyday experience at Hull-House took on symbolic resonance and an ability to evoke the romantic "world in a grain of sand."

Addams's theories of rhetorical persuasion were more and more grounded in this Emersonian belief that the "moral fact" could represent otherwise incomprehensible "moral ideas" or "abstract virtues" to essentially good but untrained common or primitive people.[11] Addams uses this developmental theory of morality, drawn from evolutionary, romantic, and Christian discourses, to reach a popular audience. As she explains:

> Morality certainly develops far earlier in the form of moral fact than in the form of moral ideas, and it is obvious that ideas only operate upon the popular mind through will and character, and must be dramatized before they reach the mass of men, even as the biography of the saints. . . .
>
> Ethics as well as political opinions may be discussed and disseminated among the sophisticated by lectures and printed pages, but to the common people they can only come through example—through a personality which seizes the popular imagination. . . . The personal example promptly rouses to emulation. ([1902] 1907, 227–28)

As a Victorian sage, or as a "representative figure," Addams certainly uses her own life, projected as a text before the American public, to effect this moral persuasion. Yet, opposed to Antzcak's description (1985) of the rhetoric of identification, she does not reject logical or enthymemic argumentation as much as she elevates the dramatistic example as being particularly suited for popular persuasion. However, most of her moral persuasion is not so much directed at the morally untrained "primitive" South Italians and others of her own neighborhood as it is to the supposedly morally advanced bourgeois she addressed in her public lectures and articles. To her, the poor are essentially kind and generous, even heroically so. Her stories aim to provoke awareness and empathy among the "moral majority."

For example, the memorable vignette of the nursing, working-class mother whose breast milk mixed with the slop water as she toiled through the night scrubbing marble floor tiles in a public building was surely designed to prick the conscience of the middle-class woman nursing comfortably at home (Addams [1910] 1968, 174). The fantastic story of the "Devil Baby at Hull-House" in *The Second Twenty Years at Hull-House* is another such parable and one on which Addams reflects at length (1930, 47–79). A rumor had spread wildly through the immigrant neighborhood, particularly among elderly women, that Hull-House was sheltering a baby boy who had been born as a devil child. The reasons given for this horrendous birth were various, but in most versions the event became a punishment of the father for some maltreatment of his wife. Addams interprets her neighbors' insistence upon the truth of this story, their persistent efforts to see the child, and their evident satisfaction in their beliefs as a tale of repressed suffering brought about by men being socially recompensed. Again, one of her motives in this tale is to make her readers aware of the disparities between their lives and those of their sisters across town.

In part because of such social disparities, she believed that morality must be relative, or more accurately contrastive, based always upon empathy. The romantic codeword "particularity" was important because human life is complex and infinitely varied, making ethical choices more than a simple choice between good and evil. Addams valued the differences of her multiethnic neighborhood and sought to preserve each group's history and heritage. This valuing of difference fed her democratic theory that morality should not be calculated by professional experts and handed down from on high. Democratic experience with the broader life of the community becomes necessary for the moral development of all classes and individuals, for "as individuals and societies we can come to know ourselves, Addams suggests, *only* to the extent that we realize the experience of others" (Elshtain 1990, 9).

In the decade after the founding of Hull-House, Addams emphasized community education, becoming an educator as much as a social worker, influencing and being influenced by the discourse of John Dewey, Herbert Mead, and William James while helping build American pragmatism.[12] Dewey, a frequent visitor to Hull-House, observed and approved of the hands-on approach to learning taking place there. Addams's theories of education in *Democracy and Social Ethics* and in *The Second Twenty Years at Hull-House* made education for democracy central, an education based upon a collapse of low and high culture and the use of public media in "Education by the Current Event" (Addams 1930, 380–413). Her orientation to processual thinking, to experimentation and action, and to whatever seemed to work (including Prohibition) made her a vital intellectual partner in the development of pragmatism.

Addams and Hull-House were as great an influence on Dewey and on James as they were on her, however rarely this is reflected in the historical record. Addams shared the podium with James, and her anti-imperialist and antiwar rhetoric had preceded and paralleled his just after the Spanish-American War. Both she and James made use of Tolstoy's communitarian Christian ideas, but both rejected his extremes of nonresistance. Both searched for a moral substitute for war, basing their discourse on the necessity of rechanneling (or re-"canaliz[ing]") natural primitive instincts (Addams [1922] 1945, 240). Addams believed these instincts, originally healthy, had been left no outlet in modern industrial society.

Always concerned with these questions of human nature and the perpetually benign human instincts, Addams, a founder and president of the Women's International League for Peace and Freedom, argued that "war is not a natural activity for mankind, that large masses of men should fight against other large masses is abnormal, both from the biological and ethical point of view" (246). She went on to explain that "it is a natural tendency of men to come into friendly relationships with ever larger and larger groups, and to live constantly a more extended life. . . . It is the very spring of life which underlies all social organizations and political association" (246).

Always, women were to be the catalysts of this peaceful, democratic world society. In this her rhetoric never changed, but it did expand to add women's unique capacities for internationalism, pacifism, and mediation of war. She continued to use her evolutionary social rhetoric, placing woman at the fulcrum as the lever of progress. Using the Progressive movement as a platform—she seconded Roosevelt's nomination at the 1912 Progressive party convention—she spoke of tapping the great "reservoir" of women's moral energy to move a lagging America to join the "worldwide movement toward juster social conditions" (Levine 1971, 191). In 1932, speaking on a Women's International League Congress on disarmament, she used a historical argument that women's instinctive nurturance of life had contributed to the progress of civilization in the past, and their rejection of war would continue that progress (originally published in *Liberty*, March 12, 1932):

> The history of one nation after another shows that it was the mothers who first protested that their children should no longer be slain as living sacrifices upon the altars of tribal gods. Women rebelled against the waste of life they had nurtured.
>
> I should like to see the women of civilization rebel against the senseless wholesale human sacrifice of warfare. I am convinced that many thousands of women throughout the world would gladly rise to this challenge. (Johnson 1960, 324)

For Addams, the moral equivalent to, or substitute for, war would be human labor—labor performed, however, in a system based on social utility rather than commercial gain. From early on at Hull-House, how much she would accept total reorganization of capitalism became an issue; this remained a sticking point between her and Hull-House cofounder Ellen Starr, and it continues to perplex feminist scholars. What is not in question is that she supported essential reforms including unionization, shorter work days, restrictions on sweatshop and child labor, a social security system, and unemployment insurance. In large measure because of her lifetime of persuasive discourse, by the time of her death in 1935 these reforms had been accepted as necessary and legislation had been enacted.

In her argument for women's suffrage in 1910, one can see the mélange of all three classes of discourse, with a resilient strand remaining the late discourse of "True Womanhood." She writes in the *Ladies' Home Journal*:

> This paper is an attempt to show that many women today are failing to discharge their duties to their own households properly simply because

they do not perceive that as society grows more complicated it is necessary that woman shall extend her sense of responsibility to many things
outside of her home if she would continue to preserve the home in its
entirety. . . .

In short, if woman would keep on with her old business of
caring for her house and rearing her children she will have to have some
conscience in regard to public affairs lying quite outside of her immediate
household. The individual conscience and devotion are no longer effective. (reprinted in Johnson 1960, 104–5)

Addams worked to persuade American women that with changes in
the country's industrial organization, they must have the vote and a
wider sphere in order to fulfill their traditional responsibilities, to
preserve the domestic sphere. This became a highly successful argument she used again and again with modifications.

In the 1918 *Journal of Home Economics*, once more in the activity of
"breadgiving," she tries to persuade home economists that women
belong in the international sphere:

But is it not quite possible that as women entered into city politics when
clean milk and sanitary housing became matters for municipal legislation, as they have consulted state officials when the premature labor of
children and the tuberculosis death rate became factors in a political
campaign, so they may normally be concerned with international affairs
when these are dealing with such human and poignant matters as food
for the starving and the rescue of women and children from annihilation?
(reprinted in Johnson 1960, 134)

This argument for a "normalized" feminist internationalism bases
itself on Addams's late discourse of True Womanhood in league with
Enlightenment's discourse of freedom and greater social justice. It
pushes toward a feminine imaginary, a horizon in which women are
free to act with all their powers to create a more just and humane
global environment. This political imaginary builds upon an assumption of a democratic public space in which women can actively pursue
world citizenship.

Urban renewal clearance to make way for the 1965 campus of the
University of Illinois at Chicago destroyed most of Hull-House's
massive, thirteen-building complex. The impressive material confirmation of Addams's effective action in the public sphere was gone, but

the public space she had helped create for the exercise of women's power had long since been dispersed. Conway faults the reformers' own unwitting capitulation to the "controlling power of the stereotype of female temperament" for this loss of power: "Acquiescence in this control was indeed the major weakness in the ideology of feminism for the stereotype of the female personality was an essentially conservative one although women reformers coupled it with social innovation and occasionally with trenchant social criticism" (1971, 166). However, as Conway concedes, Addams and other reformers had first to construct "the very institutions which were their vehicle from middle-class feminine life" (174). To create these institutions, they used existing rhetorics, complete with their old assumptions about the sexes and their roles. An underlying assumption of the "cult of True Womanhood" was that men were not women's moral or intellectual equals. But without seeing men and women as equals, women reformers could find no way out of the traditional masculine stereotype of the female temperament; thus they had to continue to deny their "masculine" traits of power-seeking or aggression, even rationality.

Whether or how the rhetoric of women reformers may have "prepared the climate" for a conservative Freudian discourse in which biology is destiny, an articulation of Freudianism to the discourse of the True (or New) Woman produced a backlash. Because of this backlash, women — despite suffrage — lost power and were even reconfined to domestic space. The 1930s' rearticulation of an old discourse of women's power to an emerging dominant discourse primarily benefiting men remains a historic example of a social transformation tied to a rearticulation and consolidation of discursive power. Women's difference was appropriated and articulated to a discourse used to undermine women's power in the public sphere. That need not mean, however, that all discourses of women's difference will always harm women or cannot again be articulated with new discourses to empower social change at strategic moments.

Nonetheless, the complexity of Addams's social democratic rhetoric and its resistance to the emergence of an individualist and professional/specialist culture have been occulted, certainly in part by early Freudian discourses of women's psychology. Indeed, what remains with the public even today is Addams's own saintly image, the imaginary ghost of True Womanhood. It is hoped that renewed attention to the constellation of conflicting discourses used by Addams will show the futility of continuing to essentialize Addams as purely a "saint," another feminine "do-gooder," or a type of "representative reformer." Although popularized and easy to access, her theories are not simplistic. She has left us a Progressive Era rhetoric that resists the ideology of the individual as primary moral arbiter in society and that attempts to maintain a wider public sphere for social action.

Even though she was constrained by her lifelong role as chief administrative officer and fund-raiser at Hull-House, a role that (as today's college presidents have shown) can be limiting and conservative, her discourse contains contradictory radical strands. Cultural critics are just now beginning to analyze and interpret her approaches to mass culture, labor, and education. By setting Addams's conflicting discourses back into play, we can read her as a more complex historical figure—one who grasped the available discourses of her day and wielded them powerfully, yet one who at the same time was grasped and used by them, as are we all.

## *Notes*

1. Also see the edition edited by Anne Firor Scott (Cambridge: Harvard University Press, 1964).

2. Conway sees Addams as mistakenly allowing herself to become entrapped in a male-defined essentialist femininity. Davis agrees that she took on the mantle of the self-sacrificing woman. In contrast, Rudnick argues that Addams's autobiographical texts create a powerful and heroic rather than a traditionally passive feminine persona. Elshtain believes that she is both a symbol *and* a social theorist and emphasizes her occluded social theory. On this point, see Conway (1971) and (1968); Rudnick (1991, 161 n. 4); Davis (1973); Elshtain (1990, 3–12).

3. Smith-Rosenberg (1985) examines nineteenth-century women's culture in terms of the "languages" that form it and has been influential in my interpretation of Addams's discourses.

4. As Addams described it: "The oration, upon Bellerophon and his successful fight with the Minotaur, contended that social evils could only be overcome by him who soared above them into idealism" ([1910] 1968, 46–47).

5. Addams, whose own mother died when she was two, may have already identified more with her father than her mother—her autobiography begins with her father, stressing his central role in her life, but makes no

mention of her stepmother, Anna Haldeman Addams, who married her father John H. Addams when Jane was eight.

6. Indeed, such a collision had precipitated her own breakdown in health after her college years and her father's death, leading to the years she calls the "snare of preparation" in her autobiography ([1910] 1968, 65–88).

7. Addams's action orientation also reiterates her paraphrase of Carlyle: "'Tis not to taste sweet things, but to do noble and true things that the poorest son of Adam dimly longs" ([1910] 1968, 45).

8. This is a valuable book despite the fact that Kimball reads the orators narrowly as if they were predecessors of a static nineteenth-century literary culture, missing the radical implications of the social constructivism identified by revisionists.

9. June Hadden Hobbs interprets Addams's discourse here as subversive of a "traditional androcentric Protestant position" in which "faith alone is the prerequisite for salvation and inevitably leads to action. . . . Thus, like many nineteenth-century women, she finds the spiritual in the concrete and reverses the usual pattern; she says action leads to faith rather than faith leads to action" (personal communication, February 9, 1992).

10. My discussion of Bellamy Nationalism is informed by Lane (1990, 161–62).

11. As Ralph Waldo Emerson writes: "The orator, as we have seen, must be a substantial personality. Then, first, he must have power of statement, — must have the fact, and know how to tell it. . . . In every company the man with the fact is like the guide you hire to lead your party up a mountain, or through a difficult country ([1867] 1883, 61–98).

12. Deegan (1988) discusses Addams's brand of "critical pragmatism"; Elshtain writes in "Return to Hull House," "The story of Addams as an intellectual influence on Dewey has yet to be told" (1990, 182 n. 7).

# 8

# The Divergence of Purpose and Practice on the Chautauqua ✳ Keith Vawter's Self-Defense ✳ *Frederick J. Antczak*

## *and Edith Siemers*

✳In a half-century that spans thalidomide, Love Canal, Three Mile Island, Chernobyl, and the Alaskan oil spill, we have grown accustomed to hearing stories of the potential horror of postmodern life—of living, working, and even succeeding in a technologizing, corporatizing, professionalizing culture. We know what it means to have a good idea institutionalized and thereby turned to a spectacular and terrible end (although we still seem oddly surprised—as with chemical waste disposal or the ravaging of the ozone layer—whenever this story plays out again). And should we ever manage to forget, we have our share of professional "futurists" to remind us.

More rarely are we treated to an account of institutional failure in which the dramatic movement goes the other direction, a story in which something is "professionalized" and made more efficient, only to have it lapse into a blandness that in the long run subverts its purpose and dissipates its goods. At first reading, the story of the American Chautauqua's decline as an institution of oratorical culture (Antczak 1985, 74–85) seems to follow this trajectory. It appears to be a story with a simple plot and a clearly identifiable villain driven by transparently bad motives and even a distinctive modus operandi. But because we are less familiar with this sort of narrative—one that chronicles a slow divergence of practice from purpose until it ends diluted and tepid rather than boiling out of control—and because some of the cultural institutions of our own day seem to be slumping more or less unrecognized along the same decline, the story of the decline of circuit Chautauqua as an oratorical culture bears, and rewards, closer inspection.[1]

The head of the Redpath Speakers Bureau and inventor of circuit Chautauqua as it reached out through the Middle West near the turn of the century was a man named Keith Vawter. He is often blamed rather flat-footedly (Antczak 1985, 76–79, for an embarrassing instance) for the increasing divergence of rhetorical purpose and practice on the Chautauqua circuit. Nowhere have we seen his self-defense represented, much less examined critically. Nor have we seen an examination of the institutional motives that constrained his range of action, nor any consideration of the ethical effect those motives had on others influenced by the institution. Perhaps this is because such examination requires a different frame than is usual today for inquiry into the institutions of oratorical culture.

The critical perspectives often applied to oratorical cultures in our own day—from television (Skornia 1965, United States Carnegie Commission 1967) all the way to undergraduate programs in higher education (Bennett 1988a, Boyer 1987, Stewart and Spille 1987, Sykes 1988)—have been remarkably author-centered. That is, they have tended to attribute declines in oratorical cultures to the actions of responsible agents who can and do act freely, but they take only marginally into account how the range of individual freedom for action might have been influenced and progressively reshaped by institutionalizing, professionalizing forces.

In some ways, the story of Chautauqua appears to lend itself to just such an account: Vawter, the responsible agent, professionalizing Chautauqua and thereby bringing it to a remarkable level of both monetary and cultural success; then—through some sudden lapse of shrewdness or uncontrolled surge of cupidity or some other strangely uncharacteristic reason—leading it astray.

We propose to offer a different account: a narrative of the tension between Keith Vawter as responsible agent and Keith Vawter as the instrument of institutional forces in interaction with those touched (and reshaped) by the institution. We want to tell Vawter's story as an ironic tale of organized social action. But to give this account, we must ask different questions about the professionalization of oratorical cultures. We must ask about how rhetorical values were institutionalized and examine what happened to them and to the people they touched when they were; here, we must pay particular attention to how local goods and ends are redefined in the process of centralization by which the institution provides for its material survival. Thus we must consider both material conditions by which Vawter's decisions and activities were constrained and key concepts and principles from which they took their meaning.

To give an account of the decline of Chautauqua, we must note material conditions such as the Chautauqua contract, the rotation of talent called "tight booking," and the monitoring of audience response and consequent adaptation of individual performances—with, of course, due attention to Vawter's refinements of them. Moreover, a balanced assessment of Vawter's role must also return, in each of these instances, to central concepts in terms of which Vawter and other participants in Chautauqua came to understand their situation and activity, especially to one concept that may have some resonance for oratorical cultures in our own day: namely, the disposition to categorize all who appeared—one-man bands and exotic zither players lumped with Eugene Debs and Thomas Edison indiscriminately—as "talent," subject to a "quality control" to fit in on a homogenizing "circuit" of public speech.

In considering such factors, we do not mean to dismiss agent-centered criticism of oratorical cultures; rather, we think that the question of Vawter's individual responsibility is rendered more interesting and accurate by the new issues that criticism of institutions opens up and places in human context. These issues do not obscure the offenses of which Vawter stands indicted and for which he reluctantly accepted partial culpability, namely that his professionalizing innovations were central influences in the dilution of public educational substance on the circuit and that, moreover, they were designed and maintained as such by Vawter himself in order to maximize receipts in an institution previously devoted more centrally to making citizens rather than making profits. But a more complicated approach allows us to appreciate more fully and fairly his intriguing self-defense: As Vawter saw it—especially as he saw the role of local leadership—this indictment had things almost exactly backwards, because it misunderstood the constraints on, perhaps the very nature of, organized social action.

Early Chautauqua could never have been accused of overprofessionalization. Reverend John Heyl Vincent and businessman Lewis Miller founded Chautauqua as a permanent settlement on the shores of New York's Lake Chautauqua in 1873. Each summer thousands came to the summer resort to be part of educational programs addressed particularly to teachers. Vincent and Miller aimed at generating an oratorical culture that brought the resources of the East— particularly Boston, New York and Washington—to those who would teach the citizens of western states. The fare ran the gamut of academic, broadly political, and nondenominationally religious topics, as well as matters specifically concerning teaching; what went on at Lake Chautauqua might be seen as an early form of extension program in education.

William James would appear to discuss psychological issues, or biologist Louis Agassiz would recount the discoveries on his latest field trip. Governors from up and down the eastern seaboard and Senators from nearly every state would be invited to hold forth on the relative merits of the gold standard, the economic prospects of the West, or the pros and cons of ideas as arcane as trust-busting and women's suffrage. Lewis Miller's son-in-law, Thomas Alva Edison, would drop by to describe his latest projects and demonstrate an invention. And at Reverend Vincent's behest, religious leaders would grapple with theological issues. About these, there may be the most misunderstanding, for the images of later Chautauqua that many retain—of camp meetings, revivals, and Elmer Gantry outlined in torchlight—depart dramatically from the kind of oratorical culture Vincent and Miller labored mightily to establish. J. B. Hurlbut, a close associate, recalled that Vincent

> was not in sympathy with the type of religious life manifested and promoted at these gatherings. The fact that they dwelt too deeply in the realm of emotion and excitement, that they stirred the feelings to the neglect of the reasoning and thinking faculties, that the crowd called together on a camp meeting ground would not represent the sober, sane, thoughtful element of church life—all these repelled Dr. Vincent. (Hurlbut 1921, 23)

After a summer or two at Chautauqua, many visitors tried to found something similar at home. Even at its best—some (Knowles 1962, 13; Bryson 1936, 13–14; Antczak 1985, 57, 199–200) say *especially* at its best—what resulted from their efforts was predictably uneven: Isolated communities on the Great Plains had limited resources, and organizers ranged wildly in taste, seriousness, and inhibition. Yet from the start, Chautauqua took on a significant mission of democratic education:

> The American of the 1870's faced . . . a bewildering number of complex problems. There was the arrogance of the railroads and the trusts, a prolonged and severe economic depression, political corruption in city, state, and federal government, a "stolen" Presidential election (Hayes-Tilden) and a wave of bitter strikes which shocked the nation and created widespread fear for the safety of democratic institutions. (Gould 1961, 98)

No assessment of Chautauqua can be complete without taking into account its involvement of ordinary people in discussions of public policy in matters of real public import: the eight-hour day, the conservation of natural resources, pure food and drug legislation, city planning, slum clearance, child labor, the establishment of national forests and parks, Prohibition, the establishment of the Federal Reserve, the union movement, the direct election of United States senators, women's suffrage. Chautauqua generated, and to some extent maintained even to the end, an oratorical culture that was substantively ambitious and publicly influential.

Nor should we overlook a subtler kind of influence. "Ultimately an even more significant contribution of Chautauqua to the democracy was a broadening, a diversification of the American intellect. The exposure of those intellects to different disciplines provided alternative ways to see and talk about and act on their world" (Antczak 1985, 85); and this exposure happened in an unusually personal way. When people attended Chautauqua,

> they saw their neighbors there. They watched the color creep up the neck of the local banker when Debs castigated the financial interests, and they planned to be present when the banker got his next shave from the barber, an unreconstructed Populist. If Debs had spoken at a political rally, the banker would not have gone, and there would have been no argument to anticipate. But everyone went to Chautauqua . . . ideas presented during

Chautauqua Week were argued and discussed in these communities a
hundred times in the ensuing year. (Gould 1961, 82)

A community's interrelations thus enabled people to reach concrete,
personal understandings of new ideas. For part of the fun was to "key
in" well enough to anticipate what would anger the banker, what
would anger the barber, and why. By identifying ideas with already
familiar people, listeners came to see how those new ideas worked in
the world and how they related to other ideas. The citizens of a small
midwestern town knew each others' characters, and that ethical
charge made the new ideas more worth listening to and talking about.
Put another way, being nested in the ethos, the way of life and
interaction in a community, actually made the new ideas easier to
grasp, more possible to learn and think and talk about and take sides
upon.

How did Chautauqua get itself into such a situation? Why did it
     Yet it also cannot be denied that the Chautauqua met a sadly
diminished end. By the time it ran out its string in the 1920s, it had
become largely a medium of specialty entertainment, crowded with
zither players and yodelers and bell ringers. Even such a medium
might still have found what we now call a market niche had it not been
for technological developments. The movies brought top-billing entertainment to town and radio later brought it home; moreover, the
automobile and the expansion of the road system made it possible to
leave home and town and go to the bright lights in person. As a
medium of democratic education, as an oratorical culture, Chautauqua had once exerted a distinctive influence, both broad and uniquely
personal; but once it was transformed into primarily a medium of
entertainment, it grew less and less able to compete.

     How did Chautauqua get itself into such a situation? Why did it
ultimately fail? Ironically, part of the problem was the professionalization of the circuit system that Keith Vawter instituted precisely in
order to make Chautauqua more efficient in the distribution and use
of its human resources.

     The first effective Chautauqua circuit system was formed by the
Redpath Chautauqua Bureau, a speaker's bureau that founder James
Redpath had formed in the 1870s to handle Chautauqua bookings. But
the system that Vawter, as Redpath's manager, pieced together in the
1890s was an increasing departure from the less-organized past. Until
then, Chautauqua had operated quite haphazardly. Speakers had

been provided by a variety of bureaus and booking agents directly to independent Chautauquas, which were organized and run by local leaders. Bureaus themselves had no systematic role in coordinating local Chautauquas, no formal control over their scheduling in terms of content or dates, nor any further monetary stake in local failure or success. Local Chautauquas competed with one another for available speakers and other acts, and the costs of advertising, the difficulties of travel, and the wild vagaries of scheduling often coupled with a small town's modest receipts to limit the talent they might compete for, which in turn made it difficult for smaller and less prosperous communities to attract the same quality and sometimes even quantity of performers. Vawter's first professionalizing innovation reshaped Chautauqua by bringing a new kind of efficiency to the institution; but it also brought a different sense of its mission.

Vawter's "circuit system" moved to group neighboring towns together and served them systematically with programs organized by the Redpath Bureau. The towns of the agrarian Midwest were quite literally few and far between; the more that could be clustered into a working loop of the circuit and the more such loops that could be established, the more travel time and other expenses could be reduced and cost-efficiency be increased.

The circuiting together of towns had homogenizing effects. Different towns had once been free to pursue different tastes; Kalona was free to indulge more philosophical, religious, and literary interests than Cedar Rapids, which could lean as it preferred to the political and economic. Existing sites also had been free to hold their Chautauquas at different times of the summer, often in conjunction with meaningful anniversaries or other local events. Now towns were circuited together, and by the system Vawter called "tight booking" were "serviced" from a centralized control on the same schedule with the same "talent."

The Kalona Chautauqua might now start on a Monday, when the "first night" talent would appear; they would go up the road to open the Cedar Rapids Chautauqua on Tuesday, and so on along the circuit. Tight booking was clearly more efficient; a speaker who might get one eastern Iowa appearance in June, another perhaps in southwestern Iowa in July, and another perhaps in north central Iowa in early September now could count on eight to fourteen bookings within a fortnight, most closely enough arranged for one day's travel. The price was an increasingly homogenizing effect with respect to both timing and topics.

Further, tight booking was a system that depended upon and promoted a certain conception of speakers. Typically referred to as the "talent," speakers and other acts came to be viewed as commodities to be "sold" and distributed in a way not much different from selling wheat or soap flakes. In fact, Vawter even initiated a system of what we might call "quality control": Local managers (and later, agents from the central office) were required to monitor audience reaction to each part of the program and to report to the home office after every performance. Chautauqua historian Theodore Morrison reported that more than one performer who "was doing something that was not entirely 'safe'" was greeted at the next stop by "a more or less strongly worded 'suggestion' from the central office." The effect of this commodifying policy on the intellectual quality of Chautauqua was prompt and unmistakeable:

> Surveillance by local managers made crowd-pleasers rather than agents of culture out of too many performers. For the men and women who seriously advocated a program of action, there was no place at all; they might offend somebody in the audience. The inspirational speakers took over, and the once-vigorous Chautauqua movement was drowned in a flood of pap. (Morrison 1974, 95, 96)

If this was quality control, the quality in question was no longer the quality of oratorical culture but rather the quality of inoffensiveness that could be put on stage and be repeated, to equally harmless effect, tomorrow night down the road. It was, if you will, culture at wholesale rather than retail; concern for quality of product came to be tempered by the systematizing emphasis on reach of distribution.

This system successfully provided bigger names—William Jennings Bryan, "Mark Twain," "Fightin' Bob" LaFollette, William Rainey Harper, George Norris, William James, Edison—to smaller places by reducing the costs of publicity, talent, and transportation for the local Chautauquas. But at the same time it effectively gave the Redpath Bureau a different financial interest: Vawter saw more and more clearly that whole legs of the circuit system could break down without enough stable and successful host towns, leaving Redpath liable for the salaries of the speakers it had assembled. And local Chautauquas failed frequently, for reasons ranging from local economic difficulty to bad weather to "hinterland" disinterest in the tastes enforced by local organizing boards.

Keith Vawter had not established his elaborate regional system only to watch it fail for local reasons. Energetic "scouting" activities to identify new host towns subsequently developed, reflecting the stake the bureau felt in maintaining and expanding the circuit. At his instigation and under his supervision, the Redpath Bureau developed an evaluation system by which to determine whether Atalissa or Ankeny or Anamosa could measure up culturally and ethically as "a real Chautauqua town." In the construction and fine-tuning of the evaluation guidelines, Vawter set out the considerations necessary to support and sustain a community qualified to be included in Chautauqua. And as Vawter systematically refined them, these considerations became more and more clearly not only cultural but also material.

An undated early draft of Vawter's guideline for agents enumerated the considerations, institutional and individual, by which the prospective Chautauqua town might be recognized. First came a "checklist" of eighteen types of organizations, from PTA to Kiwanis and Rotary clubs to the YMCA and the Boy Scouts. Vawter regarded such organizations as essential because they demonstrated civic involvement and unity. But it was clear to Vawter that such involvement could not be long sustained without identifiable community leadership. Vawter believed that ultimately a Chautauqua "can be put on anywhere given the strong leadership of that town"; conversely, Vawter often found the absence of an identifiable and unifying ethos of leadership by itself a sufficient reason to explain why a particular Chautauqua failed. Agent Halley Kinney reported Vawter as explaining one such failure in just these terms. "This whole community is so devoid of leadership, so ripped and shattered with factions, racial, religious, social and economic that they cannot get to getheron [sic] the simple matter of reorganizing . . . I admit this is an aggravated case, but it illustrates the fading away of a community center" (Kinney 1952, 6). Vawter institutionalized this value of local leadership in the distinctive Chautauqua contract he developed.

> The noteworthy feature of the contract was the guarantee. Each community that bid for a Chautauqua had to form a committee that would be

responsible to raise a stipulated amount, the guarantee, by selling season tickets. The "hook" was that each member of the committee agreed to be legally liable for the amount of the guarantee. It was of course an unimpeachable sign of eminence in one's community to be a sponsor of culture, and those who saw themselves as their community's leading citizens contended zealously for the honor of membership in the Chautauqua committee. In binding this caliber of citizen, the guarantee gave the most prominent and responsible citizens at each stop along the circuit, a peronal stake—in terms of the loss of money and also the loss of personal face—in the chautauqua's success in their town. (Antczak 1985, 76–77)

Vawter trained his agents to recruit prospective committee members primarily in terms of explicit appeal to civic motives, not motives of monetary gain. Chautauqua was said to promote "a united community, progressive and inspiring." But again, as Redpath agent T. A. Wildman described it in an untitled agent bulletin, private leadership from "the better element of the community" was crucial to such public accomplishment. Thus, such leadership was to be presented as nothing less than a public duty: "A clear moral obligation rests upon them [community leaders] in conserving the morals and advancing the prospects of the young people" (1).

Again, the successes resulting from such notions of leadership for education and self-improvement should not be underestimated; they did, for a time, generate an oratorical culture guided and driven to a significant extent by civic motives. Certainly speakers were regularly contracted to speak to such motives on the circuit, whether in attempting to advance the knowledge of literature or the appreciation of art or equipping the local citizens to grasp and take thoughtful positions on the issues of the day. Communities themselves responded by making these issues part of their own discourse, as is manifest not only in editorials and political campaigns but in the private diaries and journals that survive from those days (see especially Briggs and Da Boll 1969, and Hurlbut 1921). Further studies of Chautauqua's oratorical culture will have much to gain in focusing on these materials and this interaction. In an age when schoolchildren are regularly reported to be unable to locate their own country on a world map and when large percentages of voting-age people cannot identify their representative or either of their senators, some of the Chautauqua's accomplishments in democratic education are worth note, perhaps envy, and certainly further examination.

But all this notwithstanding, the leadership appeals were only part of what became increasingly clearly the story of a commoditization and consumption of culture; the structure of the Redpath Chautauqua contract made it clear to prospective committee members that Chautauqua and the imperatives to which, for efficiency's sake, it was to respond were also to be viewed in business terms. By centralizing and commoditizing both the fare and the motives, the material survival of the institution was to be guaranteed.

Vawter's undated guidelines for booking agents instructed them to "sell" Chautauqua as "a business builder and a business getter, making the town a center for merchandising" (6). Moreover, once "signed on," sponsors had a stake in seeing Chautauqua as a financial entity. A town's "contract holders" in effect contracted to underwrite the Chautauqua in case it ended in a deficit. While a successful Chautauqua represented profits of a variety of educational and social kinds, a failure very specifically meant bottom-line losses shared among the sponsors. Thus, Vawter's contract institutionalized an economic stake in material, as distinct from cultural, "success."

Because the committee members did not want the price of an unsuccessful Chautauqua coming out of their pockets, they became a more dependably active promotion committee. When local Chautauquas nonetheless did draw disappointing crowds, contract holders in their correspondence with the bureau typically attributed the failure to inaccessibly highbrow fare. Invariably, committee members then began to take on a more active role in selecting talent they thought was more broadly promotable. Gradually, this local appropriation of an institutional motive does appear to have changed the kinds and balances of bookings that committees were willing to risk. The inoffensive and banal gradually crowded out the more intellectually demanding, as the Chautauqua programs vividly illustrate.

Even as late as the Belle Plaine Chautauqua of 1909, six and a half of the program's fifteen pages are devoted to the lecturers. Each has a half-page spread of four or five paragraphs containing general information and background as well as the standard plug for the lecturer's matchless oratorical ability:

> His power over an audience is nothing short of marvelous. One moment, the people are convulsed, the next moment they are in tears. One moment they are lost in self-condemnation, the next they are lifted to the heights

of moral vision that makes it absolutely impossible to descend to the old planes of common and sordid living. (*Redpath-Vawter Chautauqua Program* 1909, 2)

Already, it would seem, oratory was being "sold" as a cultural commodity whose noteworthiness lay to some extent in its entertainment value. But still, oratory is treated differently—praised for its capacity to induce, however histrionically, some kind of moral and intellectual effect. And it is treated at greater length and given more detailed attention; the entertainment, which made up the rest of the Chautauqua, takes up only five pages.

By the 1925 Cedar Rapids Chautauqua, however, we can see a distinct change. In a seven-page program, only one page is delegated to the speakers. Nine lecturers are noted on this one page, each receiving at most three or four descriptive sentences. In contrast, the entertainment gets four and a half pages; the Tyrolean Alpine Singers and Yodelers rate a half-page spread while the governor of North Carolina gets two sentences. This "overtaking" of the programs suggests how thoroughly the actual Chautauquas were commensurately overtaken by the drive for entertainment.

The center was not holding; civic leadership more and more often—and not necessarily or even often because of outright financial compulsion—played it financially safe. Hence an oratorical culture that had always "balanced in" a measure of lighter material now tilted dramatically in that direction. It was not long after—with, of course, the also very significant arrivals of radio, the movies, and the mobility that automobiles could provide—that the Chautauqua withered and died.

It seems this can all be explained rather tidily. People were gaining more and more access to more and more convenient entertainment alternatives, so they had more and more reason to reject another institution that existed increasingly just to give them the lowest common denominator along these lines and that increasingly betrayed the more public purpose of educating those wants. In this telling of the story, the villain—both to the local contract holders who lost money and to the retrospective critic—was clearly Vawter, who failed the local communities by redefining the motives that drove and guided the institution as primarily economic and not educational. As the system grew more centralized and efficient and professionalized, it lost touch with its raison d'être and consequently lost its once-distinctive hold on its local audiences. It's a rather simple story, with a plot and characters as clear as the goose and the golden egg.

What disrupts this tidy narrative is that, as his papers reveal, Vawter was himself keenly aware of the decline and was surprisingly torn between his desire on the one hand to turn the kind of profit that would sustain the circuit and on the other hand his genuinely civic and educational motives. In all his contractual dealings, throughout his voluminous correspondence, Vawter never once failed to insist that Chautauquas best served the common good of communities first through education and only after that through entertainment; his papers provide substantial evidence that this was more than lip service.

Of course it can't be denied that Vawter was a businessman, and a very sharp one. Before joining the bureau, he had a profitable private business as a booking agent for independent Chautauquas. But he claimed he made the move to Redpath specifically because he saw a way of running the business on another scale, one that could benefit not only the investors monetarily but also the host towns culturally. His first year as manager of Redpath was hardly an unambiguous example of profiteering, since the process of retooling led the bureau into a substantial deficit. Only through his dedication to his vision of a circuit Chautauqua did he manage to recoup the losses the next year and to remain thereafter in workably good standing with his creditors.

"Making the circuit run smoothly was Vawter's job, and he was evidently quite good at it," said Redpath agent for Iowa Halley Kinney, "whether he was building a program or arranging a promotion" (Kinney 1952, 6). Here again it's possible to tell the story too simply; to characterize Vawter as some sort of prairie Frank Lorenzo, single-mindedly maximizing profits without attention to or conscience for other concerns would be to miss the complicating side of his character that emerges again and again in his papers. Vawter—who over the course of his involvement with Chautauqua had many offers to go into other kinds of work—believed rather passionately not only in the profitability but also in the cultural value of what he was doing. He seems always to have explained Chautauqua not simply in business terms but also in civic terms as "an influence for good in a community" as he puts it in his pamphlet "What of the Chatauqua?" and as "a united effort for the common good" in his phrase from the pamphlet

"Reasons Why." That is to say, beyond the break-even point his concern for profit was tempered with repeatedly expressed and some times enforced concern for the ongoing cultural needs of the individual community.

Interestingly, it was not in terms of lost profits but rather of his commitment to the cultural value and possibilities of Chautauqua that Vawter bemoaned its decline. A journalist quotes Vawter as saying, "The strange thing is that, while the people really want to be instructed, they imagine they do not want instruction so much as entertainment. If you ask a man whether he desires to be entertained or instructed, he will tell you he wishes only to be entertained" (Kelly 1919, 32). It is worth speculating what Vawter could have meant by "want" in talking about the people's "wanting instruction." The evidence of his receipts—and Keith Vawter was never inattentive to receipts—ran unambiguously away from "desiring" or "wishing for" instruction. The sentence does make grammatical sense if we substitute the older sense of "want" as "need" or "lack"; but it only makes psychological sense—only makes sense as a thing for Vawter to bother saying—if he saw himself at least partly in principled service to communities, serving their needs, ministering to what, their own tastes notwithstanding, they might lack.

Such a concept imposes a sense of a community's goods and ends from the outside, just as much as the centralization involved in "circuiting" did. It particularly chagrined Vawter that this was necessary—that local leadership was not insistently educational leadership, not resistant to the decline but apparently content and sometimes eager to be complicit in it: Vawter's system had so effectively commodified culture that it had inured its audiences to respond as consumers. Vawter for a time tinkered with taking back control of certain programs, shifting within his sense of the possible the balance of education and entertainment:

> At first, Keith Vawter would frequently let the local committee select the various items to go on the Chautauqua. Whenever this was done the meeting fell short of success. For the local committee did not even know what they themselves wished to hear; they only thought they knew. Vawter then made it a flat rule that, instead of giving the people what they imagined they wanted, he would make up the program himself and the local committee might take it or leave it. (Kelly 1919, 32)

For a short time and to a limited extent, this worked. In Vawter's somewhat romanticized conceit, "old towns"—towns once initiated into the circuit under a traditional set of motives that had to do with democratic education and self-improvement—were more comfortable with "a higher grade of program . . . sufficiently high-brow or cultured." But new towns—the towns that founded their Chautauquas not so much out of the old motives of self-improvement but rather in an attempt to keep up with the Joneses, or rather the Clarindas and the Clear Lakes, the very towns that Vawter's system had driven him to recruit—insisted on more "popular numbers" (Kelly 1919, 32).

Certainly Vawter's old town/new town distinction begs further examination by Chautauqua scholars; it seems unlikely by itself to explain the whole decline, and itself understates the transformatory effects of professionalization and centralization on the "wants" of even old towns. But it is nonetheless ironic that Redpath agents themselves had used these "keep up with the neighbors" appeals in recruiting new towns that did not respond immediately to the prospects of education and self-improvement. And here was the rub: The old towns by themselves were not enough in size, number, or geographical closeness to support much of a circuit. The circuit system's very structure, institutionalizing values of efficiency and scale, depended on balancing programs so as to keep the new towns.

Vawter saw himself, then, in a tragic position somewhat of his own making. It was both his job and his duty to keep circuit Chautauqua alive; failure to turn some profit imperiled the very cultural benefits Chautauqua could bring, not only to the unprofitable town itself but also to all the others circuited to it. Indeed, Vawter had left a cushy personal niche and entered the business at this level specifically because he saw how his circuit system could bring more of those benefits more efficiently (and also profitably) to more communities. But it was concurrently the strength and the weakness of that system that the loss of even a few sponsoring towns could imperil the whole. So Vawter ultimately felt compelled to give local committees what they chose and to put his chips (quite literally) on the quality of those choices. To try another metaphor, he had loomed a whole system whose weave depended on a certain kind of local leadership, and in his view it was precisely that leadership that kept unraveling.

Note how the story of Chautauqua as an oratorical culture both affirms and complicates the usual stories of institutionalization—how institutionalization centralizes and commodifies purposes of social action in order to ensure first the material survival of the institution itself; how the centralization of the defining of goods and ends requires that they be defined to some extent by forces outside at least some of the communities for which they are being defined; and how such external definition must be inferior to local preferences. A more complex picture of Vawter and a more interesting story of the Chautauqua's decline emerge from his papers and the Redpath correspondence: We find there a person of some courage and persistence as well as some financial inventiveness, a businessman who looked often and closely above the bottom line. In Vawter's eyes, the decline of the Chautauqua actually reversed the typical ironic stories of organized social action, casting the antagonists tragically at odds with their own interests and the protagonist tragically at odds with himself in mutually contradictory but practically inseparable roles.

He was a citizen who had a cultural commitment to the towns he served, one that went demonstrably beyond the commitment of the very leaders of some of those towns. And if he was complicit, more or less inadvertantly, in the decline of Chautauqua's later years, he had been the central figure in the growing successes of its middle years, bringing to many places that weren't much more than crossroads the likes of William Rainey Harper, Thomas Edison, George Norris, Eugene Debs, and Robert Ingersoll. Vawter lifted his nose from his account books to note the decline and for a time fought it with real conviction and caginess. Ultimately he was overcome in these efforts, but only after significant clashes and mainly by the very scope and nature of his own creation—the circuit system's insatiable need for more towns.

Vawter had gradually put himself in a position where he could not discriminate except on financial bases among kinds of towns, kinds of motives for which they joined, kinds of leaderships. For that, surely, he must be held culpable. Further, Vawter designed Chautauqua's homogenizing innovations—the Chautauqua contract, tight booking, the monitoring system of quality control, the scouting procedure for new host towns—and he must be held responsible for them and their effects also. Perhaps in the end his most serious culpability lay in failing to create (or to see early enough a need for) a counterbalance to the institutional motive of material survival—failing to establish some principle of cultural discrimination along with all his concentration on cultural dissemination, some way to distinguish need from want and civic leadership from penny-pinching.

But if Vawter's self-defense is not wholly vindicating, it does hold some promising implications for inquiry into oratorical cultures. It suggests that we need to ask how rhetorical values are in fact institutionalized and to examine what happens to them—independent of authorial intention—when they are. It suggests that author-centered perspectives must be supplemented, especially insofar as institutions and audiences determine the range of individual autonomy. Surely one way we must continue to inquire into oratorical cultures is to examine the external institutions and internal dynamics that form them; Burkean scholars especially will have more to tell us about how such institutions are "goaded with a spirit of hierarchy" and grow "rotten with perfection" (Burke 1966, 15–20) and perhaps even about what it would be to view the patterns of institutionalization themselves as a kind of language, an ethically transformatory language both about and of the oratorical culture they define. This would at least discourage future scholars from attributing the declines of oratorical culture too narrowly.

And what are we to say of Vawter? Keith Vawter was to a demonstrable degree culpable for the divergence of purpose and practice on the Chautauqua. But he was also to some extent correct that institutionalizing the Chautauqua, for all the goods it brought over a considerable scope and time, had left him with little room to maneuver between his conflicting self-assigned roles as morally responsible agent and instrument of institutional forces. Thus he was also at least partly right in holding the local leaders complicit in Chautauqua's ultimate demise. This perhaps leads to a further implication for critics: that we must complicate our stories—stories of the tensions between the roles of the individual and stories of the tensions between principles of cultural discrimination and the interests of institutions in their own material survival—when it comes to the maintenance of oratorical cultures.

## Note

1. For the purposes of such research, the Redpath Chautauqua Collection of the University of Iowa is an unmined treasure. Beyond very extensive coverage of Iowa Chautauquas, the collection includes materials on Chautau-

quas in Illinois, Michigan, Indiana, Kentucky, and Canada. It is a sizable collection: The University of Iowa library claims that the Redpath Chautauqua Collection is the most extensive collection of circuit Chautauqua material anywhere, containing over 900 linear feet of papers, business correspondence, contracts and financial reports, programs and handbills of a rich and intriguing variety, and even agent reports on the status of existing Chautauqua communities and scouting reports on prospective locales.

One reason the collection is so exceptional is that the majority of it was donated by people directly involved with the Chautauqua for much of their lives. Most of the Redpath Chautauqua Bureau's records were provided by Henry P. Harrison, long a key manager in the agency. More pertinent to this study were the donations made by Keith Vawter's wife; after his death, Mrs. Vawter donated a huge gift of invaluable personal records to the collection.

Also held in Iowa City is the Chautauqua Pamphlet Collection of the Historical Society of Iowa, which contains a wealth of pamphlets, photos, and records of Redpath agents. We acknowledge with warm thanks the able and tireless assistance of the librarians at both the Historical Society and the Special Collections Department at the University of Iowa Library.

# 9

# The Rhetoric of
# Picturesque Scenery ❋
# A Nineteenth-Century
# Epideictic ❋ *S. Michael Halloran*

❋In the late 1940s, my parents used to take me on long Sunday afternoon drives through the western New England countryside. The route I recall best is Route 2 in Massachusetts, especially the stretch running east from North Adams, up Hoosic Mountain, and down through the Pioneer Valley toward Northampton. There were frequent stops at scenic overlooks, many of them with high viewing towers, pedestal-mounted binoculars that cost a dime to use, and shops featuring wooden tomahawks, silver Indian-head rings, and tom-toms made from tin cans and inner tubes. This was "the Mohawk Trail." We were following in the footsteps of Indians and pioneers.

Often we would stop for dinner at Wiggins Tavern, a "colonial-style" restaurant in the basement of the Hotel Northampton, and then inspect the buggies, blacksmith shop, and old-fashioned outhouse on display behind the hotel, and buy penny candy and copies of James Whitcomb Riley's "The Passing of the Backhouse" at the country store. It used to puzzle me that my mother, who was otherwise loud in her condemnation of all things "vulgar," would tolerate this mildly scatological broadside. I think the antiqueness of the poem and the mode of plumbing it celebrated somehow reversed their moral polarity, transforming what otherwise would have qualified as vulgarity—and thus, in one of my mother's favorite maxims, "amusing, but only to the vulgar"—into a sort of homily.[1]

In fact, the whole trip was something like an edifying discourse. In retracing the supposed path of pioneers and viewing the scenes and artifacts of their time, we were rehearsing an American ethos, participating in a rite of the civic religion. Outhouses, buggies, the Mohawk Trail itself, even the ersatz Indian artifacts were tokens of a revered past, some of it quite alive in the experiences of my parents, more of it as legendary for them as it was for me, all of it significant in defining who we believed ourselves to be as Americans of the mid-twentieth century. And central to that understanding was the land-scape itself. The rolling and picturesque Berkshire hills were the central appeal in these Sunday afternoon discourses. The scenic vistas that punctuated the winding mountain road were conventionally beautiful and, beyond this, resonant with a mythical past. We could imagine pioneers clearing this forest, farming these valleys, main-taining an uneasy peace with the Mohawk Indians.

The sensibility that drew us to the Berkshire hills, and that early in this century had led to the construction of the highway called "the Mohawk Trail," has roots in a nineteenth-century fascination with "picturesque" scenery. My purpose in this essay is to explore some nineteenth-century representations of the picturesque, with a spe-cific emphasis on their rhetorical significance. I will try to show that the picturesque in literature and art served a purpose traditionally associated with the kind of oratory practiced at public ceremonials, such as Pericles' funeral oration, Daniel Webster's Bunker Hill Monu-ment Address, and Lincoln's Gettysburg Address. Rhetorical theo-rists offer varied analyses of this "epideictic" genre of rhetoric, but they agree that it attempts to foreground and celebrate values as-sumed to be central to the identity of a group or people (Perelman and Olbrechts-Tyteca 1969; Rosenfield 1980; Oravec 1976). An epideictic speech is an effort to say in public who "we" are. My thesis, then, is that nineteenth-century picturesque representation was an attempt to articulate an American identity. The landscape—in colonial times a wilderness to be subdued and cultivated for use—became a mystical repository of Americanness and a locus of praise for the young nation. Myra Jehlen develops at length the more general claim that "the physical fact of the continent" more than any abstract ideas has been crucial in defining an American identity (1986, 3). I focus here on a particular style of representing the landscape and treat it as part of a rhetorical transformation, in which the representation and contemplation of scenery took on a function traditionally associated with public ceremonials and the oratory appropriate to them.

The word *picturesque* entered the English language toward the end of the seventeenth century. During the eighteenth century there developed around the term a fairly elaborate aesthetic theory of natural scenery and landscape gardening (Hipple 1957). It appears alongside "the sublime" and "the beautiful" in the works of many eighteenth-century British writers on aesthetics and rhetoric, who developed elaborately theorized distinctions among the terms. These distinctions were of less concern to nineteenth-century Americans, and they have little bearing on my argument here; while most of my examples would have been recognized as "picturesque" by the eighteenth-century British theorists, some might more properly be called "sublime."

My first point of reference will be *A Wonder Book for Girls and Boys* (1852) by Nathaniel Hawthorne, who had studied with and boarded in the home of Samuel P. Newman at Bowdoin College during a period when Newman was undoubtedly working on what would become the first commercially successful American rhetoric text (Stewart 1948, 14). Newman's *A Practical System of Rhetoric* characterizes "picturesque" as a term that,

> when applied to natural scenery, relates primarily and principally to the harmoniousness of effect produced on the mind, and implies such a prominence and combination of objects as give an expression or character to the scene. Nature seems in such instances to perform that work of combination, which, when represented to us on canvass by the skilful [*sic*] painter, we say he has designed by the aid of imagination and taste. ([1827] 1842, 58)

This notion of the picturesque is fairly conventional for the period and expresses well the sensibility apparent in the scenes from Hawthorne's work I will characterize below as "picturesque."

*A Wonder Book* is a collection of classical myths told to a group of children by a college student named Eustace Bright, who presumably draws upon his studies at Williams College in the Berkshire hills of western Massachusetts. The book shows us something of the classical tradition as seen through nineteenth-century eyes. As Eustace Bright's uncle puts it in *A Wonder Book*, "These stories appear to be an attempt to render the fables of classical antiquity into the idiom of modern fancy and feeling" (Hawthorne [1852] 1982, 1235). One aspect of that idiom turns out to be picturesque description, as illustrated in the following passage from Eustace Bright's version of the legend of Philemon and Baucis:

> Their cottage stood on a rising ground, at some short distance from a village, which lay in a hollow valley, that was about half a mile in breadth. This valley, in past ages, when the world was new, had probably been the bed of a lake. There, fishes had glided to and fro in the depths, and water-weeds had grown along the margin, and trees and hills had seen their reflected images in the broad and peaceful mirror. But as the waters subsided, men had cultivated the soil, and built houses on it, so that it was now a fertile spot, and bore no traces of the ancient lake, except a very small brook, which meandered through the midst of the village, and supplied the inhabitants with water. The valley had been dry land so long, that oaks had sprung up and been succeeded by others, as tall and stately as the first. Never was there a prettier or more fruitful valley. The very sight of the plenty around them should have made the inhabitants kind and gentle, and ready to show their gratitude to Providence by doing good to their fellow-creatures. (1260)

Three qualities mark this passage as picturesque in the broad meaning I am attaching to the term. First, it depicts an inviting natural landscape touched lightly by human cultivation; the scene is pastoral. Second, it conveys a strong sense of harmonious visual composition; in this case, the scene recalls a great number of nine-teenth-century paintings, particularly of the so-called Hudson River School, depicting a village nestled comfortably alongside a stream in a sunlit valley. (It also recalls the actual scenery of the Berkshire hills, including a couple of the major scenic overlooks of the Mohawk Trail.) Third, the scene is supposed to excite a moral response in the viewer.

The connection between aesthetic harmony in nature and spiri-tual harmony in the people who view it is not always made so explicit as in this passage, but it is one of the basic assumptions of picturesque representation, and it gives to it a special rhetorical import. The scene in nature is presented as if it were addressed to an audience. The harmonious composition that makes the scene seem like a painting — picturesque — is understood as a mode of appeal eliciting the best moral qualities of the audience/viewers. It foregrounds values understood to be uncontroversial and thus serves to increase the intensity of the audience's adherence to those values. Perelman and Olbrechts-Tyteca attribute this function to the epideictic genre and argue further that much of education is epideictic, in that it serves to inculcate commonly held values (1969, 47–54). Sullivan (1988) extends this line of thinking into an understanding of children's literature generally as a form of epideictic.

In Hawthorne's version of the Philemon and Baucis tale the appeal of the picturesque countryside has failed almost completely. With the exception of the old couple, all the villagers prove inhospitable to the two gods who visit them in the guise of human travelers, as they have been to each other and to Philemon and Baucis. They are punished by a sort of instant reversal of evolution, which Hawthorne records in another strikingly picturesque passage:

> Philemon and his wife turned towards the valley, where, at sunset, only the day before, they had seen the meadows, the houses, the gardens, the clumps of trees, the wide, green-margined street, with children playing in it, and all the tokens of business, enjoyment, and prosperity. But what was their astonishment! Even the fertile vale, in the hollow of which it lay, had ceased to have existence. In its stead, they beheld the broad, blue surface of a lake, which filled the great basin of the valley, from brim to brim, and reflected the surrounding hills in its bosom, with as tranquil an image as if it had been there ever since the creation of the world. For an instant, the lake remained perfectly smooth. Then, a little breeze sprang up, and caused the water to dance, glitter, and sparkle in the early sunbeams, and to dash, with a pleasant rippling murmur, against the hither shore. ([1852] 1982, 1272–73)

A few paragraphs later, we learn that the villagers have all been changed into fish, and Mercury comments, "There needed but little change, for they were already a scaly set of rascals, and the coldest-blooded beings in existence" (1273).

Hawthorne made frequent use of picturesque description in his fictions and sketches, and I want to consider one more example that suggests something of its relationship as a rhetorical mode to American oratorical culture. "The Old Manse," first published as a preface to the collection *Mosses from an Old Manse* (1846), is an account of the three years (1842–1845) during which Hawthorne lived and worked in a house in Concord owned by the Emerson family. It is replete with what amount to visual commonplaces of picturesque representation—orchards and fields bordered by old stone walls, the Concord and Assabeth rivers flowing lazily between banks lush with trees, and the slightly dilapidated old manse itself, its walls rich with the tradition of Puritan divines who had lived and worked there, whose manuscripts and books Hawthorne pores over eagerly. These descriptive passages and a relaxed, meandering style give it a deeply personal tone, yet "The Old Manse" is both more and less than a personal memoir: more in that it has much to say about Hawthorne's work, and is in this sense a kind of professional credo as well; less in that it is reticent on what was clearly the most important aspect of his "personal" life during this period—his relationship with Sophia Peabody, the bride he had married immediately before moving into the manse.

Hawthorne begins with his arrival at the manse, drawing the scene in picturesque terms and using a plural "we" that is one of the few hints in the essay of his bride's presence: "Between two tall gateposts of rough-hewn stone, (the gate itself having fallen from its hinges, at some unknown epoch,) we beheld the gray front of the old parsonage, terminating the vista of an avenue of black ash trees" ([1846] 1982, 1123). By the opening of the second paragraph, the occasion has become "that memorable summer-afternoon when *I* entered it as *my* home" (1123; emphasis added), and for the remainder of the essay, "we" will refer most often to Hawthorne and the reader. He then places himself in relation to a literary tradition and literary invention in relation to the picturesque scene:

> It was awful to reflect how many sermons must have been written there. The latest inhabitant alone—he, by whose translation to Paradise the dwelling was left vacant—had penned nearly three thousand discourses, besides the better, if not the greater number, that gushed living from his lips. How often, no doubt, had he paced to-and-fro along the avenue, attuning his meditations to the sighs and gentle murmurs, and deep and solemn peals of the wind, among the lofty tops of the trees! In that variety of natural utterances, he could find something accordant with every passage of his sermon, were it of tenderness or reverential fear. (1124)

It is worth pausing here to note that Hawthorne attributes to the minister a process of rhetorical invention he almost certainly would not have employed or understood. The idea of drawing "inspiration"

from direct communion with nature, while not wholly unprecedented, was unusual prior to the transformation of nineteenth-century rhetoric from an art based in the wisdom of communal consensus
to one based in the individual's unique personal experience. Rather
than listening to the wind in the trees for sermonic inspiration, the
Puritan preacher would have scanned the established wisdom of his
community, most likely using the traditional method of topical invention to organize the process.

Hawthorne continues, turning now to his own literary efforts:

> The boughs over my head seemed shadowy with solemn thoughts, as
> well as with rustling leaves. I took shame to myself for having been so
> long a writer of idle stories, and ventured to hope that wisdom would
> descend upon me with the falling leaves of the avenue; and that I should
> light upon an intellectual treasure in the old Manse, well worth those
> hoards of long-hidden gold, which people seek for in moss-grown
> houses. Profound treatises of morality;—a layman's unprofessional, and
> therefore unprejudiced views of religion;—histories, (such as Bancroft
> might have written, had he taken up his abode here, as he once pur-
> posed,) bright with picture, gleaming over a depth of philosophic
> thought;—these were the works that might fitly have flowed from such a
> retirement. In the humblest event, I resolved at least to achieve a novel,
> that should evolve some deep lesson, and should possess physical sub-
> stance enough to stand alone. (1124)

He notes further that Emerson had written "Nature" in the room he
takes as his study and that he finds the room gloomy with soot and
"the grim prints of Puritan ministers." He brightens the room with a
coat of paint, a vase of flowers, and "the sweet and lovely head of one
of Raphael's Madonnas, and two pleasant little pictures of the Lake of
Como" to replace the portraits of ministers (1124–25).

Hawthorne thus sets up in the beginning of the essay a skewed
opposition between his own work as a teller of "idle stories" and the
tradition of sermons, histories, and "profound treatises of morality"—a tradition that is clearly "oratorical" within the meaning we are
giving that term in this volume. But in place of the method of
invention associated with that tradition, he affirms a process of
inspiration through direct communion with nature, a process more
appropriately associated with "idle stories." In the pages that follow he
takes the reader on a tour of the picturesque countryside, records a

rainy week spent poring over old books and manuscripts in the attic in search of some "intellectual treasure," then returns to the countryside and an idyllic day spent fishing on the Assabeth with Ellery Channing. The books prove dull and sterile, the countryside rich with lessons in history, morality, and happiness—a contrast that underscores Hawthorne's preference for inspiration over methodical invention. In concluding the essay, he notes that he has produced neither moral tome nor novel but only more tales and sketches, "idle weeds and withering blossoms" as he calls them (1148). Yet he no longer feels shame as a writer of tales and sketches, and—even more significantly—he has developed a jaundiced eye for the tracts and sermons of his Puritan forebears. He has learned that "thought grows mouldy. What was good and nourishing food for the spirits of one generation, affords no sustenance for the next" (1136). He has also learned to accept his own literary gift and to take the "sustenance" he had formerly sought in dusty tomes from a day spent fishing on the Assabeth or simply walking in the orchards and fields.

There is reason to doubt that Hawthorne actually harbored the ambition he imputes to himself in the opening pages of "The Old Manse." He had studied the Puritan past closely before moving into the manse and would continue to do so, but the use he made of that tradition shows no inclination to participate in it as a writer of moralizing tracts. The Puritan past was to Hawthorne matter for literary tales, such as "My Kinsman, Major Molineux" (1832), "Young Goodman Brown" (1835), and "The May-Pole of Merry Mount" (1836). And when he did finally produce a novel, any "deep lesson" one might draw from it would be at odds rather than in keeping with the Puritan tradition it chronicled.[2] Roger Chillingworth is in many ways the consummate Puritan, but it is he if anyone who is damned in *The Scarlet Letter* (1850). And when the Reverend Arthur Dimmesdale tries to confess his guilt as father of Hester Prynne's illegitimate child, the traditional oratorical forum of the pulpit proves antithetical to his purpose. The more he tries to confess his guilt, the more saintly the congregation takes him to be. It becomes virtually impossible for him to tell the truth from the pulpit, and he must mount the scaffold to bare his breast and *show* his guilt to the community. Dimmesdale's efforts to reveal his sin might serve as a figure of a declining oratorical tradition giving way to an aesthetic of showing, a literary aesthetic such as Henry James would later articulate.

Hawthorne's professed "shame" as a teller of tales can thus be taken as a rhetorical contrivance to underscore the opposition between two sensibilities, the one of explicit moral principles that can be codified in treatises and sermons, the other of a joyful and deeply personal morality drawn from communion with nature and friends. Within the Puritan sensibility, Hawthorne's tales might well be idle and shameful, but the Puritanism he articulates in both "Young Goodman Brown" and *The Scarlet Letter* ends in a misanthropic unhappiness quite alien to the persona of Hawthorne in "The Old Manse." By portraying himself at the outset as a would-be Puritan moralist, he emphasizes the power of picturesque scenery to teach a higher morality of freedom and contentment. Of his fishing idyll with Channing, for example, he says that

> the chief profit of those wild days, to him and me, lay—not in any definite idea—not in any angular or rounded truth, which we dug out of the shapeless mass of problematical stuff—but in the freedom which we thereby won from all custom and conventionalism, and fettering influences of man on man. We were so free to-day, that it was impossible to be slaves again tomorrow. When we crossed the threshold of a house, or trod the thronged pavements of a city, still the leaves of the trees, that overhung the Assabeth, were whispering to us—'Be free! Be free!' ([1846] 1982, 1141)

Upon arriving at the manse he had hoped those same leaves would descend on him with a wisdom that would produce "profound treatises of morality" and "deep lessons" (1124). They have taught him instead that there are heights in life before which the profundities pale.

Yet the leaves of the trees may only figure another source of inspiration, one too intensely personal to be spoken openly. "My conscience," he says toward the end of "The Old Manse,"

> does not reproach me with betraying anything too sacredly individual to be revealed by a human spirit, to its brother or sister spirit. How narrow— how shallow and scanty too—is the stream of thought that has been flowing from my pen, compared with the broad tide of dim emotions, ideas, and associations, which swell around me from that portion of my existence! How little have I told! . . . I have appealed to no sentiment or sensibilities, save such as are diffused among us all. So far as I am a man

of really individual attributes, I veil my face; nor am I, nor have ever been, one of those supremely hospitable people, who serve up their own hearts delicately fried, with brain-sauce, as a tidbit for their beloved public. (1147)

What was "too sacredly individual" to be revealed was undoubtedly the intensity of Hawthorne's relationship with his young wife, Sophia—and his reticence on this subject becomes all the more fascinating in light of his selection for the first story in *Mosses*: "The Birth-mark" (1843), a tale of a man who kills his bride in an effort to perfect her beauty. But for purposes of this essay I want only to underscore the sharply skewed opposition he establishes between "individual attributes" and the "sentiment or sensibilities . . . such as are diffused among us all." The transcendent value Hawthorne gives to those individual attributes he is still unwilling to make public places him on the cusp of an individualist literary culture emerging from the neoclassical oratorical culture in which he had been schooled. Private experience was supplanting communally rehearsed principle as the ground of civic virtue, and Hawthorne straddled the divide.

Examples of the sort of description I am calling picturesque abound in the work of such nineteenth-century writers as Emerson, Thoreau, Whittier, Longfellow, William Cullen Bryant, James Fenimore Cooper, Francis Parkman, and others. Among painters, Asher Durand, Frederick Church, Thomas Cole, John F. Kensett, and Jasper Cropsey (to name only the most famous) are in varying degrees "picturesque." I use quotation marks around the term here to emphasize the circularity of the idea that painters produce paintings that are "like a picture." But of course it is *to us*, and largely because of our familiarity with their work, that the images of Cole, Cropsey, and others seem almost to define what a "picture" should look like and conversely what makes a landscape "as pretty as a picture." The pedestal-mounted binoculars of the Mohawk Trail and the millions of cameras that have been pointed at mountain streams and fertile valleys and slightly dilapidated old barns and houses were trained by painters of the Hudson River School and writers such as Hawthorne, Thoreau, and Longfellow. And if their images seem to us somewhat commonplace, it is testimony to the great power of their vision. The lakes and woods and mountains of Hudson River School paintings reappear in illustrations for travel books, in the "View Master" stere-opticons popular in the 1940s and 1950s, in settings for magazine and television advertisements, in "sofa-sized" mass-produced paintings for suburban homes. These and similar picturesque images continue to draw countless vacationers to the lakes and mountains that were favorite subjects of the painters who first represented their appeal. We have learned from those painters and writers that we ought to be moved by specific features of the landscape.

From their imitators we have learned a degree of numbness, making the appeal sometimes difficult to respond to. Hawthorne, for example, recorded experiencing the numbness that can result from previous exposure to representations of a "sublime" scene as early as 1832 in "My Visit to Niagara," a sketch of his initial view of America's first famous tourist attraction. Sublime scenery may present a special problem in that it is supposed to excite feelings of awe or terror, in contrast to the more tranquil emotions associated with the pictur-esque. To represent a scene in a painting or a literary vignette is immediately to place it in a human perspective and in this sense to assert power over it and rob it of the strangeness and menace that made it sublime.

The nineteenth-century enthusiasm for picturesque scenery was on one level simply an American manifestation of Romanticism, and in this sense it derived from such sources as Wordsworth, Coleridge, and Schiller as well as the belletristic critics and rhetoricians. But it happened to occur simultaneously with an American move to estab-lish a national literature and culture, and, partly in consequence, it took on some peculiarly American characteristics and a special Amer-ican significance. The picturesque strand in the Romantic sensibility tended to be both narrative and nostalgic. It represented the natural world as a scene for life lived at a simpler and more tranquil pace. In American picturesque imagery, this tendency was expressed in refer-ences to colonial and Revolutionary times and in mythologized por-traits of native Americans. Hawthorne, for example, finds in the countryside around the old manse reminders of the colonial and British soldiers who had fought at Concord and of the Indians who had preceded them, as well as of the Puritans and their tradition of oratorical literature. Longfellow's "Song of Hiawatha" (1855) and "The Courtship of Miles Standish" (1858) are more aggressive efforts to construct an American past set in a picturesque landscape. These references, and the scenic images that were their tokens, in turn entered the developing national culture. The writings of Longfellow, Hawthorne, Bryant, and Cooper became standard fare for school-children, and places like Concord and Plymouth and Lake George—the last a frequent subject of Hudson River School painters that was called an "American Como"—became shrines of the civic religion.

An 1829 sonnet by William Cullen Bryant suggests the pride in American scenery that was shared by many writers and painters of the picturesque tradition, giving their work a distinct epideictic function. Addressed "To Cole, the Painter, Departing for Europe," the poem praises both painter and the landscape he depicts and by implication the nation identified with both:

> Thine eyes shall see the light of distant skies:
>   Yet, Cole! thy heart shall bear to Europe's strand
>   A living image of our own bright land,
> Such as upon thy glorious canvas lies;
> Lone lakes—savannas where the bison roves—
>   Rocks rich with summer garlands—solemn streams—
>   Skies, where the desert eagle wheels and screams—
> Spring bloom and autumn blaze of boundless groves.
> Fair scenes shall greet thee where thou goest—fair,
>   But different—everywhere the trace of men,
>   Paths, homes, graves, ruins, from the lowest glen
> To where life shrinks from the fierce Alpine air,
>   Gaze on them, till the tears shall dim thy sight,
>   But keep that earlier, wilder image bright.
>                               (Bryant [1829] 1914, 116)

Thomas Cole was himself a writer as well as a painter, and after returning from Europe he echoed Bryant's sonnet in an essay defending American scenery against those who would dismiss it for lacking the centuries-old buildings and ruins that give the European landscape its own characteristic picturesqueness. In "Essay on American Scenery," Cole argued that "the most distinctive, and perhaps the most impressive, characteristic of American scenery is its wildness" ([1835] 1965, 102), and his work was influential in shaping a tradition that emphasized the "wildness" of the American landscape—ironically, at the moment when it was being transformed by the industrial revolution.

Asher Durand would still later represent the bond between Cole and Bryant in the painting *Kindred Spirits* (1849), which shows the two men standing on a rocky crag overlooking a mountain stream in the translucent light of a typically picturesque woodland. According to Kenneth Myers (1987), *Kindred Spirits* draws on specific geographic features in the area of Kaaterskill Clove, a region Cole had painted in a set of early landscapes that quickly made both the Catskill mountains and Thomas Cole famous. Durand was one of the early discoverers of Cole's work and was later influenced by Cole to specialize in landscape painting. Art historian Barbara Novak points out a specifically political import of *Kindred Spirits* and of the whole American tradition of picturesque representation: "Man can also commune with *man* through nature. . . . This picture is evidence not only of a singular contemplation after a transcendental model, but of a sharing through communion, of a potential community" (1980, 15). But note that the potential community represented would be grounded in each individual's communion with the "wilder image" of an American landscape and thus free of the "custom and conventionalism, and fettering influences of man on man" of which Hawthorne had written. Picturesque representation in America thus celebrates the vision of a political community that no longer needs the public standards and values articulated in traditional oratorical modes. As Bryant's sonnet suggests, America was coming to understand itself as "different," free of "the trace of men" that was everywhere in the Old World.

A further elaboration of the picturesque sensibility is developed in *Picturesque America* (1874), a multivolume book of engravings and essays edited by Bryant nearly half a century after he wrote "To Cole, the Painter." The engravings depict pastoral scenes in various areas of the country, with heavy emphasis on the kinds of images favored by Cole and other Hudson River School painters—waterfalls, woodland streams and lakes, mountain peaks, slightly dilapidated buildings—and the essays frequently stress the historic associations of the scenes depicted. The essay by O. B. Bunce on Lake George, for example, records both its discovery by the Jesuit Isaac Jogues and a number of incidents from the French and Indian War. The essay also refers to the adventures of Cooper's Leatherstocking on Lake George. As its title suggests, the book quite explicitly makes picturesque beauty a locus of praise for the nation. Bryant writes warmly in his introduction of the unspoiled beauties of "our continent," "our Republic," "our White

Mountains," "our Catskills," and so forth. Viewing the landscape has taken on a purpose traditionally associated with ceremonial oratory. It has become a celebration of the country's greatness.

In a number of ways, *Picturesque America* represents the increasing stratification by class of American society. Its lavish physical quality clearly made it a luxury item for an economic elite, for whom it served as a guide to one of the rituals of wealth. Travel for the purpose of enjoying scenic beauty had been increasingly common among the well-to-do since the 1820s, and by the 1870s sites such as Niagara Falls and the Hudson River valley were frequented by an aspiring middle class as well. Visiting what John Sears (1989) calls our "sacred places" had become a celebration of one's success in the meritocracy as well as of one's identity as an American. The scenes depicted in *Picturesque America* sometimes included figures who might be fellow members of the meritocracy at play, as fishermen or hikers for example. More often they included farmers, boatmen, and former slaves who could be seen by readers as inferior others. The book offers rustic scenes as a commodity for consumption by an urban elite and in this way celebrates their difference. Thoreau had made explicit in *Walden* the connection between the picturesque and social class three decades before the publication of *Picturesque America*, though he viewed the class hierarchy quite differently:

> The most interesting dwellings in this country, as the painter knows, are the most unpretending, humble log huts and cottages of the poor commonly; it is the life of the inhabitants whose shells they are, and not any peculiarity in their surfaces merely, which makes them *picturesque*; and equally interesting will be the citizen's suburban box, when his life shall be as simple and as agreeable to the imagination, and there is as little straining after effect in the style of his dwelling. ([1854] 1985, 360)

It was not sufficient for the new elite just to go to the right places. To distinguish themselves from the hoi polloi, who might also have access to the sacred places, they had to experience the right emotional responses, to exhibit what the rhetoricians called "taste." The essayists and engravers of *Picturesque America* had learned to see actual landscapes in the by-then conventional terms set by painters such as Cole and Cropsey and writers such as Hawthorne and Longfellow. But unlike the "first generation" picturesque writers and painters, the artists of *Picturesque America* articulate this visual sensibility as a social obligation. In an essay on the beauties of the Maine coast, for example, we read:

> People in search of the picturesque should understand the importance of selecting suitable points of view. The beauty or impressiveness of a picture sometimes greatly depends on this. It is often a matter of search to discover the point from which an object has its best expression; and probably only those of intuitive artistic tastes are enabled to see all the beauties of a landscape, which others lose in ignorance of how to select the most advantageous standing-place. To the cold and indifferent, Nature has no charms; she reveals herself only to those who surrender their hearts to her influence, and who patiently study her aspects. The beauty of an object lies partly in the capacity of the spectator to see it, and partly in his ability to put himself where the form and color impress the senses most effectively. Not one man in ten discerns half the beauty or a tree or a pile of rocks, and hence those who fail to discover in a landscape the charm others describe in it, should question their own power of appreciation rather than the accuracy of the delineation. The shores of Mount Desert must be studied with this appreciation and taste, if their beauties are to be understood. (Bunce [1874b] 1974, 8–10)

The contrast with Thoreau's egalitarian vision could hardly be more stark.

One way of understanding classical epideictic is as a simple display of eloquence. By demonstrating power to move the audience through praise of appropriate cultural icons, the orator brings honor upon himself. In *Picturesque America*, we see a curious and typically late-nineteenth-century inversion of this principle. Here it is not the orator's power that is being put on display, but the audience's. By demonstrating what Hugh Blair had characterized as "the power of receiving pleasure from the beauties of nature and of art" — taste (1783, 1:16) — viewers bring honor upon themselves. But it is a private display, an honor in one's own eyes. Only I can know whether I am really appreciating the beauties of Mount Desert — though of course I might fake the correct responses, particularly with the aid of a book like *Picturesque America*. And if I do respond correctly, if I achieve the status of that one in ten who discerns and appreciates the beauty of a landscape, I can feel superior to the nine who inevitably fail. This version of the picturesque thus reflects some troubling qualities of the new middle-class ethos: a nagging mistrust of the individual sensibility and—partly in consequence—an increasingly strong sense of social stratification.

Mistrust of the individual moral sense was of course not new in the 1870s. Hawthorne's idyll on the Assabeth of three decades before had given him a vision of moral and aesthetic autonomy, of an ability to hear for oneself the unmediated whispering of the trees. Others had envisioned a similar spirit of moral independence. "Trust thyself," wrote Emerson; "every heart vibrates to that iron string" ([1841] 1983, 260); Thoreau's "experiment" at Walden Pond was but the most famous of many efforts to live on that principle. Yet Hawthorne also tells of the "hobgoblins of flesh and blood" who flocked to Emerson for "the clue that should guide them out of their self-involved bewilderment," and he admits to having had this same impulse himself: "There had been epochs of my life, when I, too, might have asked of this prophet the master-word, that should solve me the riddle of the universe; but now, being happy, I felt as if there were no question to be put, and therefore admired Emerson as a poet of deep beauty and austere tenderness, but sought nothing from him as a philosopher" ([1846] 1982, 1145–46). As a source of moral authority, the trees overhanging the Assabeth were even for Hawthorne a counsel of perfection for use in privileged moments only, and Emerson, having told his reader to "trust thyself," would paradoxically continue offering advice for decades to come.

Any doubts Hawthorne had about the individual moral sense were thus acknowledged *self*-doubts and not just suspicion of an inferior class. This is not to say that Hawthorne was free of class prejudice. His early travel sketches include deeply offensive portraits of recent immigrants as "the scum which every wind blows off the Irish shores" ([1832d] 1989, 49; see also [1832a] 1989 for evidence of Hawthorne's anti-Irish prejudice). But he concludes with a chauvinistic vision of an America that can elevate such people:

> It was cheering, also, to reflect, that nothing short of settled depravity could resist the strength of moral influences, diffused throughout our native land;—that the stock of home-bred virtue is large enough to absorb and neutralize so much of foreign vice;—and that the outcasts of Europe, if not by their own choice, yet by an almost inevitable necessity, promote the welfare of the country that receives them to its bosom. ([1832d] 1989, 54–55)

A similar egalitarian optimism can be seen in Thoreau, Fuller, and many of the other transcendental idealists. But by the last quarter of the century, the middle-class ethos had produced a new elite whose sense of status was nervous and unstable and who were consequently jealous of the outward signs of status. Popular lecturers such as William Graham Sumner and Russell Conwell were preaching economic opportunism to large and enthusiastic audiences who shared their social Darwinist views, and even reformers such as Henry George tended to accept the view of society as an arena of fierce and remorseless competition. For the insecure elite of this society, the expressions of taste catalogued in a book like *Picturesque America* would be means of signifying, and thus clinging to, their hard-won and precarious standing. And part of the expression would be feeling superior, being aware of a great unwashed who lack the capacity to receive pleasure from the beauties of nature and art. The "sharing through communion" celebrated in Durand's *Kindred Spirits* and Hawthorne's "The Old Manse" had given way to a competitive individualism that desperately needed inferiors to sneer at and shun. Yet the imagery of the picturesque could represent either social impulse equally well.

In a 1953 essay on "The Spaciousness of Old Rhetoric," Richard Weaver asks why we no longer practice or appreciate the sort of grandiloquent oratory that delighted many Americans of the nineteenth century. His answer is that such oratory rests upon the use of broad generalizations that are part of a common ideological heritage formerly shared by most Americans but no longer alive among us. As one of many examples, he quotes part of an 1858 speech to the Valley Agricultural Society of Virginia, which concludes with the assertion that the ancient Romans had a "high standard of moral virtue which made them the easy masters of their race" (279). A nineteenth-century audience, according to Weaver, would have granted without question the sweeping claim that moral virtue makes one master, enabling the speaker to move forward with grander and more stirring claims. Weaver does not note that if slaves overheard the speech they might have attributed qualities other than moral virtue to the masters of *their* race. In fact, Weaver associates the willingness to grant such broad cultural assumptions with a "universal enlightened consensus" (280). The narrowness of this alleged consensus—which excluded women, native Americans, Irish immigrants, and other people of the free working class as well as African-American slaves—should make us wary of more recent arguments for the teaching of "cultural literacy."

The rhetoric of the picturesque arose in the same period as the "spacious" oratory admired by Weaver, and in many cases picturesque representation was an important strategy of the oratory. Webster's celebrated "Bunker Hill Monument Address" of 1825, for example, relies heavily on depictions contrasting the peaceful hillside and harbor of the present with the battle they had witnessed some fifty years before, thus investing the landscape with the sense of history and moral significance that is a hallmark of the picturesque. The oratorical style favored by Webster is, as Weaver notes, quite dead, and many of the literary masters of picturesque representation are likewise in full eclipse. Who reads Longfellow these days? Neither Bryant's name nor any of his works appears in E. D. Hirsch's famous list of what literate Americans are supposed to know. Yet as I suggested at the beginning of this essay, our taste for picturesque scenery remains alive and continues to influence some of the rituals of family life. We go to camping and picnic grounds situated in "picturesque" locales that carry an aura of an American past and are sometimes associated with specific historical events. The site of the Battle of Saratoga, often referred to as the turning point of the Revolution, is a national park where we can drive through the scenes of the battle in sequence, retracing its progress while enjoying vistas of the Hudson River and the Green Mountains of Vermont and maybe picnicking near the monument to the leg in which Benedict Arnold, then still a committed revolutionary, was wounded at Saratoga. For the price of a ticket, we can enjoy simulacra of a picturesque colonial life at Old Sturbridge Village and Plimouth Plantation in Massachusetts; or camp at the Lake George Battlefield, where Sir William Johnson slept the night before the battle of Fort William Henry; or tour the Old Manse at Concord and look out from the windows of Hawthorne's study on the site where "the shot heard round the world" was fired.[3] And of course we market everything from environmental activism to instant coffee through the use of picturesque imagery.

I think our taste for picturesque scenery survives for essentially the same reason that the oratory of Webster and Edward Everett and the poetry of Longfellow and Bryant does not: It suits a postromantic moral sense that prizes individual choice above all things, a moral sense that feels imposed upon by the sorts of broad general claims that constitute the "spaciousness" admired by Richard Weaver. Like Hawthorne's fishing trip on the Assabeth or the communion between Bryant and Cole depicted by Asher Durand, an afternoon spent contemplating the scenery of Lake George leaves us free of all "custom and conventionalism, and fettering influences of man on man." It can give us the sense of an enlarged moral vision and connection with an American past, yet it imposes no specific construction of what that past might mean. And in doing so it allows us to forget some of the less heroic aspects of our past and evade some of the resulting conflicts in our present.

As a transformation of the traditional epideictic practiced by Webster, Everett, Longfellow, Bryant, and others, the rhetoric of the picturesque thus illustrates a central point of the story Gregory Clark and I told in our introductory essay: There were both losses and gains in the transformation of nineteenth-century oratorical culture. The neoclassical oratorical culture was exclusionary and its rhetoric morally presumptuous, but it had the virtue of articulating its presumptions with some clarity and in that way creating the possibility of debate. For example, arguing that it was the moral virtue of the Romans that made them "masters of their race" entails a tacit acknowledgment that a reasonable person could believe the contrary — else why bother making the argument? A more complex example is offered by the many ceremonial speeches, including Webster's Bunker Hill Monument Address, in which nineteenth-century white Americans extolled the spirit of liberty, the Declaration of Independence, and other icons of the Revolution. These invited many contrary speeches by abolitionists, such as Frederick Douglass's eloquent denunciation of Independence Day celebrations as "mere bombast, fraud, deception, impiety, and hypocrisy — a thin veil to cover up crimes which would disgrace a nation of savages" ([1852] 1988, 374).

The ceremonial rhetoric of Webster, Douglass, and others was thus "spacious" in a sense not recognized by Richard Weaver: It could constitute a space in which to debate important issues. The rhetoric of the picturesque can in this sense be paradoxically cramped; if, as often happens, it gives us images without arguments, it offers no space for debate, no vector for passion. The same picturesque image could celebrate both the egalitarian vision of radical transcendentalists and the elitist spirit of *Picturesque America*, and an epideictic thus unfocused risks being "ceremonial" in the most pejorative sense—the celebration of nothing more than a passing occasion.

Yet in spite of O. B. Bunce's sneering dismissal of those who "fail to discover in a landscape the charm others describe in it," the rhetorical celebration of picturesque scenery defined an America with the potential of a radical equality. Indeed, his strained assertion of an ineffable experience available to that fortunate one in ten might be taken as an effort to prop up the principle of hierarchy in the face of an inexorable democratizing force. The landscape was there for all to see. If, as Myra Jehlen claims, *that* is the essence of America, and if, as Hawthorne imagined, one could draw inspiration directly from the stones and the foliage, then the traditional rituals of exclusion would be powerless. One could be ignorant of the classical languages, of the rhetorical figures and tropes, even of "our" literature and oratory and art, and yet know all it takes to be American.

Ceremonials that celebrate the picturesque landscape—hiking, camping, the Sunday afternoon drive on the Mohawk Trail—seem thus to be the ultimate transformation of the epideictic genre, in which we dispense entirely with rhetorical forms and forums to make immediate contact with values that constitute us as a people. In the face of such an experience, "rhetoric" can seem a poor and even pernicious thing. But of course there is no unmediated experience of the landscape or of "American values," and the power of the experience is testimony to the power and subtlety of the rhetorics that construct it. We have learned to hear the whispering of the trees from writers and artists such as Hawthorne, Bryant, Cole, and Durand, from the mass-produced prints and boilerplate prose of their imitators. The complex story of what happened to rhetoric in the nineteenth century should include some consideration of these many figures who deserve, though they might not claim, the title of rhetorician.

## Notes

1. The entire maxim went like this: "Vulgarity is amusing, but only to the vulgar, and they are not worth amusing." Whatever my mother may have meant by "vulgarity," my own understanding of the term was narrower than that of Sarah Josepha Hale, as recorded in this volume by Nicole Tonkovich; it meant blunt reference to or ostentatious performance of certain bodily functions, usually for humorous effect. My brother and I revelled in our vulgarity.

2. Hawthorne had published a novel, *Fanshawe* (1828), fourteen years before moving into the Old Manse, but he was not proud of this youthful creation and preferred to think of *The Scarlet Letter* as his "first" novel.

3. The late Donald Stewart has pointed out that I betray in this catalogue of scenery and throughout the essay my northeastern provincialism, and my friend Ronald Reid puts a sharper point on it: None of the places I mention is in the United States of America, he says. Well, I grew up thinking that west of Syracuse was terra incognita, and while I have since marveled at the Utah desert and the Rocky Mountains, the landscape of my youth will always be the heartland of *my* United States of America. This may also be true of Ronald Reid, who grew up in the Midwest, though he has resided for some years now on a picturesque mountainside overlooking the Pioneer Valley in central Massachusetts. Perhaps we are all regionalists at heart.

# Afterword ❉ *Gregory Clark and*

## *S. Michael Halloran*

❉In *Nineteenth-Century Rhetoric in North America*, Nan Johnson argues that "an account of the nature of the 19th century rhetorical tradition implies an investigation of the philosophical assumptions, theoretical models, and cultural mandates that shaped 19th century theory and practice" (1991, 7). The perspective developed in this collection of essays supports that argument but with a significant modification: Philosophy and theory are not, in our view, of the same order as "cultural mandates" but are rather manifestations of culture, perhaps epiphenomena of deeper cultural forces. Together these essays attempt to demonstrate how changes in the theory and practice of rhetoric can be understood in the larger context of cultural change.

Read in terms of the historiographical notion of transformation developed in our introductory essay, these essays also attempt to show that while rhetoric continued to function throughout the nineteenth century as public discourse—that is, as a means of constructing and enacting citizenship—the nature of the American public(s) changed. And so, consequently, did the forms and forums of rhetoric, in ways that problematize the very idea of "public discourse." We will return to question of what is to count as public discourse, but first we must turn once more to theoretical language provided by Kenneth Burke.

In *A Grammar of Motives*, Burke defines transformation as referring to "a qualitative shift in the nature of motivation" that occurs through the process of changing identifications ([1945] 1969, 357). In *A Rhetoric of Motives*, he notes that such changes in identification often occur when "a specific activity makes one a participant in some social or economic class" ([1950] 1969, 28). The example he delights in using is the shepherd who cares for the sheep: "The shepherd, qua shepherd, acts for the good of the sheep, to protect them from discomfiture and harm. But he may be 'identified' with a project that is raising the sheep for market" (27). Burke's point is that the social and economic context of a person's actions can identify her or him with purposes at odds with those of the actions regarded abstractly, or, to put it another way, that "one's morality as a specialist cannot be allowed to do duty for one's morality as a citizen" (31). If we raise the further question of the nature of the market for which the sheep are being raised, this example also offers an instance of transformation—a portrayal of change not as "a leap from one state to another" but as a movement through the "common ground" of both. The nurturing function of the shepherd is the same whether the sheep are being raised for their wool or for their meat, but the purposes served by that nurturing are significantly different—at least in terms of the lifespan of the sheep.

The common ground shared by the rhetoric of an oratorical culture and the rhetoric of a professional culture of expertise is the socially constitutive function of public discourse. Rhetoric through-out the century, as these essays describe it, functions as a means by which American communities were defined and maintained. At the beginning of the century, these essays suggest, the public purposes that American rhetoric served had mostly to do with establishing and maintaining coherent moral and political parameters for the new nation-state. By the end of the century, we are arguing, they had mostly to do with establishing and maintaining the efficient economic authority of rational and technical expertise. What changed through the century was not so much the theory of rhetoric or the function of its practice—it was always to persuade, to bind people together in their assent to a common cause. What changed was the nature of the cause to which they gave their assent and the forms taken by the discourse that served to bind them to it. The change was driven by what Johnson calls "cultural mandates" that, according to these essays, themselves changed with the advent of populist politics, the expansion of literacy and easy access to books and magazines, and the increasingly specialized academy and private and public sectors of what we have called a professionalized economy. Rhetoric in both theory and practice appears to have changed gradually and un-selfconsciously in response to these and other cultural mandates.

The historiography of transformation we adumbrate in this collection is the study of a dynamic through which culture constructs discourse and discourse constructs culture. Embedding rhetoric deeply in its social contexts, this historiography necessarily pays as much attention to rhetorical practice as it does to rhetorical theory — it may in fact blur the distinction between "theory" and "practice" as it examines the symbiotic interaction of discourse and the communities in which it develops and works. The essays presented in this collection point toward historical studies of rhetoric that focus on a variety of practices and theories, that probe the theoretical implications of practice, and problematize what is to count as "rhetoric."

First, these essays point toward histories that avoid teleological subtexts that would privilege one rhetoric over another and, in doing so, trace a neatly plotted course of ascent or decline to the present. Such histories will trace what Foucault calls "descent" in contrast to "origins" (1977, 145), a project that "disturbs what was previously considered immobile" and "fragments what was thought unified" (147). History, in his terms, should not "recount the necessary birth of truth and values; it should become a differential knowledge of energies and failings, heights and degenerations, poisons and antidotes. Its task is to become a curative science" (156). It can do that by tracing the descent of rhetorical theories and practices we have inherited in ways that foreground the cultural forces to which they were responses and the social purposes they served. Another way is to expose in particular cases the general principles involved in the relation of public discourse and its culture, principles that can help us be more judicious in our own rhetorical theory and practice.

Second, these essays point toward what Susan C. Jarratt describes as "a comprehensive historical practice unfettered by strict disciplinary boundaries," one that offers "an expanded range of materials: not only the pedagogical treatises summarized in traditional histories, but any literary artifact as it operates to shape knowledge and effect social action." In such a practice, Jarratt notes, "The identification of materials at an active site becomes as much the work of the revisionary historian as her commenting on them" (1991, 13). We would go farther to suggest that the range of materials may extend beyond the literary to embrace symbolic expression in nonverbal media, such as painting and social ritual, insofar as these function to construct and enact citizenship.

Finally, these essays point toward studies that give special emphasis to "public" discourse, while recognizing how hard it is to delimit a public sphere in the modern world. The feminist idea that "the personal is political" highlights the difficulty of sustaining a clear distinction of the sort made by George Kennedy (1980, 4–5) between civic and personal realms, and studies in this volume show on the one hand how ostensibly "personal" or "private" or "domestic" discourse could have public significance (Rouse, Tonkovich, Halloran) and on the other how overtly public discourse could become politically ineffectual (Reid, Antczak and Siemers). The nature of citizenship was complicated by the transformation of oratorical culture, in ways that raise deep questions about how discourse can function to construct and enact citizenship. The connection between rhetorical studies and this specifically public function of discourse is nonetheless worth preserving—is indeed that much more important because of the intellectual challenge it presents. It may be that in an individualist and professionalized culture there is no discourse that is not in some sense "public." Histories that reveal the public function of many discourses, including those not traditionally recognized as "rhetorical," can serve Foucault's "curative" purpose by making us aware of possibilities for improving our public life.

# Works Cited ✳ Contributors ✳ Index

# Works Cited

Abbott, Andrew. 1988. *The System of Professions: An Essay on the Division of Expert Labor*. Chicago: University of Chicago Press.

Adams, John Quincy. 1810. *Lectures on Rhetoric and Oratory*. Cambridge, Mass.: Hilliard and Metcalf.

Addams, Jane. 1880. "Opening Address of the Junior Exhibition." *Rockford Seminar Magazine* 8:4 (April): 110–11.

———. 1881. "Cassandra." In *Rockford Seminary, Thirtieth Commencement, Essays of Graduating Class, Wednesday June 22, 1881*. De Kalb, Ill.: *News* Steam Press.

———. [1902] 1907. *Democracy and Social Ethics*. New York: Macmillan.

———. [1910] 1968. *Twenty Years at Hull-House*. New York: Signet.

———. 1916. *The Long Road of Woman's Memory*. New York. Macmillan.

———. [1922] 1945. "Peace and Bread in Time of War." In *Anniversary Edition, Women's International League for Peace and Freedom, 1915–1945*. New York: King's Crown Press.

———. 1930. *The Second Twenty Years at Hull-House*. New York: Macmillan.

———. 1960. *Jane Addams: A Centennial Reader*. Ed. Emily Cooper Johnson. New York: Macmillan.

Albert, Judith Strong. 1980. "Margaret Fuller and Mary Ware Allen: 'in Youth an insatiate Student'—A Certain Kind of Friendship." *Thoreau Journal Quarterly* 12.3: 9–22.

Alcoff, Linda. 1988. "Cultural Feminism Versus Post-Structuralism: The Identity Crisis in Feminist Theory." *Signs: Journal of Women in Culture and Society* 13.3: 405–36.

Allen, Margaret. 1973. "The Political and Social Criticism of Margaret Fuller." *South Atlantic Quarterly* 72: 560–73.

Allibone, S. Austin. 1858. *A Critical Dictionary of English Literature and British Authors Living and Deceased from the Earliest Accounts to the Latter Half of the Nineteenth Century*. Philadelphia: Charles and Peterson.

Aly, Bower, and Grafton P. Tanquary. 1943. "The Early National Period: 1788–1860." In *A History and Criticism of American Public Address*, ed. William Norwood Brigance, 1:55–110. New York: McGraw-Hill.

Anderson, Dorothy L. 1949. "Edward T. Channing's Teaching of Rhetoric." *Speech Monographs* 16: 69–81.

Antczak, Frederick J. 1985. *Thought and Character: The Rhetoric of Democratic Education*. Ames: Iowa State University Press, 1985.

Armstrong, Nancy. 1987. *Desire and Domestic Fiction: A Political History of the Novel*. New York: Oxford University Press.

Augustine. 1987. *De Doctrina Christiana*. Trans. D. W. Robertson, Jr. New York: Macmillan.

Austin, Gilbert. [1806] 1966. *Chironomia: or a Treatise in Rhetorical Delivery*. Ed. Mary Margaret Robb and Lester Thornssen. Carbondale: Southern Illinois University Press.

Baker, George M. 1876. *The Handy Speaker*. New York: Charles T. Dillingham.

Baker, George Pierce. 1895. *Principles of Argumentation*. Boston: Ginn.

Beecher, Henry Ward. 1902. *Yale Lectures on Preaching, First, Second, and Third Series*. Boston: Pilgrim.

Bell, Alexander Melville. 1878. *The Principles of Elocution*. Salem, Mass.: Burbank.

Bender, Thomas. 1984. "The Erosion of Public Culture: Cities, Discourse and Professional Disciplines." In *The Authority of Experts: Studies in History and Theory*, ed. Thomas L. Haskell, 84–106. Bloomington: Indiana University Press.

Bennett, William J. 1988a. *American Education. Making It Work: A Report to the President and the American People*. Washington, D.C.: Department of Education.

————. 1988b. *Our Children and Our Country: Improving America's Schools and Affirming the Common Culture*. New York: Simon and Schuster.

Berlin, James A. 1984. *Writing Instruction in Nineteenth-Century American Colleges*. Carbondale: Southern Illinois University Press.

Bitzer, Lloyd. 1978. "Rhetoric and Public Knowledge." In *Rhetoric, Philosophy, and Literature: An Exploration*, ed. Don M. Burks, 67–93. West Lafayette, Ind.: Purdue University Press.

Blair, Hugh. [1783] 1965. *Lectures on Rhetoric and Belles Lettres*. 2 vols. Ed. Harold F. Harding. Carbondale: Southern Illinois University Press.

Bledstein, Burton. 1976. *The Culture of Professionalism: The Middle Class and the Development of Higher Education in America*. New York: W. W. Norton.

Bourdieu, Pierre. 1971. "Systems of Education and Systems of Thought." In *Knowledge and Control: New Directions for the Sociology of Education*, ed. Michael D. F. Young, 189–207. London: Collier-Macmillan.

———. 1977. *Reproduction in Education, Society, and Culture*. Trans. Richard Nice. London: Sage.

———. 1984. *Distinction: A Social Critique of the Judgment of Taste*. Trans. Richard Nice. Cambridge: Harvard University Press.

Boyer, Ernest L. 1987. *College: The Undergraduate Experience in America*. New York: Harper and Row.

Braden, Waldo W. 1948. "The Lecture Movement, 1840–1860." *Quarterly Journal of Speech* 34: 206–12.

Briggs, Irene, and Raymond Da Boll. 1969. *Recollections of the Lyceum and Chautauqua Circuits*. Freeport, Maine: Bond Wheelwright.

Broadus, John. [1870] 1909. *A Treatise on the Preparation and Delivery of Sermons*. 26th ed., ed. Edwin Charles Dargan. New York: A. C. Armstrong and Son.

Brown, Charles Walter. 1902. *The American Star Speaker and Model Elocutionist*. Chicago: M. A. Donohue & Co.

———. 1911. *Brown's Standard Elocution and Speaker*. Chicago: Laird and Lee.

Brown, Isaac Hinton. 1845. *Common School Elocution and Oratory*. New York: Fowler & Wells Co.

Bryant, William Cullen. [1829] 1914. "To Cole, the Painter, Departing for Europe." In *Poems of William Cullen Bryant*. Oxford: Oxford University Press.

Bryson, Lyman. 1936. *Adult Education*. New York: American Book.

Buck, Gertrude. 1899. *A Course in Argumentative Writing*. New York: H. Holt and Co.

Buell, Lawrence. 1986. *New England Literary Culture from Revolution through Renaissance*. Cambridge: Cambridge University Press.

*Buffalo Morning Express*, November 27, 1861, 3.

Bulkin, Elly, Minnie Bruce Pratt, and Barbara Smith. 1984. *Yours in Struggle: Three Essays on Racism and Anti-Semitism*. New York: Long Haul Press.

Bunce, O. B. [1874a] 1974. "Lake George and Lake Champlain." In *Picturesque America*, ed. William Cullen Bryant, 2:252–75. New York: Appleton.

———. [1874b] 1974. "On the Coast of Maine." In *Picturesque America*, ed. William Cullen Bryant, 1:1–16. New York: Appleton.

Burgess, Theodore C. 1902. *Epideictic Literature*. Chicago: University of Chicago Press.

Burke, Kenneth. [1945] 1969. *A Grammar of Motives*. Berkeley: University of California Press.

———. [1950] 1969. *A Rhetoric of Motives*. Berkeley: University of California Press.

———. [1961] 1970. *The Rhetoric of Religion*. Berkeley: University of California Press.

———. 1966. *Language as Symbolic Action*. Berkeley: University of California Press.

Caldwell, Merritt. 1845. *A Practical Manual of Elocution: Embracing Voice and Gesture*. Philadelphia: Sorin and Ball.

Calhoun, Daniel. 1973. *The Intelligence of a People*. Princeton: Princeton University Press.

Capper, Charles. 1987. "Margaret Fuller as Cultural Reformer: The Conversations in Boston." *American Quarterly* 39.4: 509–28.

Channing, Edward T. [1856] 1968. *Lectures Read to the Seniors at Harvard College*. Ed. Dorothy I. Anderson and Waldo W. Braden. Carbondale: Southern Illinois University Press.

Charvat, William. 1959. *The Origins of American Critical Thought, 1810–1835*. Philadelphia: University of Pennsylvania Press.

Chevigny, Bell Gale. 1976. *The Woman and the Myth: Margaret Fuller's Life and Writings*. New York: The Feminist Press.

Clark, Gregory. 1987. "Timothy Dwight's Moral Rhetoric at Yale, 1795–1818." *Rhetorica* 5: 149–61.

Cole, Thomas. [1835] 1965. "Essay on American Scenery." In *American Art 1700–1960: Sources and Documents*, ed. John W. McCoubrey, 98–110. Englewood Cliffs, N.J.: Prentice-Hall.

Commager, Henry Steele. 1936. *Theodore Parker*. Boston: Little, Brown.

Conley, Thomas M. 1990. *Rhetoric in the European Tradition*. New York: Longman.

Conway, Jill K. 1964. "Jane Addams: An American Heroine." *Daedalus* 93.2 (Spring): 761–80.

———. [1968] 1987. *The First Generation of American Woman Graduates*. Ph.D. diss., Harvard University, reprinted in Higher Education, Culture and Professionalism, 1850–1950 series. New York: Garland.

———. 1971. "Women Reformers and American Culture, 1870–1930." *Journal of Social History* 5.2: 164–77.

Coulter, John. [1901] 1902. *The New Century Perfect Speaker*. Chicago: n.p.

Crowley, Sharon. 1990. *The Methodical Memory: Invention in Current-Traditional Rhetoric*. Carbondale: Southern Illinois University Press.

Cumnock, Robert McLain. 1878. *Choice Readings for Public and Private Entertainment*. Chicago: Jansen, McClurg & Co.

Curry, S. S. 1891. *The Province of Expression*. Boston: School of Expression.

———. 1907. *Foundations of Expression*. Boston: The Expression Company.

Dall, Caroline Healey. 1895. *Margaret and Her Friends*. Boston: Roberts.

Davis, Allen F. 1973. *American Heroine: The Life and Legend of Jane Addams*. New York: Oxford University Press.

Deegan, Mary Jo. 1988. *Jane Addams and the Men of the Chicago School, 1892–1912*. New Brunswick, N.J.: Transaction Books.

Dexter, Franklin B. 1917. "Student Life at Yale College Under the First President Dwight (1795–1817)." *Proceedings of the American Antiquarian Society* 27: 318–35.

Douglas, Ann. 1977. *The Feminization of American Culture*. New York: Avon Books.

Douglass, Frederick. [1852] 1988. "What to the Slave Is the Fourth of July?" In *Three Centuries of American Rhetorical Discourse: An Anthology and a Review*, ed. Ronald F. Reid, 371–74. Prospect Heights, Ill.: Waveland Press.

Dwight, Timothy. 1786a. "The Friend, No. XI." *The New Haven Gazette, and Connecticut Magazine* 1:19 (June).

———. 1786b. "The Friend, No. XII." *The New Haven Gazette, and Connecticut Magazine* 1:21 (July).

———. [1794] 1969. *Greenfield Hill*. In *The Major Poems of Timothy Dwight*, ed. William J. McTaggart and William K. Bottorf, 367–541. Gainesville, Fla.: Scholars' Facsimiles and Reprints, 1969.

———. 1795. *The True Means of Establishing Public Happiness, a sermon, delivered on the 7th of July 1795, before the Connecticut Society of Cincinnati*. New Haven, Conn.: Thomas and Samuel Green.

———. 1798. *The Duty of Americans at the Present Crisis, illustrated in a discourse, preached on the Fourth of July, 1798*. New Haven, Conn.: Thomas and Samuel Green.

———. 1808. *A Sermon Preached at the Opening of the Theological Institution in Andover; and at the Ordination of Rev. Eliphalet Pearson, LL.D.* Boston: Farrand, Mallory, and Co.

———. 1810. "Lectures on the Evidences of Divine Revelation: Lecture III." *The Panoplist and Missionary Magazine* 3.3 (August): 101–11.

———. 1818. *Theology; Explained and Defended*. 5 vols. Middletown, Conn.: Clark and Lyman.

———. [1821] 1969. *Travels; in New-England and New-York*. 4 vols. Ed. Barbara Miller Solomon. Cambridge: The Belknap Press of Harvard University Press.

———. 1828. *Sermons*. 2 vols. New Haven, Conn.: Hezekiah Howe and Durrie and Peck.

Dwyer, John. 1987. *Virtuous Discourse: Sensibility and Community in Late Eigh-*

*teenth-Century Scotland*. Edinburgh: John Donald Publishers.

Eakin, Paul John. 1976. *The New England Girl: Cultural Ideals in Hawthorne, Stowe, Howells and James*. Athens: University of Georgia Press.

"Editor's Table." *Russell's Magazine* 3 (1858): 181–83.

Edwards, Jonathan. [1746] 1959. *A Treatise Concerning Religious Affections*. Ed. John Smith. New Haven, Conn.: Yale University Press.

———. [1765] 1989. *The Nature of True Virtue*. In *Ethical Writings*, ed. Paul Ramsey, 537–627. New Haven, Conn.: Yale University Press.

Elshtain, Jean Bethke. 1990. *Power Trips and Other Journeys: Essays in Feminism as Civic Discourse*. Madison: Wisconsin University Press.

Emerson, Ralph Waldo. [1841] 1983. "Self Reliance." In *Ralph Waldo Emerson: Essays and Lectures*, 257–82. New York: The Library of America.

———. [1867] 1883. "Eloquence." In *Society and Solitude*, vol. 7 of *The Works of Ralph Waldo Emerson*, 61–98, Standard Library Edition. Cambridge, Mass.: Riverside Press.

Entrikin, Isabelle Webb. 1946. *Sarah Josepha Hale and Godey's Lady's Book*. Philadelphia: Lancaster Press.

Everett, Edward. 1827a. "Porter on Rhetorical Delivery." *United States Review and Literary Gazette* 2: 333–39.

———. 1827b. "Speeches of Henry Clay." *North American Review* 25: 425–51.

———. 1835. "Webster's Speeches." *North American Review* 41: 231–51.

———. [ca. 1847.] "List of books recommended to be read by students while at the university." Manuscript, Harvard University Archives.

———. 1878. *Orations and Speeches on Various Occasions*. 9th ed. Boston: Little, Brown.

———. 1878. Papers. Massachusetts Historical Society, Boston, Mass. Fenno, Frank H. *The Science and Art of Elocution*. New York: Hinds, Noble & Eldredge.

———. 1900. *The Peerless Speaker*. Chicago: Thompson & Thomas. Fergenson, Laraine R. 1987. "Margaret Fuller in the Classroom: The Providence Period." In *Studies in the American Renaissance*, ed. Joel Myerson, 131–42. Charlottesville: University Press of Virginia.

Ferguson, Robert A. 1984. *Law and Letters in American Culture*. Cambridge: Harvard University Press.

Finley, Ruth E. 1932. *The Lady of Godey's: Sarah Josepha Hale*. Philadelphia: Lippincott.

Fisher, Philip. 1985. *Hard Facts: Setting and Form in the American Novel*. New York: Oxford University Press.

Foucault, Michel. 1977. "Nietzsche, Genealogy, History." In *Language, Counter-*

*Memory, Practice*, ed. Donald F. Bouchard, 139–64. Ithaca: Cornell University Press.

Fox-Genovese, Elizabeth. 1988. *Within the Plantation Household: Black and White Women of the Old South*. Chapel Hill and London: University of North Carolina Press.

Freimarck, Vincent. 1966. "Rhetoric at Yale in 1807." *Proceedings of the American Philosophical Society* 110: 235–55.

Friedson, Eliot. 1986. *Professional Powers: A Study of the Institutionalization of Formal Knowledge*. Chicago: University of Chicago Press.

Frothingham, Paul Revere. 1925. *Edward Everett: Orator and Statesman*. Boston: Houghton, Mifflin.

Fuller, Margaret. 1843. "The Great Lawsuit: Man vs. Men; Woman vs. Women." *The Dial* 4: 1–47.

———. 1845a. "Fourth of July." *New York Tribune* 4 July: 2.

———. 1845b. "Prevalent Idea that Politeness is too Great a Luxury to be Given to the Poor." *New York Tribune* 7 June: 3.

———. [1845c] 1971. *Woman in the Nineteenth Century*. New York: W. W. Norton.

———. 1846. "American Literature; Its Position in the Present Time, and Prospects for the Future." In *Margaret Fuller, Essays on American Life and Letters*, ed. Joel Myerson, 381–400. New York: College and University Press.

———. 1852. *Memoirs of Margaret Fuller Ossoli*. Ed. W. H. Channing, J. F. Clarke, and R. W. Emerson. 2 vols. London: Richard Bentley, New Berlington Street.

Gadamer, Hans-Georg. 1975. *Truth and Method*. New York: Continuum.

Garrett, Phineas. 1866. *One Hundred Choice Selections for Readings and Recitations*. Chicago: P. Garrett & Co.

———. 1870–1926. *The Speakers Garland and Literary Bouquet*. Vol. 2. Philadelphia: P. Garrett & Co.

Gere, Anne Ruggles. 1987. *Writing Groups: History, Theory, and Implications*. Carbondale: Southern Illinois University Press.

Giddings, Paula. 1984. *When and Where I Enter: The Impact of Black Women on Race and Sex in America*. Toronto and New York: Bantam.

*Godey's Lady's Book* (under various titles). 1837–1877. Vols. 14–95.

Gossett, Suzanne, and Barbara Ann Bardes. 1990. *Declarations of Independence: Women and Political Power in Nineteenth-Century American Fiction*. New Brunswick, N.J.: Rutgers University Press.

Gould, Joseph E. 1961. *The Chautauqua Movement: An Episode in Continuing*

*American Revolution*. New York: State University of New York Press.

Graff, Gerald. 1987. *Professing Literature: An Institutional History*. Chicago: University of Chicago Press.

Graff, Gerald, and Michael Warner, eds. 1989. *The Origins of Literary Studies in America: A Documentary Anthology*. New York: Routledge.

Gunderson, Robert Gray. 1957. *The Log-Cabin Campaign*. [Lexington]: University of Kentucky Press.

Guthrie, Warren. 1947. "The Development of Rhetorical Theory in America, 1635–1850, II." *Speech Monographs* 14: 38–54.

———. 1949. "The Development of Rhetorical Theory in America, 1635–1850, IV." *Speech Monographs* 16: 98–113.

Gwynn, Aubrey. 1964. *Roman Education from Cicero to Quintilian*. New York: Russell and Russell.

[Hale, Edward Everett.] 1859. "Edward Everett." *American Journal of Education* 7: 325–66.

Hale, Sarah Josepha. [1852] 1970. *Northwood: or, Life North and South*. New York: Johnson Reprint.

Halloran, S. Michael. 1982. "Rhetoric in the American College Curriculum: The Decline of Public Discourse." *PreText* 3: 245–69.

———. 1990. "From Rhetoric to Composition: The Teaching of Rhetoric in America to 1900." In *A Short History of Writing Instruction from Ancient Greece to Twentieth-Century America*, ed. James J. Murphy, 151–82. Davis, Calif.: Hermagoras.

Hatch, Nathan O. 1989. *The Democratization of American Christianity*. New Haven, Conn.: Yale University Press.

Hawthorne, Nathaniel. [1832a] 1989. "The Inland Port." In *Nathaniel Hawthorne's American Travel Sketches*, ed. Alfred Weber, Beth L. Luecke, and Dennis Berthold, 43–45. Hanover and London: University Press of New England.

———. [1832b] 1982. "My Kinsman, Major Molineux." In *Nathaniel Hawthorne: Tales and Sketches*, 68–87. New York: The Library of America.

———. [1832c] 1982. "My Visit to Niagara." In *Nathaniel Hawthorne: Tales and Sketches*, 244–50. New York: The Library of America.

———. [1832d] 1989. "An Ontario Steam-Boat." In *Nathaniel Hawthorne's American Travel Sketches*, ed. Alfred Weber, Beth L. Luecke, and Dennis Berthold, 49–55. Hanover and London: University Press of New England.

———. [1835a] 1982. "The May-Pole of Merry Mount." In *Nathaniel Hawthorne: Tales and Sketches*, 360–70. New York: The Library of America.

———. [1835b] 1982. "Young Goodman Brown." In *Nathaniel Hawthorne: Tales and Sketches*, 276–89. New York: The Library of America.

————. [1843] 1982. "The Birth-mark." In *Nathaniel Hawthorne: Tales and Sketches*, 764–80. New York: The Library of America.

————. [1846] 1982. "The Olde Manse." In *Nathaniel Hawthorne: Tales and Sketches*, 1142–49. New York: The Library of America.

————. [1850] 1983. *The Scarlet Letter*. In *Nathaniel Hawthorne: Novels*, 115–345. New York: The Library of America.

————. [1852] 1982. *A Wonder Book for Girls and Boys*. In Nathaniel Hawthorne: Tales and Sketches, 1159–1302. New York: The Library of America.

Heath, Shirley Brice. 1981. "Toward an Ethnohistory of Writing in American Education." In *Writing: The Nature, Development, and Teaching of Written Communication*. Vol. 1, *Variation in Writing: Functional and Linguistic-Cultural Difference*, ed. Marcia Farr Whiteman, 25–45. Hillsdale, N.J.: Lawrence Erlbaum.

Hipple, Walter John, Jr. 1957. *The Beautiful, the Sublime, and the Picturesque in Eighteenth-Century British Aesthetic Theory*. Carbondale: Southern Illinois University Press.

Hoffman, Nicole Tonkovich. 1990. "Scribbling, Writing, Author(iz)ing: Nineteenth-Century Women Writers." Ph.D. diss., University of Utah.

Hofstadter, Richard, and DeWitt Hardy. 1952. *The Development and Scope of Higher Education in the United States*. New York: Columbia University Press.

Hoppin, James M. 1881. *Homiletics*. New York: Dodd, Mead & Co.

Horowitz, Helen Lefkowitz. 1984. *Alma Mater: Design and Experience in the Women's Colleges from Their Nineteenth-Century Beginnings to the 1930s*. Boston: Beacon Press.

Hoyt, Edward A., and Loriman S. Brigham. 1956. "Glimpses of Margaret Fuller: The Greene Street School and Florence." *New England Quarterly* 29 (March): 87–98.

Hudspeth, Robert N., ed. 1983. *The Letters of Margaret Fuller*. 5 vols. to date. Ithaca and London: Cornell University Press.

Hurlbut, J. L. 1921. *The Story of Chautauqua*. New York: G. P. Putnam.

Hutcheson, Francis. 1728. *Essays on the Nature and Conduct of the Passions and Affections*. London: J. Osborn and T. Longman.

Jamieson, Alexander. 1820. *A Grammar of Rhetoric and Polite Literature*. New Haven, Conn.: A. H. Maltby.

Jarratt, Susan C. 1991. *Rereading the Sophists: Classical Rhetoric Refigured*. Carbondale: Southern Illinois University Press.

Jehlen, Myra. 1986. *American Incarnation: The Individual, the Nation, the Conti-*

*nent*. Cambridge: Harvard University Press.

Jensen, Joan M. 1986. *Loosening the Bonds: Mid-Atlantic Farm Women 1750–1850*. New Haven, Conn., and London: Yale University Press.

Johnson, Harriet Hall. [1910] 1980. "Margaret Fuller as Known by Her Scholars." In *Critical Essays on Margaret Fuller*, ed. Joel Myerson, 134–40. Boston: G. K. Hall and Co.

Johnson, Nan. 1991. *Nineteenth-Century Rhetoric in North America*. Carbondale: Southern Illinois University Press.

Kames, Henry Home, Lord. 1751. *Essays on the Principles of Morality and Natural Religion*. Edinburgh: Printed by R. Fleming, for A. Kincaid and A. Donaldson.

――――. [1785] 1972. *Elements of Criticism*, 6th ed., 2 vols. New York: Garland.

Kant, Immanuel. [1790] 1952. *A Critique of Judgment*. Oxford: Clarendon Press.

Kelley, Mary. 1984. *Private Woman, Public Stage: Literary Domesticity in Nineteenth Century America*. New York: Oxford University Press.

Kelly, Fred C. 1919. "What 20,000,000 People Like to Hear." *American Magazine* 9 June: 32.

Kennedy, George A. 1980. *Classical Rhetoric in Its Christian and Secular Tradition from Ancient to Modern Times*. Chapel Hill: University of North Carolina Press.

Kerber, Linda. 1980. *Women of the Republic: Intellect and Ideology in Revolutionary America*. Chapel Hill: University of North Carolina Press.

――――. 1986. *Women of the Republic: Intellect and Ideology in Revolutionary America*. New York: Norton.

――――. 1988. "Separate Spheres, Female Worlds, Woman's Place: The Rhetoric of Women's History." *Journal of American History* 75 (June): 9–39.

Kervane, Eugene. 1966. "Augustine's *De doctrina christiana*: A Treatise on Christian Education." *Recherches Augustiniennes* 4: 99–133.

Kimball, Bruce. 1986. *Orators and Philosophers: A History of the Idea of Liberal Education*. New York: Teachers College, Columbia University.

Kinney, Halley. 1952. "Report." Unpublished essay. Redpath Chautauqua Collection, University of Iowa.

Kitzhaber, Albert R. [1953] 1990. *Rhetoric in American Colleges, 1850–1900*. Dallas: Southern Methodist University Press.

Kloppenberg, James T. 1987. "The Virtues of Liberalism: Christianity, Republicanism, and Ethics in Early American Political Discourse." *Journal of American History* 74: 9–33.

Knowles, Malcolm. 1962. *The Adult Education Movement in the United States*. New York: Holt, Rinehart & Winston.

Knox, Samuel. 1809. *A Compendious System of Rhetoric*. Baltimore: Swain and Matchett.

Kolodny, Annette. 1984. *The Land Before Her: Fantasy and Experience of the American Frontiers, 1630–1860*. Chapel Hill: University of North Carolina Press.

*The Ladies' Magazine* (under various titles). 1828–1833. Vols. 1–9.

Lane, Ann J. 1990. *To "Herland" and Beyond: The Life and Work of Charlotte Perkins Gilman*. New York: Meridian.

Lerner, Gerda. 1972. *Black Women in America: A Documentary History*. New York: Vintage Books.

Levine, Daniel. 1971. *Jane Addams and the Liberal Tradition*. Madison: State Historical Society of Wisconsin.

Longfellow, Henry Wadsworth. [1855] 1893. "The Song of Hiawatha." In *The Complete Poetical Works of Henry Wadsworth Longfellow*, 113–64. Boston and New York: Houghton, Mifflin and Company.

———. [1858] 1893. "The Courtship of Miles Standish." In *The Complete Poetical Works of Henry Wadsworth Longfellow*, 164–84. Boston and New York: Houghton, Mifflin and Company.

Loring, James Spear. 1853. *The Hundred Boston Orators Appointed by the Municipal Authorities and Other Public Bodies, from 1770 to 1853; Comprising Historical Gleanings, Illustrating the Principles and Progress of our Republican Institutions*. Boston: John P. Jewett.

Loveland, Ann C. 1971. *Emblem of Liberty: The Image of Lafayette in the American Mind*. Baton Rouge: Louisiana University Press.

Lowth, Robert. [1763] 1815. *Lectures on the Sacred Poetry of the Hebrews*. Trans. G. Gregory. Boston: Joseph T. Buckingham.

Lumm, Emma Griffith. 1898. *The New American Speaker*. Chicago: C. W. Stanton Co.

McCall, Laura. 1989. "'The Reign of Brute Force is Now Over': A Content Analysis of *Godey's Lady's Book*, 1830–1860." *Journal of the Early Republic* 9: 217–36.

McCormick, Richard P. 1966. *The Second American Party System: Party Formation in the Jacksonian Era*. Chapel Hill: University of North Carolina Press.

McGuffey, W. H. 1857. *McGuffey's New Sixth Eclectic Reader*. Cincinnati: Wilson, Hinkle & Co.

McIlvaine, J. H. 1870. *Elocution: The Sources and Elements*. New York: Charles Scribner and Company.

MacIntyre, Alasdair. 1984. *After Virtue: A Study in Moral Theory*. 2nd ed. Notre Dame, Ind.: University of Notre Dame Press.

———. 1988. *Whose Justice? Which Rationality?* London: Duckworth.

Magoon, E. L. 1849. *Living Orators in America*. New York: Baker and Scribner.

Martin, Lawrence. 1928. "The Genesis of *Godey's Lady's Book.*" *New England Quarterly* 1:41–70.

Martin, Theodora Penny. 1987. *The Sound of Our Own Voices: Women's Study Clubs 1860–1910*. Boston: Beacon.

Miller, Susan. 1989. *Rescuing the Subject: A Critical Introduction to Rhetoric and the Writer*. Carbondale: Southern Illinois University Press.

———. 1991. *Textual Carnivals: The Politics of Composition*. Carbondale: Southern Illinois University Press.

Miller, Thomas P. 1990a. Editor's Introduction. *The Selected Writings of John Witherspoon*. Carbondale: Southern Illinois University Press.

———. 1990b. "Where Did College English Studies Come From?" *Rhetoric Review* 9 (Fall): 50–71.

Morgan, Anna. 1889. *An Hour with Delsarte: A Study of Expression*. Boston: Lee and Shepard.

Morrison, Theodore. 1974. *Chautauqua*. Chicago: University of Chicago Press.

Mott, Frank Luther. 1930–1968. *A History of American Magazines*. 5 vols. New York: Appleton.

Mouffe, Chantal. 1983. "The Sex-Gender System and the Discursive Construction of Women's Subordination." In *Rethinking Ideology: A Marxist Debate*, ed. Sakari Hanninen and Leena Paldan, International Socialism Discussion 3, 139–43. New York: International General/IMMRC.

Myers, Kenneth. 1987. *The Catskills: Painter, Writers, and Tourists in the Mountains 1820–1895*. Yonkers, N.Y.: The Hudson River Museum of Westchester.

Myerson, Joel. 1974. "Caroline Dall's Reminiscences of Margaret Fuller." *Harvard Library Bulletin* 22: 414–18.

Myerson, Joel, ed. 1985. *Studies in the American Renaissance*. Charlottesville: University Press of Virginia.

Newman, Samuel P. [1827] 1842. *A Practical System of Rhetoric*. New York: Dayton and Newman, 1842.

Northrop, Henry Davenport. 1910. *The Ideal Speaker and Entertainer*. Chicago: Geo. W. Berthon.

Novak, Barbara. 1980. *Nature and Culture: American Landscape Painting 1825–1875*. New York: Oxford University Press.

Nye, Russel. 1970. *The Unembarrassed Muse: The Popular Arts in America*. New York: Dial.

Olmsted, Denison. 1858. "Timothy Dwight as Teacher." *The American Journal of*

*Education* 5: 567–85.

Ong, Walter J. 1971. "Latin Language Study as a Renaissance Puberty Rite." In *Rhetoric, Romance, and Technology: Studies in the Interaction of Expression and Culture*. Ithaca: Cornell University Press.

Oravec, Christine. 1976. "'Observation' in Aristotle's Theory of Epideictic." *Philosophy and Rhetoric* 9: 162–74.

———. 1986. "The Democratic Critics: An Alternative American Rhetorical Tradition in the Nineteenth Century." *Rhetorica* 4.4: 395–421.

Parker, Edward G. 1857. *The Golden Age of Oratory*. Boston: Whittemore, Niles, and Hall.

Parker, Richard Greene, and J. Madison Watson. 1870. *The National Fifth Reader*. New York: A. S. Barnes & Co.

Parker, William Riley. 1967. "Where Do English Departments Come From?" *College English* 28 (February): 339–51.

Parton, James. 1873. *Fanny Fern: A Memorial Volume, Containing Her Select Writings and a Memoir*. New York: G. W. Carleton.

Perelman, Ch., and L. Olbrechts-Tyteca. 1969. *The New Rhetoric: A Treatise on Argumentation*. Trans. John Wilkinson and Purcell Weaver. Notre Dame, Ind.: University of Notre Dame Press.

Phelps, Austin. 1857. *The Theory of Preaching: An Oration Before the Porter Rhetorical Society of the Theological Seminary at Andover*. Andover, Mass.: Warren F. Draper.

———. 1861. *The Relations of the Bible to the Civilization of the Future: A Sermon Delivered Before His Excellency Nathaniel P. Banks, Governor, His Honor Eliphalet Trask, Lieut. Governor, The Honorable Council, and The Legislature of Massachusetts, at the Annual Election, Wednesday, January 2, 1861*. Boston: William White, Printer to the State.

———. 1867. *The New Birth, or The Work of the Holy Spirit*. Boston: Gould and Lincoln.

———. 1881. *The Theory of Preaching*. New York: Scribner's.

———. 1882. *Men and Books; or, Studies in Homiletics*. New York: Scribner's.

———. 1883. *English Style in Public Discourse with Special Reference to the Usages of the Pulpit*. New York: Scribner's.

———. 1884. "The New England Clergy and the Anti-Slavery Reform." *The Congregationalist*, April 24. Boston: W. L. Greene & Co.

Plato. 1956. *Phaedrus*. Trans. W. C. Helmbold and W. G. Rabinowitz. The Library of Liberal Arts. Indianapolis: Bobbs-Merrill.

Porter, Ebenezer. [1827] 1830. *Analysis of the Principles of Rhetorical Delivery*. Andover, Mass.: Mark Newman.

_____. 1834. *Lectures on Homiletics and Preaching, and on Public Prayer*. Andover, Mass.: Flagg, Gould and Newman.

Potter, David. 1944. *Debating in the Colonial Chartered Colleges: An Historical Survey, 1642–1900*. Teachers College Contributions to Education no. 899. New York: Teachers College, Columbia University.

Press, Gerald A. 1984. "Doctrina in Augustine's *De doctrina christiana*." *Philosophy and Rhetoric* 17: 98–120.

Quintilian. 1980. *Institutio Oratoria*. Trans. H. E. Butler. Loeb Classical Library. Cambridge: Harvard University Press.

Ravitz, Abe C. 1956. "Timothy Dwight: Professor of Rhetoric." *New England Quarterly* 29: 63–72.

Raymond, George L. 1879. *The Orator's Manual*. New York: Silver, Burdett & Co.

*Redpath-Vawter Chautauqua Program* [Belle Plaine, Iowa]. 1909. Redpath Chautauqua Collection, University of Iowa.

*Redpath-Vawter Chautauqua Program* [Cedar Rapids, Iowa]. 1925. Redpath Chautauqua Collection, University of Iowa.

Reid, Ronald F. 1956. "Edward Everett: Rhetorician of Nationalism, 1824–1855." *Quarterly Journal of Speech* 42: 273–82.

_____. 1957. "Edward Everett's 'The Character of Washington.'" *Southern Speech Journal* 22: 144–56.

_____. 1959. "The Boylston Professorship of Rhetoric and Oratory, 1806–1904: A Case Study in Changing Concepts of Rhetoric and Pedagogy." *Quarterly Journal of Speech* 45: 239–57.

_____. 1960. "John Ward's Influence in America: Joseph McKean and the Boylston Lectures on Rhetoric and Oratory." *Speech Monographs* 27: 340–44.

_____. 1967. "Newspaper Response to the Gettysburg Addresses." *Quarterly Journal of Speech* 53: 50–60.

_____. 1990. *Edward Everett: Unionist Orator*. New York: Greenwood Press.

Reingold, Nathan. 1964. *Science in Nineteenth-Century America: A Documentary History*. New York: Hill and Wang.

Rezneck, Samuel. 1968. *Education for a Technological Society: A Sesquicentennial History of Rensselaer Polytechnic Institute*. Troy, N.Y.: Rensselaer Polytechnic Institute.

Robinson, David M. 1982. "Margaret Fuller and the Transcendental Ethos: *Woman in the Nineteenth-Century*." *PMLA* 97.1: 83–98.

Rosenfield, Lawrence W. 1980. "The Practical Celebration of Epideictic." In *Rhetoric in Transition: Studies in the Nature and Uses of Rhetoric*, ed. Eugene

E. White, 131–55. University Park: Pennsylvania State University Press.

Rosenthal, Bernard. 1970. "*The Dial*, Transcendentalism, and Margaret Fuller." *English Language Notes* 8: 28–36.

Rouse, P. Joy. 1990. "Positional Historiography and Margaret Fuller's Public Discourse of Mutual Interpretation." *Rhetoric Society Quarterly* 20.3: 233–41.

Rudnick, Lois. 1991. "A Feminist American Success Myth: Jane Addams's *Twenty Years at Hull House.*" In *Tradition and the Talents of Women*, ed. Florence Howe, 145–67 Urbana: Illinois University Press.

Rush, James. 1827. *The Philosophy of the Human Voice*. Philadelphia: Grigg and Elliott.

Russell, William. 1846. *American Elocutionist*. Boston: Jenks and Palmer.

———. 1892. *Orthography: The Cultivation of the Voice in Elocution*. Boston and New York: Houghton Mifflin.

Ryan, Mary P. 1990. *Women in Public: Between Banners and Ballots, 1825–1880*. Baltimore: Johns Hopkins University Press.

Satterwhite, Joseph N. 1956. "The Tremulous Formula: Form and Technique in Godey's Fiction." *American Quarterly* 8: 99–113.

Scott, Donald M. 1978. *From Office to Profession: The New England Ministry 1750–1850*. Philadelphia: University of Pennsylvania Press.

Sears, John F. 1989. *Sacred Places: American Tourist Attractions in the Nineteenth Century*. New York: Oxford University Press.

Sennett, Richard. 1977. *The Fall of Public Man*. New York: Alfred A. Knopf.

Shaver, Claude. L. 1954. "Steele MacKaye and the Delsartian Tradition." In *History of Speech Education in America*, ed. Karl R. Wallace, 202–18. New York: Appleton-Century-Crofts, Inc.

Shedd, William G. T. 1855. *The Education of a Ministry*. Boston: Marvin.

———. 1859. *Eloquence a Virtue; or, Outlines of a Systematic Rhetoric*. Trans. of Theremin, *Eloquence a Virtue*. Andover, Mass.: Warren F. Draper.

———. 1867. *Homiletics and Pastoral Theology*. New York: Charles Scribner and Co.

Sheridan, Thomas. 1762. *Lectures on Elocution*. London: W. Strahan for A. Millar.

Shoemaker, J. W. 1873. *The Elocutionist's Annual*. Philadelphia: National School of Elocution and Oratory.

———. 1886. *Practical Elocution; For Use in Colleges and Schools and by Private Students*. Philadelphia: National School of Elocution and Oratory.

Shuffelton, Frank. 1985. "Margaret Fuller at the Greene Street School: The Journal of Evelina Metcalf." In *Studies in the American Renaissance*, ed. Joel

Myerson, 29–46. Charlottesville: University Press of Virginia.

Silliman, Benjamin. 1817. *A Sketch of the Life and Character of President Dwight, Delivered as an Eulogium.* New Haven, Conn.: Maltby, Goldsmith and Co.

Skornia, Harry Jay. 1965. *Television and Society: An Inquest and Agenda for Improvement.* New York: McGraw-Hill.

Sloan, Douglas. 1971. *The Scottish Enlightenment and the American College Ideal.* New York: Teacher's College, Columbia University.

Smith, Adam. [1759] 1976. *The Theory of Moral Sentiments,* ed. D. D. Raphael and A. L. Macfie. Oxford: Clarendon Press.

Smith-Rosenberg, Carroll. 1985. *Disorderly Conduct: Visions of Gender in Victorian America.* New York: Alfred A. Knopf.

Stearns, Bertha M. 1929. "Early New England Magazines for Ladies." *New England Quarterly* 2: 420–57.

Stearns, Foster. 1928. "Edward Everett: Secretary of State, November 6, 1852, to March 3, 1853." In *The American Secretaries of State and Their Diplomacy,* ed. Samuel Flagg Bemis, 6: 117–41. New York: Alfred A. Knopf.

Stebbins, Genevieve. 1886. *Delsarte System of Dramatic Expression.* New York: E. S. Werner.

Sterling, Dorothy. 1984. *We Are Your Sisters: Black Women in the Nineteeth Century.* New York: W. W. Norton.

Stewart, David W., and Harry A. Spille. 1988. *Diploma Mills: Degrees of Fraud.* New York: Macmillan.

Stewart, Randall. 1948. *Nathaniel Hawthorne: A Biography.* New Haven, Conn.: Yale University Press.

Sullivan, Dale. 1988. "A Rhetoric of Children's Literature as Epideictic Discourse." Ph.D. diss., Rensselaer Polytechnic Institute.

Sweet, Warren. 1963. *Religion in the Development of American Culture, 1765–1840.* Gloucester, Mass.: Scribner's.

Sykes, Charles J. 1988. *Profscam: Professors and the Demise of Higher Education.* New York: Kampmann and Co.

Thompson, Eleanor Wolf. 1947. *Education for Ladies, 1830–1960: Ideas on Education in Magazines for Women.* New York: King's Crown Press.

Thoreau, Henry David. [1849] 1990. "Resistance to Civil Government." In *The Heath Anthology of American Literature,* ed. Paul Lauter et al. Vol. 1. Lexington, Mass.: D. C. Heath and Company.

———. [1854] 1985. *Walden.* In *Henry David Thoreau,* 321–587. New York: The Library of America.

Tompkins, Jane. 1985. *Sensational Designs: The Cultural Work of American Fiction, 1790–1860.* New York: Oxford University Press.

United States Carnegie Commission on Educational Television. 1967. *Public Television, A Program for Action: The Report and Recommendations of the Carnegie Commission on Educational Television*. New York: Harper and Row.

Vawter, Keith. n.d. "Reasons Why." *The Chautauqua Herald*, 5:3. Redpath Chautauqua Collection, University of Iowa.

———. n.d. Untitled draft of agent guidelines. Keith Vawter's private papers, Redpath Chautauqua Collection, University of Iowa.

———. 1923. "What of the Chautauqua?" *Redpath-Vawter Chautaugua Program*, Redpath Chautauqua Collection, University of Iowa.

Walker, John. [1781] 1810. *Elements of Elocution*. Boston: D. Mallory & Co.

———. 1808. *Elements of Speaking*. New York: Smith and Forman.

Ward, Elizabeth Stewart Phelps. 1892. *Austin Phelps: A Memoir*. New York: Scribner's.

Ward, John. 1759. *A System of Oratory*. London: J. Ward.

Weaver, Richard. [1953] 1965. "The Spaciousness of Old Rhetoric." In *The Province of Rhetoric*, ed. Joseph Schwartz and John A. Rycenga, 275–92. New York: The Ronald Press Company.

———. 1963. "Language Is Sermonic." In *Dimensions of Rhetorical Scholarship*, ed. Robert E. Nebergall, 49–64. Norman: University of Oklahoma Press.

Webster, Daniel. [1825] 1988. "Bunker Hill Monument Address." In *Three Centuries of American Rhetorical Discourse: An Anthology and a Review*, ed. Ronald F. Reid, 207–55. Prospect Heights, Ill.: Waveland Press.

Welter, Barbara. 1966. "The Cult of True Womanhood: 1820–1860." *American Quarterly* 18.2: 151–74.

———. 1976. *Dimity Convictions: The American Woman in the Nineteenth-Century*. Athens: Ohio University Press.

Werner, Edgar S. 1890. *Werner's Readings and Recitations*. No. 1. New York: Edgar S. Werner.

Whately, Richard. [1828] 1969. *Elements of Rhetoric: Comprising an Analysis of the Laws of Moral Evidence and of Persuasion, with Rules for Argumentative Conposition and Elocution*. 7th ed., rev., ed. Douglas Ehninger. Carbondale: Southern Illinois University Press.

Wichelns, Herbert A. 1943. "Ralph Waldo Emerson." In *A History and Criticism of American Public Address*, ed. William Norwood Brigance, 2:501–25. New York: McGraw-Hill.

Wildman, T. A. n.d. "Getting Lyceum Business." Untitled agent bulletin.

Williams, Daniel Day. 1970. *The Andover Liberals: A Study in American Theology*. New York: Octagon Books.

Williams, Raymond. 1961. *The Long Revolution*. New York: Columbia University Press.

Wilson, Marcius. 1861. *The Fifth Reader of the School and Family Series*. New York: Harper & Brothers.

Witherspoon, John. [1810] 1990. *Lectures on Moral Philosophy and Eloquence*. In *The Selected Writings of John Witherspoon*, ed. Thomas P. Miller, 152–318. Carbondale: Southern Illinois University Press.

Woods, William S. 1985. "The Reform Tradition in Nineteenth-Century Composition Teaching." *Written Communication* 2.4: 377–90.

Woodward, Helen. 1960. *The Lady Persuaders*. New York: Ivan Obolensky.

Woody, Thomas. 1929. *A History of Woman's Education in the United States*. 2 vols. New York: Science Press.

Wright, Richardson. 1928. *Forgotten Ladies: Nine Portraits from the American Family Album*. Philadelphia: Lippincott.

Zophy, Angela Marie Howard. 1981. *For the Improvement of My Sex: Sarah Josepha Hale's Editorship of "Godey's Lady's Book," 1837–1877*. Ann Arbor: UMI.

# Contributors

*Frederick J. Antczak* is an associate professor and chair of rhetoric at the University of Iowa in Iowa City, where he teaches the basic rhetoric course, courses in American public address, rhetorical theory, and the ethics of rhetoric. His book *Thought and Character: The Rhetoric of Democratic Education* won the University of Virginia's Phi Beta Kappa award. His work has appeared in the *Quarterly Journal of Speech*, *The Rhetoric Society Quarterly*, and in several books on political communication. He is currently editor of the *Iowa Journal of Speech Communication*.

*Gregory Clark* is an associate professor of English at Brigham Young University in Provo, Utah. He is the author of *Dialogue, Dialectic, and Conversation: A Social Perspective on the Function of Writing*. His current work examines rhetorical practice in early American narratives of travel and settlement.

*S. Michael Halloran* is a professor of rhetoric and associate dean of humanities and social sciences at Rensselaer Polytechnic Institute. His essays on rhetorical theory and criticism, the rhetoric of scientific discourse, and the history of American rhetoric have appeared in several edited collections and in journals such as *College English*, *Quarterly Journal of Speech*, *Pre/Text*, *Rhetoric Review*, and *Rhetoric Society Quarterly*.

*Russel Hirst*, a graduate of Rensselaer Polytechnic Institute's Ph.D. program in rhetoric and technical communication, is an assistant professor of English at the University of Tennessee, Knoxville, where he teaches technical communication and rhetorical theory. He has published in *The Journal of Technical Writing and Communication* and is currently coauthoring a textbook on business writing, as well as working on a book about homiletic theory in America.

*Nan Johnson* is an associate professor of English at Ohio State University, where she teaches the history of rhetoric, rhetorical theory, critical theory, and writing. She is the author of *Nineteenth-Century Rhetoric in North America* and numerous book chapters, articles, and reviews on nineteenth-century rhetoric and general topics in the history of rhetoric and composition. Currently her research focuses on the popular rhetoric movement in nineteenth-century America and cultural attitudes in this period regarding rhetorical performance and gender.

*Catherine Peaden* is an assistant professor of English at the University of Oklahoma where she teaches courses in the Composition, Rhetoric, and Literacy Program. Her historical work has appeared in a special feminist issue of *Rhetoric Society Quarterly* and in the Rhetoric Society of America volume *Rhetoric and Ideology: Compositions and Criticisms of Power*. She is currently editing a collection entitled *Nineteenth-Century Women Learn to Write: Past Cultures and Practices of Literacy*.

*Ronald F. Reid* is professor emeritus, University of Massachusetts (Amherst), where he served as professor and head in the Department of Speech. Prior to that time, he taught at Washington University (St. Louis) and Purdue. His research, which has earned him Winans-Wichelns and Golden Anniversary Monograph awards from the Speech Communication Association, deals with the history of American political discourse and rhetorical theory. He is currently writing a history of early American presidential campaign rhetoric.

*P. Joy Rouse* is an assistant professor of writing/English and textual studies at Syracuse University in Syracuse, New York, where she teaches undergraduate rhetoric courses and graduate seminars in the history of rhetoric. Her work has appeared in *Rhetoric Society Quarterly*, *Writing Lab Newsletter*, and *English Language Arts Bulletin*.

*Edith Siemers*, having completed her master's degree in communication studies at the University of Iowa in 1988, is currently an instructor at Wisconsin Lutheran College in Milwaukee, Wisconsin, where she teaches courses in both philosophy and communication.

*Nicole Tonkovich* is an assistant professor of literature at the University of California, San Diego, where she teaches courses in nineteenth-century U.S. literature and women's studies. She also directs the Fifth College Writing Program. She is completing a book entitled *Scribbling, Writing, Author(iz)ing: Nineteenth-Century Women Writers and the Professionalization of Authorship*.

# Index